COMPARATIVE REGIONALISMS FOR DEVELOPMENT IN THE 21ST CENTURY

A sensible, informative and thought-provoking collection emphasizing the importance of regionalism in Africa and beyond. Human capital development, technological innovation and good governance are critical for the long-term economic success of the Global South.

Zolani Dyosi, National Research Foundation Technology and Human Resources and Industry Programme, South Africa

The International Political Economy of New Regionalisms Series

The International Political Economy of New Regionalisms Series presents innovative analyses of a range of novel regional relations and institutions. Going beyond established, formal, interstate economic organizations, this essential series provides informed interdisciplinary and international research and debate about myriad heterogeneous intermediate-level interactions.

Reflective of its cosmopolitan and creative orientation, this series is developed by an international editorial team of established and emerging scholars in both the South and North. It reinforces ongoing networks of analysts in both academia and think-tanks as well as international agencies concerned with micro-, meso- and macro-level regionalisms.

Recent titles in the series *(continued at the back of the book)*

Mapping Agency
Comparing Regionalisms in Africa
Edited by Ulrike Lorenz-Carl and Martin Rempe

The EU and the Eurozone Crisis
Policy Challenges and Strategic Choices
Edited by Finn Laursen

China-Africa Relations in an Era of Great Transformations
Edited by Li Xing with Abdulkadir Osman Farah

The European Union Neighbourhood
Challenges and Opportunities
Edited by Teresa Cierco

Comparative Regionalisms for Development in the 21st Century

Insights from the Global South

Edited by

EMMANUEL FANTA
Université Libre de Bruxelles, Belgium

TIMOTHY M. SHAW
University of Massachusetts, Boston, USA

VANESSA T. TANG
University of KwaZulu-Natal, South Africa

UNITED NATIONS UNIVERSITY
CRIS
Comparative Regional Integration Studies

netris

Routledge
Taylor & Francis Group
LONDON AND NEW YORK

First published 2013 by Ashgate Publishing

Published 2016 by Routledge
2 Park Square, Milton Park, Abingdon, Oxon OX14 4RN
711 Third Avenue, New York, NY 10017, USA

Routledge is an imprint of the Taylor & Francis Group, an informa business

British Library Cataloguing in Publication Data
A catalogue record for this book is available from the British Library

The Library of Congress has cataloged the printed edition as follows:
Fanta, Emmanuel.
Comparative regionalisms for development in the 21st century : insights from the Global South / by Emmanuel Fanta, Timothy M Shaw and Vanessa T Tang.
pages cm.—(The international political economy of new regionalisms series)
Includes bibliographical references and index.
ISBN 978-1-4094-6520-1 (hardback)
1. Developing countries—Economic integration.
2. Developing countries—Foreign economic relations. 3. Regionalism—Developing countries. 4. Developing countries—Politics and government. 5. Developing countries—Social conditions, I. Title.

HC59.7.F33 2013
338.9009172'4—dc23

2013007975

ISBN 9781409465201 (hbk)

Contents

List of Figures and Tables

List of Figures

List of Tables

List of Appendices

Notes on Contributors

Andrea Cofelice PhD Researcher at Universities of Sienna & Padua in Italy

Melissa Dalleau previously Policy Officer, Trade & Economic Governance, ECDPM, Maastricht, The Netherlands

Emmanuel Fanta previously Researcher at UNU-CRIS in Bruges, Belgium, PhD student at Université Libre de Bruxelles, Belgium

Merle Holden Emeritus Professor, School of Accounting, Economics & Finance, UKZN, Durban, South Africa

Tiru K. Jayaraman Professor, Department of Economics, Fiji National University

Jean Kenfrack IRIC, University of Yaounde, Cameroon

Stephen Kingah Research Fellow at UNU-CRIS in Bruges, Belgium

Mark Kirton Senior Lecturer, IIR at UWI, St Augustine, Trinidad & Tobago

Maria Cristina Macovei Project Manager, Development Office, College of Europe; previously Project Coordinator for NETRIS

Jean-Bosco Ngendahimana PhD Researcher in School of Law, University of Dar es Salaam, Tanzania

Timothy M. Shaw Visiting Professor, University of Massachusetts Boston, USA

Richard Simson (deceased) was Lecturer in School of Accounting, Economics & Finance, UKZN, Durban, South Africa

Vanessa T. Tang Lecturer in School of Accounting, Economics & Finance, UKZN, Durban, South Africa

Rodrigo Tavares Associate Research Scholar at UNU-CRIS in Bruges, Belgium & Professor Getulio Vargas Foundation in Brazil (FGV-SP)

Kathleen van Hove Programme Manager, Trade & Regional Integration, ECDPM, Maastricht, The Netherlands

Luk Van Langenhove Director, UNU-CRIS in Bruges, Belgium

Foreword

The present volume is the specific outcome of a major project, called 'NETRIS'. This project focused upon the establishment and coordination of a network of African, Caribbean and Pacific (ACP) higher education institutions (HEIs) within the field of comparative regional integration. NETRIS was funded by EDULINK, the ACP-EU partnership in higher education. The coordination of the project was jointly assumed by two institutions, based in Bruges: the College of Europe and the United Nations University Institute on Comparative Regional Integration Studies (UNU-CRIS).

The specific purpose of NETRIS was to strengthen the research and training capacities of institutions in the six sub-regions by stimulating mutual learning, shared practices and collective dissemination. The NETRIS target group was researchers and research centres. The ultimate beneficiaries were students that focused upon regional integration as well as ACP policy-makers.

The NETRIS network included Addis Ababa University (AAU) (Ethiopia), Institute des Relations Internationales du Cameroun (IRIC) (Cameroun), Université Cheikh Anta Diop (UCAD) (Senegal), University of Dar es Salaam (UDSM) (Tanzania), University of KwaZulu-Natal (UKZN) (South Africa), University of South Pacific (USP) (Fiji), and University of the West Indies (IIR/UWI) (Trinidad and Tobago), together with two associated partners: European Centre for Development Policy Management (ECDPM) (Maastricht, The Netherlands) and Southern Africa Political Economy Series (SAPES) Trust (Harare, Zimbabwe).

From 2009 to 2011, NETRIS provided assistance and consultations to reinforce the capacity of ACP-based researchers to conduct multidisciplinary research on regional integration. The establishing of a network linking ACP researchers allowed for increased exchange among academics working on similar topics. The seminars improved the capacity of ACP HEIs to conduct research, and provided researchers with the adequate methodological tools to undertake comparative research on regional integration. Mobility of research staff ensured optimal usage of the available expertise from each member institution and favoured the mutual enrichment of the network members. A knowledge database was established to resolve the problem of access to information and facilitate the exchange of ideas and the dissemination of research results.

The NETRIS project has demonstrated that the study of regional integration, especially comparative studies that examine the phenomenon of regional integration across different regions and academic disciplines, is at an early stage in ACP, although of growing interest. In response to demonstrable gaps in the ability of isolated and financially constrained ACP researchers to enjoy the benefits of academic networks enjoyed by their more developed peers, the project has helped to broaden the knowledge of HEI participants on the different methodological approaches, disciplinary dimensions and contexts of regional integration in different ACP regions.

The NETRIS project was unquestionably a very ambitious endeavour, both in terms of its scope and objectives. The project aimed at bringing together these carefully selected numbers of HEIs from three different regions of the globe that face fundamentally different realities and with marked differences in research cultures and priorities in spite of their shared belonging to the ACP group. Hence the enormous challenge of dealing with a multiplicity of actors, disaggregating differences in realities and contexts and how they impact on the realization of project goals and objectives.

Comparative Regionalisms for Development in the 21st Century is a book that takes stock of the similarities and challenges with regional integration processes in the ACP regions. It builds upon contributions from the different NETRIS partners and associates. Indeed, the NETRIS activities have reflected important issues, such as:

1. Governance and political leadership forces as determinants to regional integration processes; constraints deriving from continental and subcontinental/ regional initiatives, as well as constraints and obstacles to provide the regional level an effective 'legitimization' process;
2. Fixing objectives, priorities and a sequence based on the feasibility of each step to be taken in economic and trade integration, such as: improvement of data and information, infrastructure, trade facilitation, integration of service markets and related obstacles; mobility of factors of production, effective dispute settlement mechanisms, community financing of solidarity mechanisms; rationalization and financing of regional institutions;
3. Overlapping and duplication of regional structures in ACP, proliferation of institutions between the continental and regional levels; coordination and coherence between national and regional levels: what efforts are needed to rationalize the structures?;
4. Involvement of civil society, political parties, social actors in regional integration process in ACP; obstacles to remove from a top-down approach, seeking a collective support and involvement to regional integration processes.

For too long, the study of regional integration has been Euro-centred. This volume shows that there are important insights to draw from the Global South.

Luk Van Langenhove
Director UNU-CRIS

Acknowledgements

As indicated in the Foreword by Luk Van Langenhove, the NETRIS project was a very collaborative affair over two years following a successful application to EDULINK. We gratefully acknowledge NETRIS coordinators, committee members, all participants in and organizers of the series of NETRIS seminars, and the authors and reviewers of this collection: our analytic legacy reflecting insights into comparative regionalisms from the global South.

The NETRIS network could not have existed without the generous support of the ACP-EU Cooperation programme in Higher Education (EDULINK). A programme of the ACP Group of States, with the financial assistance of the European Union. And we are grateful for permissions to publish an article and a chapter in revised form here, such as Chapters 11 and 12, respectively, as indicated. Tim Shaw also thanks the editors of *The Contemporary Caribbean* (Shipra 2013), Priti Singh & Raymond Izarali, for permission to publish a revised, extended version of his original chapter as Chapter 5.

We acknowledge with sadness in particular the valuable contribution of Dr Richard Simson (UKZN, Pietermaritzburg, RSA) who passed away during the compilation of this book, reflected in the dedication on page xix. We further acknowledge his support and active participation in NETRIS seminars.

Emmanuel Fanta, Timothy M. Shaw and Vanessa T. Tang

List of Abbreviations

ACBF	African Capacity Building Foundation
ACC	Arab Cooperation Council
ACCP	Assembly of Caribbean Community Parliamentarians
ACP	African, Caribbean & Pacific countries (associated with the EU)
ACS	Association of Caribbean States
ADB	Asian Development Bank
AEBR	Association of European Border Regions
AEC	African Economic Community
AfDB	African Development Bank
AfT	Aid for Trade
AFTA	ASEAN Free Trade Area
AGOA	African Growth & Opportunity Act (US)
ALBA	Bolivarian Alliance for the Americas
AMU	Arab Maghreb Union
ANZ	Australia and New Zealand
APEC	Asia Pacific Economic Cooperation
ASEAN	Association of Southeast Asian Nations
ASEM	Asia-Europe Meeting
ATT	Arms Trade Treaty
AU	African Union
BASIC	Brazil, South Africa, India, China (re. COP/climate change)
BLNS	Botswana, Lesotho, Namibia, Swaziland
BLS	Botswana, Lesotho, Swaziland
BRIC	Brazil, Russia, India, China
BRICS	Brazil, Russia, India, China, South Africa
CAADP	Comprehensive Africa Agriculture Development Programme
CARICOM	Caribbean Community
CDB	Caribbean Development Bank
CELAC	Community of Latin American & Caribbean States
CEMAC	Central African Economic & Monetary Community
CEN-SAD	Community of Sahel-Saharan States
CEPGL	Economic Community of the Great Lakes Countries
CIMA	Conférence Interafricaine des Marchés de l'Assurance
CMI	Chiang Mai Initiative

CoE	Council of Europe
COMESA	Common Market for Eastern & Southern Africa
COP	Conference of the Parties (re. climate change)
CSO	civil society organization
CSR	corporate social responsibility
CUFTA	Canada-US Free Trade Agreement
DAC	Development Assistance Committee (of the OECD)
DBSA	Development Bank of Southern Africa
DfID	Department for International Cooperation (UK)
DRC	Democratic Republic of the Congo
EAC	East African Community
EAEG	East Asia Economic Group
EACSO	East African Common Services Organisation
EALA	East African Legislative Assembly
EAP	East Asia & Pacific
ECCAS	Economic Community of Central African States
ECDPM	European Centre for Development Policy Management
ECOMOG	ECOWAS Monitoring Group
ECOWAS	Economic Community of West African States
EITI	Extractive Industries Transparency Initiative
EMU	European Monetary Union
EP	European Parliament
EPA	Economic Partnership Agreement (with the EU)
EPADP	EPA Development Programme
EU	European Union (of 27 countries)
FAO	Food & Agriculture Organization
FBOs	faith-based organizations
FOCAC	Forum on China-Africa Cooperation
FTA	free trade agreement/area
FTAA	Free Trade Area of the Americas
G8	Group of Eight
G20	Group of Twenty
GATT	General Agreement on Tariffs & Trade
GCC	Gulf Cooperation Council
GEF	Global Environmental Facility (World Bank)
GIGA	German Institute of Global & Area Studies
GLR	Great Lakes Region
GSP	Generalized System of Preference
GT	Growth Triangle
IBRD	World Bank
IBSA	India, Brazil & South Africa
ICC	International Criminal Court
ICT	information and communications technology

IDB	Inter-American Development Bank
IGAD	Inter-Governmental Authority for Development
IMF	International Monetary Fund
INGOs	international NGOs
IPCC	Inter-governmental Panel on Climate Change
IPE	international political economy
IPI	International Parliamentary Institution
JPA	Joint Parliamentary Assembly (ACP-EU)
LAS	League of Arab States/Arab League
LDCs	least developed countries
LPA	Lagos Plan of Action
MDC	Maputo Development Corridor
MDGs	Millennium Development Goals (UN system)
MERCOSUR	Common Market of the South
MFN	most favoured nation
MNCs	multinational corporations
NADBank	North American Development Bank
NAFTA	North American Free Trade Agreement
NATO	North Atlantic Treaty Organization
NEPAD	New Partnership for Africa's Development
NETRIS	Network of Regional Integration Studies
NGOs	non-governmental organizations
NSC	North-South Corridor
OAS	Organization of American States
OAU	Organization of African Unity
ODA	Official Development Assistance (in OECD)
OECD	Organization for Economic Cooperation & Development
OECS	Organization of Eastern Caribbean States
OHADA	Organisation pour l'Harmonisation en Afrique du Droit des Affaires
PAP	Pan African Parliament
PICS	Pacific Island Countries
PIIGS	Portugal, Ireland, Italy, Greece & Spain (in Eurozone)
PTA	preferential trade agreement
RAFT	Regional Aid for Trade
RECs	regional economic communities
SA	South Africa
SAARC	South Asian Association for Regional Cooperation
SACU	Southern African Customs Union
SADC	Southern African Development Community
SALW	small arms and light weapons
SCO	Shanghai Cooperation Organization
SICA	Central American Integration System

SSA	Sub-Saharan Africa
TDCA	Trade, Development & Cooperation Agreement (EU-SA)
TOC	transnational organized crime
TPP	Trans-Pacific Partnership
TRALAC	Trade Law Centre for Southern Africa
UAE	United Arab Emirates
UDEAC	Union Douanière et Economique d'Afrique Centrale
UEMOA	Union Economique et Monétaire Ouest-Africaine
UK	United Kingdom
UN	United Nations
UNASUR	Union of South American States
UNCTAD	UN Conference on Trade & Development
UNECA	UN Economic Commission for Africa
UNECLA	UN Economic Commission for Latin America & the Caribbean
UNESCAP	UN Economic & Social Commission for Asia & the Pacific
UNU-CRIS	UNU Institute for Comparative Regional Integration Studies
US	United States of America
WAEMU	West African Economic and Monetary Union
WEF	World Economic Forum
WFS	World Food Summit
WSF	World Social Forum
WTO	World Trade Organization

This book is dedicated to the memory of the late Richard Simson (1959-2012), a selfless humanist, who apprehended the complexities and concerns of the world economy with compassion, wit and dazzling insight.

Introduction

Comparative Regionalisms for Development in the 21st Century: Insights from the Global South

Timothy M. Shaw and Emmanuel Fanta

> [T]he rise of emerging societies is a major turn in globalization and holds significant emancipatory potential. North-South relations have been dominant for 200 years and now an East-South turn is taking shape. The 2008 economic crisis is part of a global rebalancing process. (Pieterse 2011: 22)

> Regions cut across every dimension of the study of world politics: for their proponents, they even constitute the study of IR. (Fawn 2009: 5)

> For a long period the study of regions and regional orders occupied a small if not insignificant place in IR theory and scholarship. Now we have [...] books which argue that regions are central to our understanding of world politics. (Acharya 2007: 629)

The global 'financial' crisis at the turn of the decade has accelerated changes in the relative standing of major regions: as the North Atlantic has faced a series of shocks, the Global South has been relatively ebullient and unscathed. Indeed, as both the US and Eurozone economies have confronted a series of setbacks so Asia, Latin America and even Africa have picked up the slack. While the North struggles to find its second breath in the aftermath of the crisis, the economies of the South have been able to maintain high levels of growth. This resilience of the Global South therefore questions whether we are witnessing an evolution from 'varieties of regions' towards regional rebalancing or even global restructuring.

The poorest continent in the Global South, Africa, faces an unanticipated 'second chance' at the start of the second decade of the 21st century (www.mckinsey.com). The unprecedented economic growth Africa has witnessed in the first decade of this century, which is also due to China's role in the region, has changed the perspective and opened up new opportunities in terms of development. And if the trend continues in the years to come, we may ask how many 'developmental' (UNECA 2011) versus 'fragile' or conflict-affected states (World Bank 2011) will there be in Africa by 2020. The interrelated prospects for both BRICs – now BRICS with the inclusion of South Africa as the fifth member – and the continent as parts of the Global South are being transformed by the current financial crisis centred in the US, EU and Japan (Hanson, Kararach and Shaw 2012). The setting up of the G20 in replacement of the G8 in fact reflects the recognition that economies from the Global South have an important role to play in the governance of world economic affairs. And as the South expands while the North contracts, will there be a rebalancing towards S-N, even E-S (Pieterse 2011), relations in future? The EU of 27 now includes the PIIGS, some of which have been bailed out by the IMF and have had to adopt austerity measures not so different from the structural adjustment programmes that were implemented in Africa. And the South has even been called upon to help in resolving the crisis in the North, whether it was China bailing out the EU economies (Financial Times 2011a) or Angola promising to increase its investment in crisis-affected Portugal (Financial Times 2011b).

Comparative Regionalisms at the Start of the 21st Century

Given the continuing problems of the North, both North Atlantic and North Pacific, at the start of the new millennium, regional development in the Global South is of increasing importance for sustainable global development. In addition to dynamic and heterogeneous varieties of private/transnational governance (Bevir 2011, Held and Hale 2011) (elaborated below), 'new regionalisms' at several levels, whether more formal or informal (elaborated below), serve as catalysts for the renaissance of both the African continent and the Global South by advancing their capacity to transcend fragility (ACBF 2011). To maximize development and security, they also need to advance 'network' or 'public' rather than traditional 'club' diplomacy, involving civil society and private companies as well as states and intergovernmental agencies (Heine 2006). But climate change may yet emerge as the spoiler, hence the importance of COP17 in Durban where the BRICS' related BASIC group was even more active and efficacious than at COP15 and 16.

Informed by the 2010 McKinsey report on Africa and the BRICS, especially China and India, *The Economist* at the start of the new decade asserted that

> Over the next five years…the average African economy will outpace its Asian counterpart […] Africa's economy will grow at an average annual rate of 7% over the next 20 years, slightly faster than China's.
>
> [A]frica's changing fortunes have largely been driven by China's surging demand […] but other factors have also counted.
>
> [W]ithout reforms, Africa will not be able to sustain faster growth. But its lion economies are earning a place alongside Asia's tigers. (Economist 2011: 73)

Acknowledging contemporary international relations (Cornelissen, Cheru and Shaw 2011, Dunn and Shaw 2001) /development studies perspectives in particular, this overview identifies emerging opportunities as well as challenges for the Global South at the start of the second decade of the 21st century. It especially focuses on whether the emergence of the BRICS/'second world' (Khanna 2009) presents unanticipated possibilities or threats to a heterogeneous group of countries, which includes burgeoning 'developmental' as well as 'fragile' or 'failed' states (ACBF 2011).

Given the varieties of capitalisms reflected in the varieties of regionalisms, we juxtapose literatures on conflict, development, IR, IPE, regionalisms etc (cf below). Increasingly, these are leading towards regional rebalancing/restructuring (Clark and Hoque 2012). Such comparative analysis of regionalisms has been advanced in the 21st century by the work of CSGR at Warwick (www.csgr.org), UNU-CRIS in Bruges (www.cris.unu.edu) and the German Institute of Global and Area Studies (www.giga-hamburg.de), facilitated by EU grants such as GARNET (www.garnet-eu.org), NETRIS (www.netris-acp.org) and now GR:EEN, also at Warwick, on Europe's Role in the Emerging Global Order (http://www2.warwick.ac.uk/fac/soc/csgr/green/).

This overview has four interrelated parts which stake out paths to a brighter future for both the African continent and Global South centred on regional innovations, including myriad diasporas; i.e. burgeoning 'transnational' relations (Brown 2012). First we explore the transformation taking place in regard to the financing of development in the Global South and the apparition of new players in the field. Secondly, the emergence of 'New Regionalisms' in the South and the usefulness of these experience for comparative studies of regional relationship will be explicated. We then turn our attention to the new forms of transnational governance that are emerging and the role that a novelty of actors play in this 'new multilateralism'. And finally, fourthly, we look into the implications of this trio of novel directions and players for our analyses and policies, for state and non-state, and for conflict, development, economic, environmental, IR (Tickner and Waever 2009) and IPE (Phillips and Weaver 2010) studies, etc.

Symptomatic of a changing global context, we turn first to novel forms of investment in the Global South, particularly in the least-developed countries (LLDCs) and continents, especially sources in the South itself.

Varieties of Innovative Sources of Finance

Even before the end-decade 'global' financial crisis, there was a looming gap in funding for African and other LLDCs' development if they are to even aspire to realizing the MDGs in 2015. In response to such deficiencies as well as the slowness of the 'Monterrey Consensus' to impact ODA effectiveness – from Accra to Paris and Busan – France animated a 'Leading Group' of states (www.leadinggroup.org) to suggest other means to advance global public goods and identify new financial sources for development. In association with major INGOs in a 'Forum on the Future of Aid' (www.futureofaid.net), a 'Taskforce on

International Financial Transactions and Development' (www.innovativefinance-oslo.no) came to advance the notion of 'taxation for the governing of globalization' at decade's end.

Among the dozen or so global levies, mainly on ubiquitous financial flows, proposed by the taskforce to advance global public goods were:

1. Global Solidarity Fund (GSF) for global public goods;
2. Currency Transaction Tax (CTT) (along the lines of the original Tobin Tax) (www.nigd.org/ctt);
3. airline ticket levy already being implemented by some governments in the North like France, Spain and Korea;
4. carbon taxes/trading (www.carbontax.org), a not uncontroversial set of measures encouraged by the UN IPCC and related to the Clean Development Mechanism (CDM) (www.cdm.unfccc.int);
5. climate change funds such as IBRD Global Environmental Facility (GEF) and UN agencies' Reducing Emissions from Deforestation and Forest Degradation in Developing Countries (REDD) (www.un-redd.org);
6. Digital Solidarity Fund (DSF) established in Geneva (www.dsf-fsn.org);
7. UNITAID, an international drug purchase facility to advance access to ATMs, now with broad inter- and non-state participation (www.unitaid.eu);
8. controls on money-laundering encouraged by the OECD and G8 – capital flight pa now some US$ 500 billion – including FATF/CFATF on OFCs over two decades (www.fatf-gafi.org) leading to PWYP and EITI; and
9. remittance taxes on N-S flows which have blossomed to over US$ 300 billion pa, larger than ODA for some states like Nigeria or Lesotho.

ODA from the OECD is of declining importance or attraction while at the same time donors from the Gulf states and BRICS have emerged and offer a new and attractive source of ODA (Kragelund 2011), the latter reflected in the Forum on China-Africa Cooperation (FOCAC) (Taylor 2011) and the India-Africa Forum Summit (Mawdsley and McCann 2011). New non-state actors also increasingly become part of the picture including faith-based organizations (FBOs) and private foundations. In fact, new private foundations have emerged around the turn of the century to parallel established ones like Carnegie, Ford and Rockefeller, notably the Gates Foundation (www.gatesfoundation.org) but now also the Blair (www.tonyblairfaithfoundation.org), Clinton (www.clintonfoundation.org) and Ibrahim Foundations (www.moibrahimfoundation.org). Similarly, FBOs increasingly span many religions, particularly the more pragmatic, mainstream dominations (e.g. Catholic Relief Services (www.crs.org), Islamic Relief (www.islamic-relief,com), Lutheran World Relief (www.lwr.org) and World Vision (www.worldvision.org)). With new as well as established private foundations, they increasingly partner with international organizations such as, for example, the Global Alliance for Vaccines and Immunization (GAVI) (www.gavialliance.org) (Rushton and Williams 2011).

Further examples of such novel forms of transnational global governance are found below.

But getting from conceptualization to policies/politics is problematic, which is where varieties of regionalisms come in to engage in such public, open diplomacy. Hence the imperative of animating a timely, extensive coalition to redefine and revive the direction of Africa and other LLDCs at the turn of the decade as suggested below.

Varieties of 'New Regionalisms'

The revived, redefined East African Community is emblematic of some of the new dynamics guiding regionalism in the Global South: five rather than the initial trio of members (and onto a half-dozen with South Sudan in 2012), with innovative civil society, parliamentary and security dimensions, qualifying as an instance of 'new regionalisms' (Shaw, Grant and Cornelissen 2012). Non-state actors, whether they are civil society, INGOs or MNCs, increasingly play a part in this regard and allow for the setting up of heterogeneous coalitions with the aim of regional development. In the field of security as well, these new actors play a role, such as the civil society organizations participating in the early warning mechanisms of ECOWAS and IGAD or the private military companies providing support to AU's 'green helmets'. And as security is increasingly privatized, so such coalitions become ever more problematic. This is also the case in regard to energy and mineral extraction and supply chains as their products attract the attention of transnational as well as local criminal networks. But these transnational organized networks and the trafficking of drugs and arms also reflects the increase of trade in legal goods and services. In fact, one of the greatest challenges of the dawning century will be how the emerging economies of the Global South feature in the regional and global arenas.

> Over the past decade six of the world's fastest-growing countries were African. In eight of the past ten years, Africa has grown faster than East Asia, including Japan. Even allowing for the knock-on effects of the northern hemisphere's slow-down, the IMF expects Africa to grow by 6% this year and nearly 6% in 2012, about the same as Asia. (The Economist 2011c: 15)

African political economies are now located in second, third and fourth worlds: will they identify with the G20 and/or the G192 (G193 now that South Sudan is independent?) and/or BRICS, now including RSA? Half of the dozen fastest-growing countries identified in *The Economist*'s *World in 2011* and *2012* are African (Economist 2010a and 2011b): from Ghana to Liberia, Ethiopia to Niger by contrast to the last two decades of the last century when only Uganda so ranked. The CGD in DC now suggests that 17 African countries are 'leading the way' (Radelet 2010); McKinsey (2010) lauds the continent's 'lion kings' and the BCG (2010) has identified 40 African corporations as global 'challengers'. Now arguably qualifying for the adjective/accolade 'miracle' (Dorr, Lund and Roxborough 2010) at the start of its second half-centenary, can Africa grow through the next decade given its quite stellar performance in the first decade (McKinsey 2010, UNECA 2011)? Such a welcome prospect poses challenges for public policy/diplomacy (Hanson, Kararach and Shaw 2012): can Africa bring its non-state – civil society and private sector – as well as state resources to bear in focused and sustained/cumulative inclusive 'new' 'network' rather than traditional exclusive 'club' diplomacy (Heine 2006)?

As suggested in the final section below, this is the welcome challenge or opportunity facing the Global South at the start of their second 50-year period. Have they learned and can they adapt after their first half-century given the significantly transformed global context at the turn of the decade: divergent regional incidences of and responses to the 'global' financial crisis with the Global South being much less negatively impacted than the established trans-Atlantic core in both 'old' and 'new' worlds (Pieterse 2011)?

Correspondingly and encouraged by growing recognition of climate change – NB the development of IBSA (Alden and Vieira 2011) into BASIC around COP 15 in Copenhagen at the end of 2009 leading to a significant role at COP 17 in Durban at the end of 2011 – river basins in the Global South are beginning to receive exponential attention as centres of biodiversity, energy, resources, food and water as well as conflict (Schnurr and Swatuk 2012): Congo (www.fauna-flora.org), Zambezi, Mekong, Aral sea etc. And increasingly ad hoc regional institutions are set up to deal with these issues; the Nile Basin Initiative (www.nilebasin.org) and Dialogue are arguably the most advanced to date. In parallel to these river valley organizations, other cross-border and less formal forms of micro-regions coexist. The Maputo Corridor has advanced growth in Southern Mozambique as well as the eastern Witwatersrand, reinforcing the cross-border dimensions of the Lesotho highlands water project for electricity and water (www.lhwp.org.ls); the latter was informed by the only global commission to be based outside the North in Cape Town (Dingwerth 2008). And while EPZs are associated with Asia and gas pipelines with Central Europe, development corridors and peace-parks are largely a function of Southern Africa's distinctive political economy.

The pattern of inter-regional relationships (Fawn 2009) is in flux. From the traditional North-South dependencies, the world is evolving towards a new axis that gives a greater role to the South, whether it evolves around new powerhouses like China and India or signifies a rapprochement between Latin America and the Arab World (Vagni 2009). Symbolically, Africa's regions' reluctance to sign EPAs with the EU at the turn of the decade, despite a mix of pressures and incentives, may mark a turning point as global rebalancing continues: Europe of the Eurozone crisis around the PIIGS and Asia of the BRICS transforms policy options and calculations for the continent as suggested in Cheru and Obi (2010). The tone of annual African-China FOCAC palavers (Taylor 2011) can be contrasted to that at the third EU-Africa summit in Tunis in November 2010.

And now South Africa is one of the five BRICS, raising questions not only about whether they can become a bloc (Shaw 2010) but also whether they are better cast as emerging powers rather than emerging economies or emerging markets. Certainly for Nel and Nolte (2010), South Africa is a regional power rather than an emerging economy, let alone emerging society. But is its recognition and elevation in the BRICS with or without the support of its region, whether more narrowly (SACU/SADC) or broadly (SSA) defined (Alden and Vieira 2011)? As Pieterse asks: emerging powers, emerging markets, emerging economies and/or emerging societies (Pieterse and Rehbin 2009 1-3)? And as MNCs, now from China and India as well as South Africa (hence the transition from IBSA to BRICS), have increased their investments in energy and minerals, franchises and shopping malls, so their logistics and supply chains have come to define their own regional networks (Modi 2011).

And all these dynamics impact differently on the various regions of the Global South, transforming them while also being transformed by them.

Africa

At the dawn of the 21st century, the African continent is undergoing profound socio-political, economic but also cultural changes, all of which are also reflected in the various existing and emerging processes of regionalism. First of all, the continent has witnessed a revival of regionalism since 1990 with the creation of new regional institutions and relationships that include innovative civil society, parliamentary and security dimensions, qualifying as an instance of 'new regionalisms' (Shaw, Grant and Cornelissen 2012). And regionalisms on the continent have come to cover the spectrum of levels – macro/meso/micro (Soderbaum and Taylor 2008) – and sectors – civil society, corporate networks, ecology, energy, security etc, while also incorporating a range of actors in heterogeneous coalitions, from INGOs to MNCs.

The continent's pattern of inter-regional relationships (Fawn 2009) is also in flux, from classic, inherited North-South dependencies towards a novel South-East axis around China and India but also Japan, Korea and the Gulf states (Modi 2011). This global rebalancing is also taking place within Africa itself with the emergence of South Africa as the latest country to join the BRICs and whose economic and political power also affects regionalism in the continent. Other transformation also impacts on the regional processes. Among others, exponential infrastructural development will further new regionalisms on the continent in the second decade of the 21st century, symbolized by the mobile-phone revolution and the roles of MTN and Airtel. The circulation of medias and culture facilitated by new technologies also means that ideas and fashion trends are circulating much faster within the region but also with the diasporas. This is notably reflected in the spread and success of Nollywood films and Ivorian *Coupé Décalé* music, but also in the fact that the African Cup now plays on mainstream TV in the Global North.

Reflective of its more than 50 states, 14 of which are landlocked, now including South Sudan, the largest percentage in the world, Africa has been the leading region in the South to advance regional innovations and institutions. In the initial, one-party nationalist period, reflective of jealousy surrounding newly realized independence, these were typically 'old' intergovernmental arrangements. But in the post-bipolar era, such regionalisms became less exclusively state and economic and more inclusive around emerging issues like ecology, energy, security, water etc (Shaw, Grant and Cornelissen 2011). Nevertheless, because of overlapping memberships and mandates and insufficient resources, macro- to micro-regionalisms have insufficient capacity, particularly in terms of ICT (ACBF 2008). As Wolfe Braude (2008: 7) argues, despite efforts at 'Joining Up Africa' and Trilateral FTA between COMESA, EAC and SADCC at the start of the second decade:

> The overlap of membership between regional integration arrangements in the wider southern and eastern African region is without parallel anywhere else in the world [...] seven regional economic communities are effectively operating in parallel within the region (SADC, COMESA, EAC, SACU, IGAD, ECCAS and CEPGL).

Caribbean

> What constitutes the Caribbean? [...] Among scholars, 'the Caribbean' is a socio-historical category [...] it embraces the islands and parts of the adjoining mainland and may be extended to include the Caribbean Diaspora overseas. As one scholar observes, there are many Caribbeans.
>
> In short, the definition of the Caribbean might be based on language and identity, geography, history and culture, geopolitics, geoeconomics, or organization. (Girvan 2005: 304)

The Caribbean, however defined, consists of many small states; most of which, but not all, are independent. So it has long been the focus of a series of regional experiments by both colonial and independent authorities along with international agencies, both global and hemispheric, like the UN and OAS (Bishop 2012); but early and late non-state actors have also defined their Caribbeans, from pirates to drug lords, airlines to internet providers, sports like cricket and higher educational institutions like UWI. Its most extensive and inclusive institution is the ACS with CARICOM being meso- and OECS micro-level. But these now compete with Venezuela's ALBA initiative. CARIOFORUM (CARICOM plus DR) is the only region thus far to sign an EPA with the EU, albeit with marginal impact to date.

The Caribbean economies are several, impacting formal and informal regionalisms: large and smaller scale, diasporic and illegal. Transnational relations are ubiquitous, including offshore financial centres along with money-laundering; in theory, these are regulated by the regional regulatory agency: the

Caribbean Financial Action Task Force (CFATF) (www.cfatf-gafic.org), a branch of the G20-sanctioned FATF. The diasporic economy stretches from familial – communications including phone/text, cable television and net/Skype – and cultural – e.g. Carnival travel and accommodation, music, costumes, cuisine etc – to illegal – TOC around drugs and guns. So CARICOM now has an agency based in TandT dedicated to treating crime and gangs: IMPACS (www.caricomimpacs.org). Alejandra Bronfman (2007: 5-6) presents a compelling perspective:

> [...] the circulation of commodities is one of the unifying aspects of Caribbean history [...] Globalization has not just happened to the Caribbean, the Caribbean has participated in the making of globalization [...] four things circulate: people, capital, drugs and information.

Latin America

> Despite all the attention placed on globalization and its processes, regional integration mechanisms continue to hold a pivotal position in world affairs [...] Although the debates surrounding European approaches and concepts maintain a privileged position, various located in other regional projects deserve closer attention. This requirement is no more apparent than in the Americas where the process of regionalization has a long history and is currently being increasingly complex, contested and fluid.
>
> In terms of intensity, inter-American regional projects bring out the contrast between the familiar and novel components. (Mace, Cooper and Shaw 2010: 1)

With the demise of the dream of an ambitious neo-liberal free-trade zone for the western hemisphere (FTAA) in the middle of the first decade of the 21st century, several post-Mercosur alternative regional schema have been proposed by emerging economies (and emerging powers?) like Brazil. The status of the OAS (Herz 2011) is increasingly problematic because of the historic presence as well as contemporary decline of the US. And the ambitions of NAFTA are under threat from the 'war' around drugs, gangs and migrants on the Mexico-US border (Morales 2011). Aside from the established Mercosur and Chavez's ALBA, reflective of its decade-old BRICS' status, Brazil has animated UNASUR, a hemispheric grouping without the two so-called 'gringo' countries to the North (Mace, Cooper and Shaw 2010).

Brazil as an emerging economy/power is impacting the hemisphere; not just the Southern cone with its growth trajectory enhanced by Chinese demand which has transformed large-scale agriculture in both Argentina and Brazil. Its global connections and ambitions are symbolized by IBSA – a trilateral, largely interstate network amongst the democracies of the BRICS and BASIC, which has been strengthened between COP 15 and COP 17 in RSA (Alden and Vieira 2011). Its larger companies are increasingly global players: Embraer, InBev with Belgium's Interbrew, Petrobras, Vale etc (www.bcg.com). And in terms of global civil society,

Porto Alegre is home to the WSF (www.forumsocialmundial.org.br). As the region celebrated its bicentennial in 2010, *The Economist* (2010b: 13) suggested that:

> [...] something remarkable is happening in Latin America. In the five years to 2008 the region's economies grew at an annual average rate of 5.5%. While Latin American squabbling politicians blather on about integration, the region's businesses are quietly getting on with the job – witness the emerging cohorts of *multilatinas*...
>
> Two things lie behind Latin America's renaissance. The first is the appetite of China and India for raw materials with which the continent is richly endowed. But the second is the improvement in economic management.

Asia(s): Central and South to South-east and East

> Asian institutions, relatively new on the international stage, have claimed uniqueness in terms of their decision-making norms and approach to socialization, but many have questioned their effectiveness in managing security dilemmas and the economic vulnerabilities of their members. (Acharya and Johnston 2007: 1)

Regionalisms in Asia are both conflictual/competitive as well as cooperative/consensual, reflecting the varieties of capitalisms in, say, China (Chu 2010) and India (Mukherjee Reed 2003). They centre on the regions' trio of BRICS and several developmental states like South Korea and Singapore, and reflect the opportunities as well as costs of a mix of globalizations and regionalisms: from 'Asian' crisis at the end of the last century (Robertson 2008) to Asia saving the global economy in the new one. They span the macro- to micro-level divide, with the late 20th-century Asia Pacific Economic Cooperation (APEC) (www.apec.org) being superseded in the current decade by the proposed Trans-Pacific Partnership (TPP).

Distinctive features:

1. Chinese and Indian dominance in the Shanghai Cooperation Organization (SCO) and South Asian Association for Regional Cooperation (SAARC), respectively;
2. BRICS affiliated to ASEAN (e.g. APT) and other groupings of smaller economies;
3. Asian contribution of regional growth 'triangles' to comparative regionalisms;
4. proliferation of FTAs in Asia, especially around China (Solis, Stallings and Katada 2009);
5. regional tensions around the South China Sea and Mekong Valley; and
6. East Asia's centrality to global container supply chains and increasingly to air-freight.

With the continuing difficulties of the EU and the Eurozone, Asian regionalisms are of increasingly global significance, especially as China and India continue to increase their shares of global trade, particularly manufactured exports and imports of raw materials. In short, the balance in the inter-regional relationship between Asia and Europe has shifted in favour of the former, both shorter and longer term (Gaens 2008 and 2012). Since 2000, Acharya *et al.* (2007 and 2009) have asserted the important contributions out of Asia's regionalism(s) and IR/IPE, advocating a return away from new regionalisms towards various institutional forms:

> We seek to restore interest in the institutional features of regionalism which has lagged due to the popularity of the 'new regionalism' literature which has little interest in the design features of regional institutions. At the same time, it is especially important that this renewed interest in institutionalization extends the range of analysis beyond the rationalist approach to institutional design to include constructivist and other approaches [...] to throw critical light on whether the claims of uniqueness and exceptionalism, found especially in the case of European and Asian institutions, hold up to scrutiny. (Acharya and Johnston 2007: 30-31)

Varieties of 'Transnational' Governance

In a post-bipolar era, the mix of fragile/failed states (ACBF 2011), proliferating 'global' issues and pressures for democratization, has generated some innovative forms of 'transnational' (Bevir 2011, Brown 2012) or 'private' (Dingwerth 2008, Held and Hale 2011) governance around both the developed countries and the Global South. Such new forms of governance are symbolized by the early Ottawa and Kimberley Processes, now augmented by the FCS/MCS, REDD and EITI. These may not yet be authoritative and their scope still fails to reach continuing scourges like SALW, but they are changing the governance landscape. Moreover, these new forms of multilateralisms and 'transnational' governance combine private companies with states and other non-state actors and may help overcome some hurdles from 'traditional' forms of multilateralisms such as coalitions over SALW and children/women's security being stalled due to US vetoes. When combined with innovative sources of finance, they begin to transform the regional policy terrain. They have served to encourage interstate international law towards the recognition of varieties of global governance, which may reflect varieties of sources of pressures which increasingly come from the Global South.

Part of the unwelcome legacy of the Cold War was fields of landmines. The comprehensive, heterogeneous International Campaign to Ban Landmines (www.icbl.org) led to the Ottawa Process, advanced by the 'celebrity diplomacy' of Princess Diana. By contrast, the subsequent Kimberley Process on conflict diamonds (www.kimberleyprocess.com) resulted from animation by a major and minor NGO: Global Witness (London) and Partnership Africa Canada (Ottawa), respectively. It has since spawned the Diamond Development Initiative to improve artisanal working conditions in the mines through formalization of labour (www.ddiglobal.org), a process that the World Bank has also encouraged through its network for Communities, Artisanal and Small-scale Mining Initiative (CACM) (www.artisanalmining.org).

More recent, comprehensive innovations include the industry-supported Forestry Certification Scheme (FCS) (www.fscus.org) and G8-supported Extractive Industries Transparency Initiative (EITI) (www.eiti.org), the latter being particularly timely given the dangers of 'resource curse' and windfall profits around BRICs' (if not BRICS') demand for energy and minerals. Meanwhile, despite the US constitution, an Arms Trade Treaty (ATT) is slowly being negotiated through the UN along with ISO 26 000 on CSR (www.iso.org). And UN Programmes of Action (PoA) such as the decade-old Resolution 1325 on women, peace and security and Resolution 1540 on SALW do at least serve to keep sensitive issues on the agenda. But despite the scourges of small arms and of violence against women and children, progress on SALW and child soldiers etc remains problematic, notwithstanding advocacy through the International Action Network Against Gun Violence (www.iansa.org). Each of these governance processes includes African regional programmes, including diasporas.

Finally, the Global South might follow Central America in advancing beyond not only national security but also human security, towards 'citizen security' (World Bank 2011). This contemporary notion seeks to combine freedom from needs/want with issues around SALW: how to keep citizens both safe and developing in sustainable ways. UNDP (2012) in the Caribbean and Central America at the turn of the decade began to explore such prospects in its regional human development research and reporting. Meanwhile, in Africa the ECOWAS has expressed its willingness to transform itself into the ECOWAS of the people.

Onto Varieties of Innovative Analyses/Policies?

> The G20 is without question the new game in town in respect of global governance.
>
> [A]ll 192 countries in the current world system have concerns about and perspectives on contemporary global governance after the financial crisis of 2008-2009, and are seeking to participate in its resolution in a variety of ways and in a number of different diplomatic and institutional arenas.
>
> [G]lobal governance – around whatever set of issues – will become even more complicated as more and more countries come to recognize the need to pursue developmental diplomacy as effectively as they can on the global stage. (Payne 2010: 729, 738 and 740)

The shake-up in the established hierarchy of global regions (Shaw, Grant and Cornelissen 2012) along with burgeoning varieties of finance, governance and regionalisms pose challenges to public policy in and for the Global South and Africa in particular (Hanson, Kararach and Shaw 2012). The analysis of these regionalisms also brings to light dynamics that are applicable to other parts of the world, and authors like Alex Warleigh-Lack *et al.* (2011) have begun to recognize the relevance of such new regional relationships for comparative studies of the EU, especially as it confronts its own financial crisis around the Euro. They also present challenges to the study of Africa (Cornelissen, Cheru and Shaw 2012) and related analyses of the Global South as they demand 'innovative' perspectives and policies that encompass both state and non-state; i.e. civil societies, private companies, media etc. As Douglas Lemke (2003: 117) cautioned:

> [...] political power is exercised by a variety of states and non-state actors in Africa. Because standard international relations research theorises about and collects data only for official states, much of Africa's international relations are left out.

Finally, we suggest at least some of the implications of comparative regionalisms for established approaches/disciplines/policies:

1. *development studies* – proliferation of issues and institutions, especially around Asian drivers, developmental and fragile/failed states, second world etc, increasingly the 'rest' (Clark and Hoque 2012);
2. *emerging economies/markets/powers/societies/states* – how compatible/ competitive these are as reflections of divergent assumptions/'disciplines'/ genres (Pieterse and Rehbein 2009);
3. *environmental studies* – impacts of climate change on different regions onto resource wars around water and land as well as energy and minerals (Schnurr and Swatuk 2012);
4. *gender studies* – gender dimensions of regional rebalancing/restructuring, especially given gender imbalances in China and India with profound implications for their respective regions;
5. *global governance/multilateralisms* – beyond interstate 'law' to global/ transnational coalitions around blood diamonds and landmines (Kimberley and Ottawa Processes), fisheries and forestry certification, initiatives like EITI etc, yet minimal momentum around, say, child soldiers or small arms (Brown 2012, Dingwerth 2008);
6. *global studies* – homogeneous actors to heterogeneous networks leading, for example, to Global Redesign Initiative (RDI) of the WEF (www.weforum.org);
7. *international political economy* – 'varieties of capitalisms'/corporations reaching beyond American existential and intellectual hegemony (Phillips and Weaver 2010);
8. *international relations* – recognition of plurality as well as diversity of states – developmental as well as fragile or failed – and analyses, hence

salience of developmental or network diplomacy (Tickner and Waever 2009);

9. *security studies* – treating both 'old and 'new' security issues along with diverse forms of privatization of security and civil-military relations.

The Global South at the turn of the second decade of the 21st century is at a crossroads in terms of growth, development, governance, regionalisms, sustainability etc: can it seize its second chance and transcend its somewhat lacklustre first half-century? In turn, can African and other regions advance inclusive public or network diplomacy – what Tony Payne (2010) suggests is 'development diplomacy' – of non-state as well as state actors?

References

ACBF. 2008. *A Survey of the Capacity Needs of Africa's Regional Economic Communities.* Harare: ACBF.

ACBF. 2011. *Africa Capacity Building Indicators 2011: capacity development in fragile states.* Harare: ACBF.

Acharya, A. 2007. Review Article: the emerging regional architecture of world politics. *World Politics*, 59(4), 629-652.

Acharya, A. 2009. *Whose Ideas Matter? Agency and power in Asian regionalism.* Ithaca: Cornell University Press.

Acharya, A. and Johnston A.I. 2007. Comparing Regional Institutions: an introduction, in *Crafting Cooperation: regional international institutions in comparative perspective* edited by A. Acharya and A.I. Johnston, Cambridge: Cambridge University Press, 1-31.

Alden, C. and Vieira, M. 2011. IBSA: South-South cooperation and the paradox of regional leadership. *Global Governance*, 17(3), 507-528.

Bevir, M. (ed.) 2011. *Sage Handbook of Governance.* London: Sage.

Bishop, M. 2012. *The Political Economy of Caribbean Development.* London: Palgrave Macmillan, forthcoming.

Braude, W. 2008. *SADC, COMESA and the EAC: conflicting regional and trade agendas, Occasional paper #57*. Midrand: IGD.

Boston Consulting Group. 2010. *The African Challengers: global competitors emerge from the overlooked continent.* Boston: BCG.

Bronfman, A. 2007. *On the Move: the Caribbean since 1989.* Halifax: Fernwood.

Brown, S. (ed.) 2012. *Transnational Transfers and Global Development.* London: Palgrave Macmillan.

Cadman, T. 2011. *Quality and Legitimacy of Global Governance: case lessons from forestry.* London: Palgrave Macmillan.

Cai, K.G. 2010. *The Politics of Economic Regionalism: explaining regional economic integration in East Asia.* London: Palgrave Macmillan.

Cheru, F. and Obi C. (eds.) 2010. *The Rise of China and India in Africa.* London: Zed.

Clark, S. and Hoque S. (eds.) 2012. *What Lies Ahead? Debating the prospects for a 'post-American world'.* Abingdon: Routledge.

Cornelissen, S., Cheru, F. and Shaw T.M. (eds.) 2012. *Africa and International Relations in the Twenty-first Century.* London: Palgrave Macmillan.

Dingwerth, K. 2008. Private Transnational Governance and the Developing World. *International Studies Quarterly*, 52(3): 607-634.

Dorr, N., Lund, S. and Roxborough, C. 2010. The African Miracle. *Foreign Policy*, December 2010: 80-81.

Dunn, K.C. and Shaw T.M. (eds.) 2001. *Africa's Challenge to International Relations Theory.* London: Palgrave.

The Economist. 2010a. *The World in 2010: 25th anniversary edition.* London: The Economist.

The Economist. 2010b. Nobody's Backyard. The Rise of Latin America. *The Economist*, 396(8699), 11 September: 13 and Special Report: 1-18.

The Economist. 2010c. Lights, Camera, Africa. *The Economist*, 397(8713), 18 December: 85-87.

The Economist. 2011a. The Lion Kings? *The Economist*, 398(8715), 8 January: 72-73.

The Economist. 2011b. *The World in 2011.* London: The Economist.

The Economist. 2011c. Africa Rising. *The Economist*, 401(8762), 3 December: 15 and 82-84.

Fawn, R. (ed.) 2009. Special Issue: globalising the regional, regionalising the global. *Review of International Studies*, 35, February: 1-261.

Financial Times. 2011a. China could play key role in EU rescue, *Financial Times* [Online], 27 October 2011, Available at: http://www.ft.com/intl/cms/s/0/7505d210-00ba-11e1-8590-00144feabdc0.html [Accessed 25 January 2012].

Financial Times. 2011b. Portugal appeals to Angola for funds, *Financial Times* [Online], 17 November 2011, Available at: http://www.ft.com/intl/cms/s/0/9c1f123e-1132-11e1-ad22-00144feabdc0.html [Accessed 25 January 2010].

Gaens, B. (ed.) 2008. *Europe-Asia Interregional Relations.* Aldershot: Ashgate.

Gaens, B. 2012. The Rise of Interregionalisms: the case of the EU's relations with East Asia, in *The Ashgate Research Companion to Regionalisms*, edited by T.M. Shaw, J.A. Grant and S. Cornelissen. Aldershot: Ashgate. 69-87.

Gale, F. and Haward, M. 2011. *Global Commodity Governance: state responses to sustainable forest and fisheries certification.* London: Palgrave Macmillan.

Girvan, N. 2005. Reinterpreting the Caribbean, in *The Caribbean Economy: a reader,* edited by D. Pantin. Kingston: Ian Randle. 304-318.

Grant, J.A. and Soderbaum, F. (eds.) 2003. *The New Regionalism in Africa.* Aldershot: Ashgate.

Hanson, K., Kararach, G. and Shaw, T.M. (eds.) 2012. *Rethinking Development Challenges for Public Policy: insights from contemporary Africa.* London: Palgrave MacMillan.

Heine, J. 2006. *On the Manner of Practising the New Diplomacy, Working Paper #11.* Waterloo: CIGI.

Held, D. and Hale, T. (eds.) 2011. *Handbook of Transnational Governance.* Cambridge: Polity.

Herz, M. 2011. *The Organization of American States.* Abingdon: Routledge.

Khagram, S. 2004. *Dams and Development: transnational strategies for water and power.* Ithaca: Cornell University Press.

Khanna, P. 2009. *The Second World: how emerging powers are redefining global competition in the twenty-first century.* New York: Random House.

Kragelund, P. 2011. Back to BASICs? The Rejuvenation of Non-traditional Donors' Development Cooperation with Africa. *Development and Change*, 42(2), 585-607.

Lemke, D. 2003. Review Article: Africa lessons from international relations research. *World Politics*, 56(1), 114-138.

Mace, G., Cooper, A.F. and Shaw T.M. (eds.) 2010. *Inter-American Cooperation at a Crossroads.* London: Palgrave Macmillan.

McKinsey. 2010. *McKinsey on Africa: a continent on the move.* New York: McKinsey.

Mawdsley, E. and McCann, G. (eds.) 2011. *India in Africa: Changing Geographies of Power.* Cape Town: Pambazuka.

Modi, R. (ed.) 2011. *South-South Cooperation: Africa on the centre stage.* London: Palgrave Macmillan.

Morales, I. (ed.) 2011. *National Solutions to Trans-border Problems? The governance of security and risk in post-NAFTA North America.* Farnham: Ashgate.

Nel, P. and Nolte, D. (eds.) 2010. Regional Powers in a Changing Global Order. *Review of International Studies*, 36(4), 877-974.

Payne, A. 2010. How many Gs are there in 'Global Governance' after the Crisis? The perspectives of the 'marginal majority' of the world's states. *International Affairs*, 86(3), 729-740.

Phillips, N. and Weaver, C. (eds.) 2010. *International Political Economy: debating the past, present and future.* Abingdon: Routledge.

Pieterse, J.N. 2011. Global rebalancing: crisis and the East-South turn. *Development and Change*, 42(1): 22-48.

Pieterse, J.N. and Rehbein, B. (eds.) 2009. *Globalization and Emerging Societies: development and inequality.* London: Palgrave Macmillan.

Radelet, S. 2010. *Emerging Africa: how 17 countries are leading the way.* Washington. DC: Center for Global Dialogue.

Ramutsindela, M. 2012. Transfrontier Conservation and the Spaces of Regionalism, in *The Ashgate Research Companion to Regionalisms*, edited by T.M. Shaw, J.A. Grant and S. Cornelissen. 361-373.

Robertson, J. (ed.) 2008. *Power and Politics after Financial Crises.* London: Palgrave Macmillan.

Rushton, S. and Williams, O.D. (eds.) 2011. *Partnerships and Foundations in Global Health Governance.* London: Palgrave Macmillan.

Schnurr, M. and Swatuk, L. (eds.) 2012. *Environmental Change, Natural Resources and Social Conflict.* London: Palgrave Macmillan.

Shaw, T.M. 2010. 'Can the BRICs become a bloc?' in The Emerging Politics of the Emerging Powers: the BRICs and the global South. *China Monitor*, 52, June: 4-6.

Shaw, T.M., Grant, J.A. and Cornelissen, S. (eds.) 2012. *Ashgate Research Companion to Regionalisms.* Farnham: Ashgate.

Soderbaum, F. and Taylor, I. (eds.) 2008. *Afro-Regions: the dynamics of cross-border macro-regionalism in Africa.* Uppsala: NAI.

Solis, M., Stallings, B. and Katada, S.N. (eds.) 2009. *Competitive Regionalism: FTA diffusion in the Pacific Rim.* London: Palgrave Macmillan.

Taylor, I.C. 2011. *The Forum on China-Africa Cooperation.* Abingdon: Routledge.

Tickner, A.B. and Waever, O. (eds.) 2009. *International Relations Scholarship around the World.* Abingdon: Routledge.

UNDP. 2012. *Citizen Security: Regional Human Development Report on the Caribbean.* Port of Spain: UNDP.

UNECA. 2011. *Economic Report on Africa 2011: governing development in Africa – the role of the state in economic transformation.* Addis Ababa: UNECA.

Vagni, J.J. 2009. La Cumbre América del Sur – Países Árabes (ASPA) Balances de un acercamiento estratégico. *Revista de Estudios Internacionales Mediterráneos*, 8, June, 185-196.

Warleigh-Lack, A., Robinson, N. and Rosamond, B. (eds.) 2011. *New Regionalism and the EU: dialogues, comparisons and research directions.* Abingdon: Routledge.

World Bank. 2011. *World Development Report 2011: conflict, security and development.* Washington, DC: World Bank.

Chapter 1

Competitive Bilateralism or Regionalism: A South African Perspective

Merle Holden and Vanessa T. Tang[1]

The global trading system is characterized by a growing and competing network of bilateral and regional trade agreements. In South Africa, while trade policy has been determined in a multilateral setting, bilateral and regional trade agreements have also been pursued as evidenced by the Southern African Development Community Free Trade Agreement (SADC FTA), the European Union-South Africa Trade, Development and Co-operation Agreement (EU-SA TDCA) and as a member of the Southern African Customs Union (SACU), a party to the SACU European Free Trade Association-Free Trade Agreement (SACU- EFTA FTA) and the SACU Common Market of the South-Preferential Trade Agreement (SACU-MERCOSUR PTA).

However, the verdict is still out on whether South African trade has benefited from preferential access into the United States under the African Growth and Opportunity Act (AGOA). Overlaying these arrangements, there are also ongoing Economic Partnership Agreement (EPA) negotiations with the European community. Policy makers in South Africa, despite multilateral commitments, continue to negotiate preferential deals with other countries. The official March 2011 entry of South Africa to the Brazil, Russia, India and China (BRIC) group illustrates this competitive trend within African regionalism.

Against this background, it is questionable therefore whether these bilateral and regional trade agreements are beneficial to South African trade in general. This chapter aims to investigate whether the two preferential free trade agreements, the SADC FTA and EU-SA TDCA, have had any significant impact on trading patterns and revealed comparative advantages for South Africa. Furthermore, this chapter also attempts to explore the merits for the co-existence of other preferential trade agreements.

---

1 This chapter is a revised version of a paper presented at the NETRIS Durban conference, September 2010.

Introduction

Discussions about international relations are focusing increasingly on bilateral and regional trade agreements. Since the 1990s, the global trading system is characterized by a growing and competing network of bilateral and regional free trade agreements (FTAs). As of January 10, 2013, the World Trade Organization (WTO) is monitoring some 546 notifications of FTAs with 354 agreements in operation. In just a decade, the number of active FTAs is up by almost 50 per cent (from 180 agreements in 2003). Most WTO members are party to one or more FTAs. Going by present trends, it is expected that the share of trade through bilateral and regional FTAs will continue to rise.

In South Africa, while trade policy has been determined in a multilateral setting, bilateral and regional trade agreements have also been pursued. After a period of phased-in aggressive trade liberalization agreed under the Uruguay Round of the General Agreement on Tariffs and Trade (GATT), bilateral and regional trade agreements began to play a larger role.

In the year 2000, South Africa concluded two major preferential FTAs: a bilateral FTA with the European Union – the European Union-South Africa Trade, Development and Co-operation Agreement (EU-SA TDCA) and a regional-plurilateral FTA with the Southern African Development Community – the Southern African Development Community Free Trade Agreement (SADC FTA). Holden and McMillan (2006) show that the EU-SA FTA stimulated both exports and imports for South Africa, but while South African exports to SADC were stimulated, the results for imports were ambiguous. The AGOA results were far less significant overall, suggesting that preferential access for South African exports into the United States had not been particularly beneficial.

Overlaying these arrangements, there are also ongoing Economic Partnership Agreement (EPA) negotiations with the European community. Policy makers in South Africa, despite multilateral commitments, continue to negotiate preferential deals with emerging trading partners. The official March 2011 entry of South Africa to the BRIC group illustrates this competitive trend within African regionalism.

It is our view, therefore, that South Africa's increasing engagement in the world economy and liberalization of trade creates competitive pressures and a potential shift in the country's comparative advantage in the international market. Also, with the EU-SA TDCA 12-year implementation horizon soon coming to an end, and taking into account the inclusion of South Africa into the SADC EPA negotiations, our analysis will make a contribution to the debate. The chapter therefore focuses on identifying whether South African trade has been affected in recent years by the granting of preferential access under these agreements. In addition, in a south-south developing mandate, given that a preferential trade agreement framework was signed by the Ministers of Trade in South Africa and Brazil in 2000, this chapter also attempts to explore the merits of the co-existence of a potential FTA with Brazil.

Our chapter proceeds as follows: In the next section, we provide some of the stylized facts concerning South Africa's trading export and import patterns. Thereafter, we discuss our methodology and data. Specifically, this study uses a modified version of the Balassa (1965) index to identify South Africa's most competitive commodities relative to the EU and SADC, in terms of the 'revealed' comparative advantage and also determine to what extent the most competitive commodities witnessed a shift in their trade competitiveness. Additionally, of added value, this study investigates the revealed competitiveness of South Africa relative to Brazil, an increasingly important emerging trading partner; and also identifies the major products that have export potential for South African producers. The last section concludes.

South Africa's Patterns of Trade: Stylized Facts

Over the last decade, when looking at South Africa's pattern of international trade, four major relevant themes are apparent: a significant increase in the country's openness, the dominance of manufacturing, a geographical diversification in its trade and an unbalanced bilateral and regional trading.

South Africa's trade has been considerably liberalized since the early 1990s (Jonsson and Subramanian 2001). South Africa is an open economy. As illustrated in Figure 1.1 below, the ratio of trade relative to GDP has increased significantly from 40 per cent in 1993 to 58 per cent in 2011. Also, South Africa's average most favoured nation (MFN) applied tariff rate is of interest, and as shown in Figure 1.1 has dropped considerably from 14.5 per cent in 1993 to 6 per cent in 2011 in line with that of an average upper-middle-income economy.

To provide more insight into this increased openness, Figures 1.2 and 1.3 show the country's composition of trade. Manufacturing is by far the main driver in exports from and imports into South Africa.

From a geographical standpoint, South Africa's trade remains concentrated with relatively high-income traditional partners in the north, but this concentration of trade is decreasing and there seems to be a reallocation of trade moving towards key emerging markets in the south, as shown in Figures 1.4 and 1.5.

Additionally, a noteworthy point is that while Germany has consistently been South Africa's major individual trading partner, since 2009, China has become the country's most important individual trading partner when total trade between the two countries amounted to about US$ 15 billion. In 2011, South Africa's total bilateral trade with China has reached almost US $30 billion, with an SA deficit of about US $2.5 billion.

Regarding South Africa's regional trade, the European Union as a bloc remains South Africa's most important regional trading partner as evidenced in Figures 1.6 and 1.7.

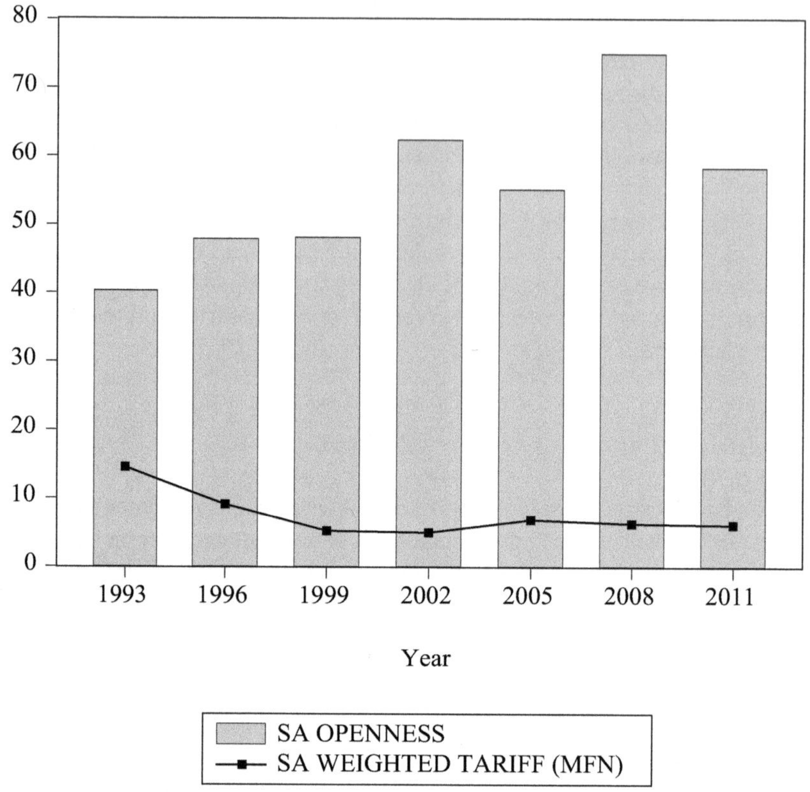

Figure 1.1 Trade Openness: 1993-2011

Source: Authors' calculations based on UNCTAD (2012) database

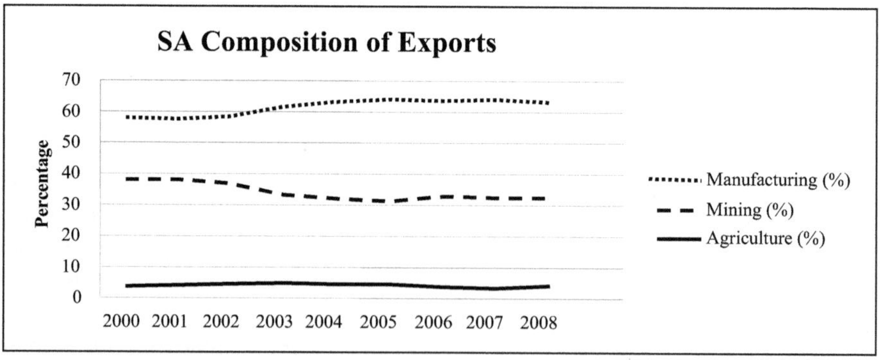

Figure 1.2 Exports Composition: 2000-2008

Source: Authors' calculations based on DTI (2010) data

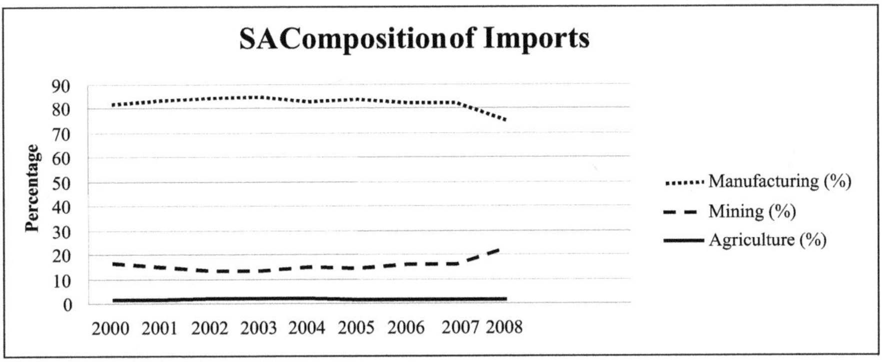

Figure 1.3 Imports Composition: 2000-2008

Source: Authors' calculations based on DTI (2010) data

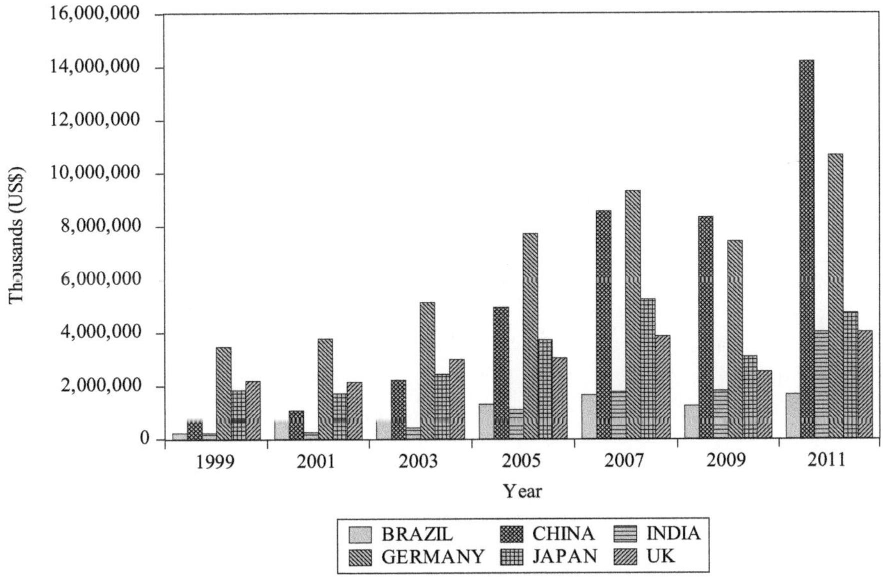

Figure 1.4 Key Trading Import Partners: 1999-2011 (US$)

Source: Authors' compilations based on UNCTAD (2012) data

Figures 1.6 and 1.7 also show that the country has slowly developed a more integrated trade with the African, Caribbean and Pacific States. According to our estimates based on UNCTAD (2012) data, South Africa's trade with Africa is focused on the SADC region and within the SADC group. Mozambique and Zimbabwe have been South Africa's two largest trading partners. However, SADC

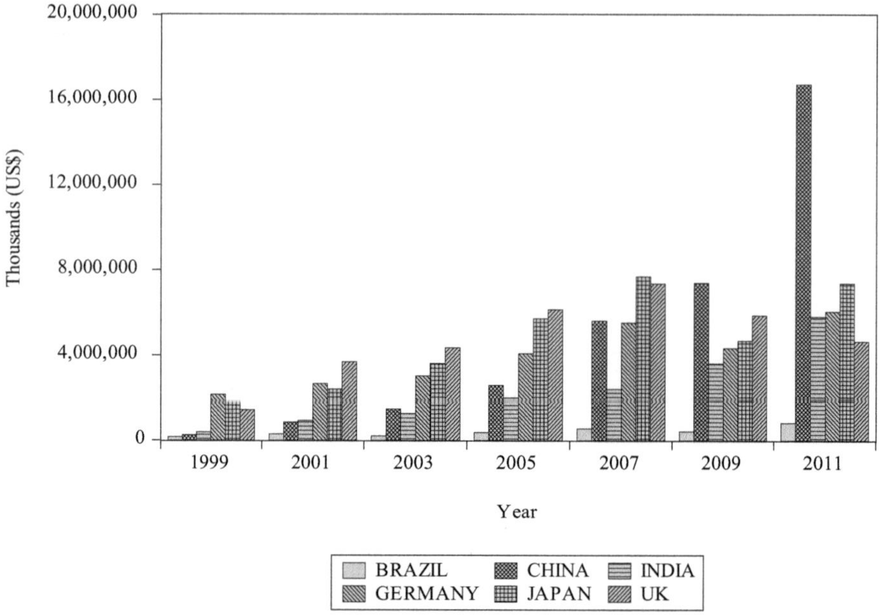

Figure 1.5 Key Trading Export Partners: 1999-2011 (US$)

Source: Authors' compilations based on UNCTAD (2012) data

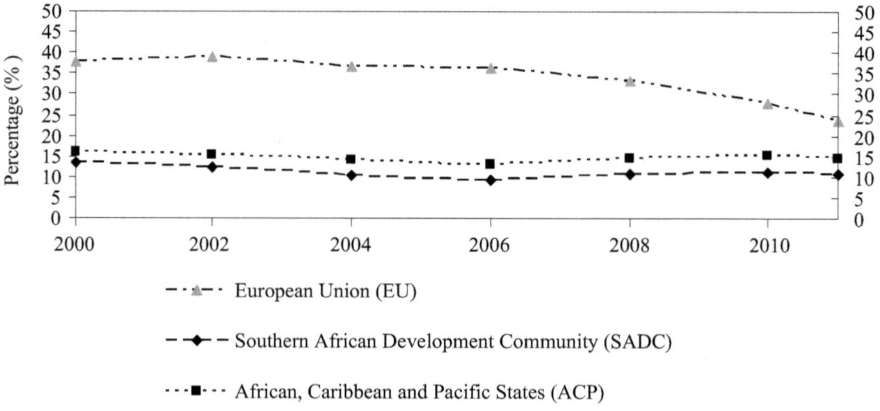

Figure 1.6 Share of South African Total Exports: 2000-2011 (%)

Source: Authors' calculations based on UNCTAD (2012) data

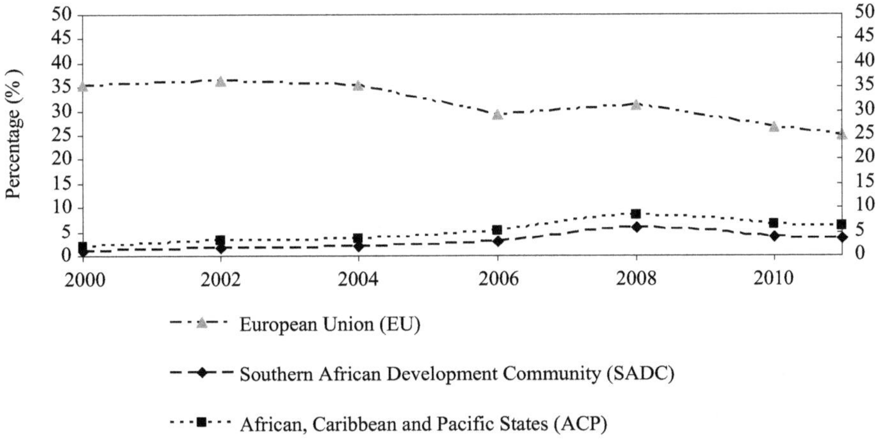

Figure 1.7 Share of South African Total Imports: 2000-2011 (%)
Source: Authors' calculations based on UNCTAD (2012) data

importance as a key export partner for South Africa is falling, accounting in 2011 for only 10.8 per cent compared to 13.4 per cent in 2000 of the country's total exports, as shown in Figure 1.6. Imports from SADC, however, have improved but are relatively marginally slimmer, accounting in 2011 for only 3.5 per cent of total imports compared to 1.1 per cent in 2000, as illustrated in Figure 1.7.

At this juncture, it is worth noting that South Africa has consistently had a trade deficit with the European Union and a trade surplus with SADC. Bilateral deficits with the European Union are potentially caused by a relatively higher propensity for South Africans to import European goods. Additionally, we feel that the relative factor endowments and lag in diversification and industrialization have been stumbling blocks for South African exports. The trade surplus with SADC is not surprising given that South Africa is economically the largest SADC member and sources the majority of its imports from the developed world. Also, in the case of SADC, this result is not surprising 'given the asymmetrical phase-in of the agreement' (Holden and Mcmillan 2006).

The Revealed Comparative Advantage: Methodology and Data

It is customary in the empirical trade literature to use the concept of revealed comparative advantage to study countries' patterns of international trade and their specialization in trade. The majority of these studies have used the Balassa (1965) index. This index is simply an index of revealed export advantage (RXA) reflecting differences in factor endowments across countries. The RXA index uses data on exports to infer competitiveness. This index can be expressed as:

Revealed Comparative Advantage: SA-SADC

The full RCA results for South Africa's revealed comparative advantages relative to the SADC-G1 are shown in Appendices 1.3 and 1.4.

In Appendix 1.3, South Africa's mean revealed comparative advantage lies in *Chemicals and related products; Machinery and transport equipment; Manufactured goods classified chiefly by material; Miscellaneous manufactured articles; Crude materials, inedible, except fuels;* and in *Commodities and transactions not elsewhere classified.*

In Appendix 1.4, South Africa's mean revealed competitiveness lies, in order of significance, in: *Chemicals and related products; Machinery and transport equipment; Miscellaneous manufactured articles; Food and live animals* and in *Manufactured goods classified chiefly by materials.*

Two significant trends are noteworthy: *Chemicals and related products, Machinery and transport equipment* and *Manufactured goods classified chiefly by material* have essentially the same pattern in the last year; *Chemicals and related products* as well as *Machinery and transport equipment* have lost shares in their RCPT. *Manufactured goods classified chiefly by materials*, on the other hand, have now gained RCPT.

Regarding the current position of South Africa's revealed exports product relative to the SADC-G1, Figure 1.9 below identifies the top five RCA export forerunners in 2009.

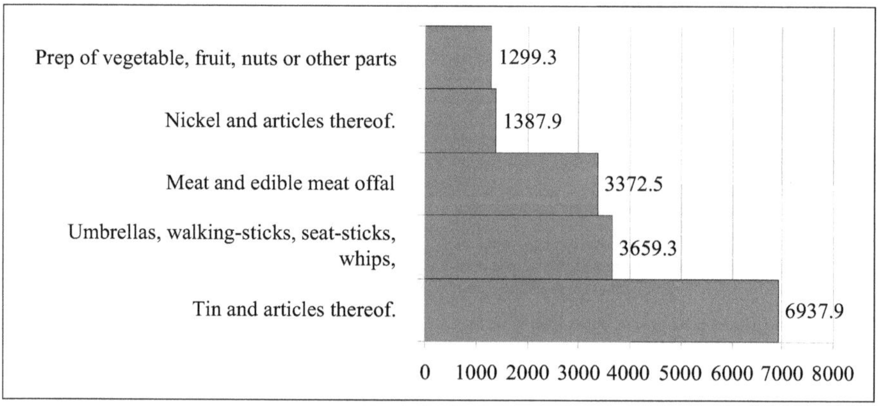

Figure 1.9 SA-SADC-G1 Export Products

Revealed Comparative Advantage: SA-Brazil

The full RCA results for South Africa's revealed competitiveness relative to Brazil are shown in Appendix 1.5.

South Africa's mean revealed competitiveness lies in only three commodity groups: *Chemicals and related products; Minerals fuels, lubricants and related materials* and in *manufactured goods classified chiefly by material.*

A point worthy of note is that in the last two years, for the commodity type *Minerals fuels, lubricants and related materials*, the country has lost its RCPT. Also, an interesting pattern has emerged for the *Machinery and transport equipment* commodity type, whereby since 2008, the country is now showing RCPT in this commodity group.

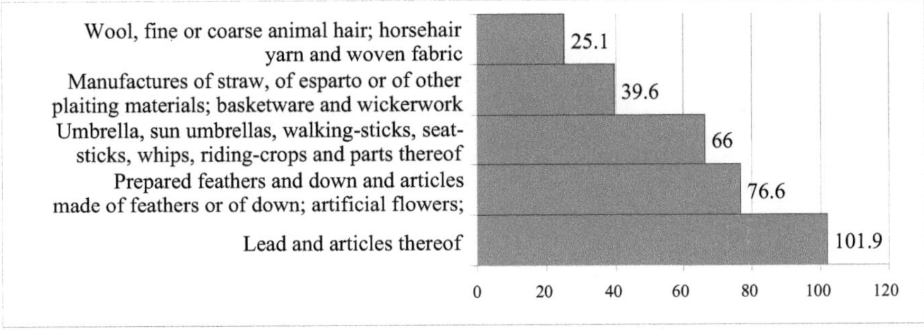

Figure 1.10 SA-Brazil Export Products

Regarding the current position of South Africa's revealed exports product relative to Brazil, Figure 1.10 below identifies the top five RCA export forerunners in 2009.

Comparative Group Revealed Export Advantages

Figure 1.11 provides a comparison of the relative RXA in 2009, of the combined top five products previously identified.

Additionally, in 2009, comparatively (three groups), within the top 10 RXA products, it is interesting to note that there is only one export product group in which South Africa's RXA lies. Explosives; pyrotechnic products; matches; pyrophoric alloys and certain combustible preparations are the only export products in the top 10 and their RXA indices are shown in Figure 1.12 below.

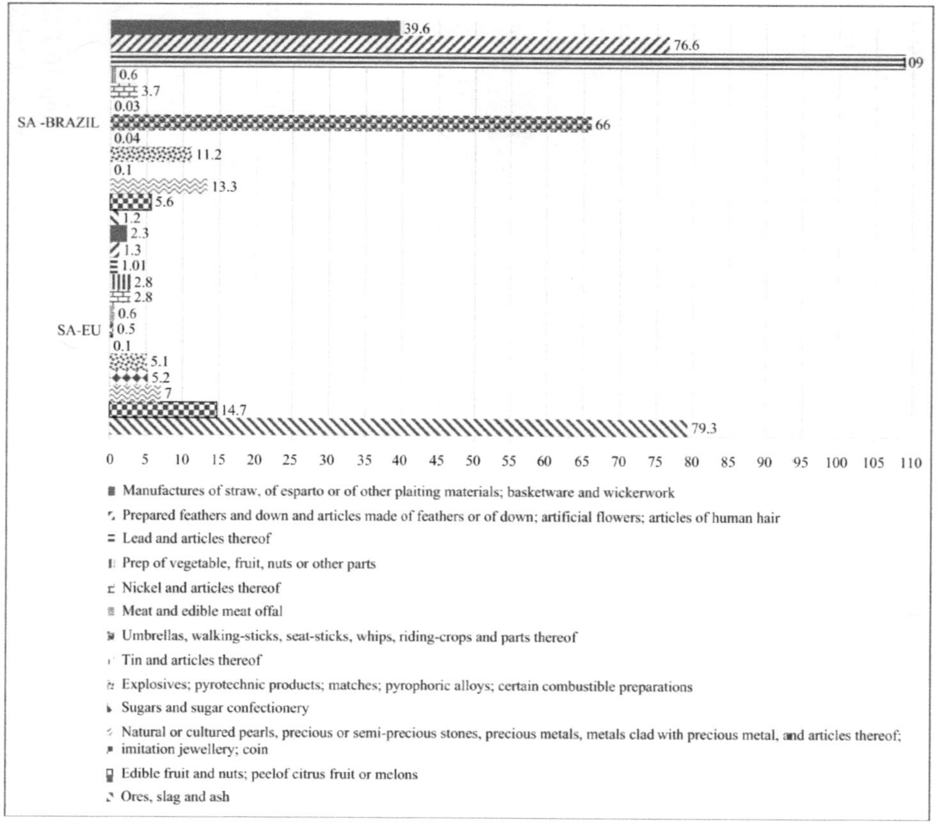

39.6
76.6
09
0.6
3.7
0.03
SA -BRAZIL
66
0.04
11.2
0.1
13.3
5.6
1.2
2.3
1.3
1.01
2.8
2.8
0.6
SA-EU
0.5
0.1
5.1
5.2
7
14.7
79.3
0 5 10 15 20 25 30 35 40 45 50 55 60 65 70 75 80 85 90 95 100 105 110
Manufactures of straw, of esparto or of other plaiting materials; basketware and wickerwork
Prepared feathers and down and articles made of feathers or of down; artificial flowers; articles of human hair
Lead and articles thereof
Prep of vegetable, fruit, nuts or other parts
Nickel and articles thereof
Meat and edible meat offal
Umbrellas, walking-sticks, seat-sticks, whips, riding-crops and parts thereof
Tin and articles thereof
Explosives; pyrotechnic products; matches; pyrophoric alloys; certain combustible preparations
Sugars and sugar confectionery
Natural or cultured pearls, precious or semi-precious stones, precious metals, metals clad with precious metal, and articles thereof; imitation jewellery; coin
Edible fruit and nuts; peelof citrus fruit or melons
Ores, slag and ash

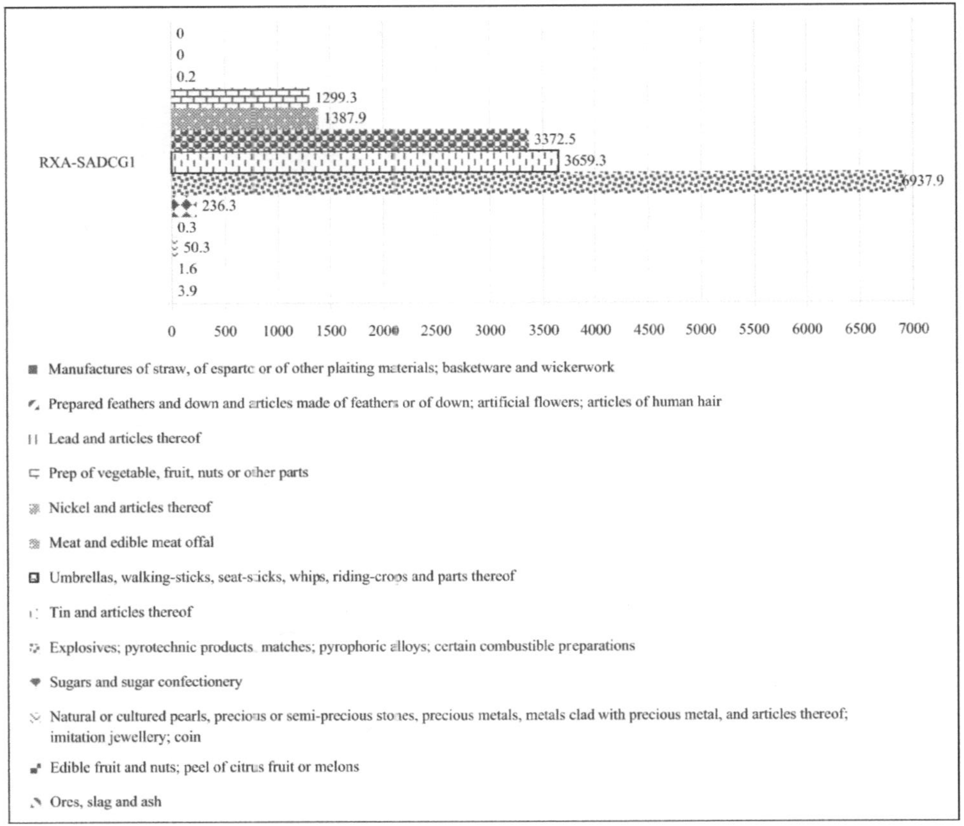

Figure 1.11 Comparative Combined Top Five RXA

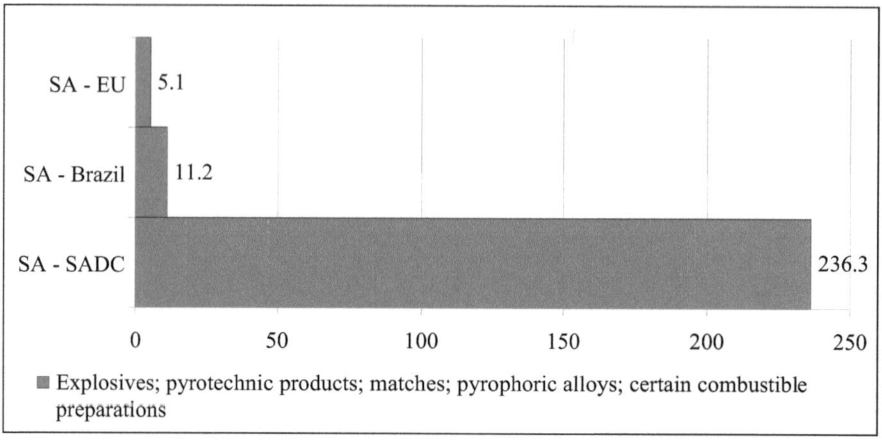

Figure 1.12 Comparative Top Ten RXA

Conclusions and Policy Recommendations

Preferential trade agreements and free trade agreements have long been an important feature in South Africa's trade policy. While their economic benefits remain a matter of contention, many developing countries including South Africa are compelled to pursue them.

In this chapter, we have provided some of the stylized facts regarding South Africa's patterns of trade. This is followed by an empirical investigation of South Africa's revealed comparative advantages in trade bilaterally and regionally.

The overall results show that the trajectory of South Africa's deepening integration has not been a linear one. Also, this study has 'revealed' changing patterns in the most recent years in the country's competitiveness in trade. A noteworthy point is that South Africa has a comparative advantage relative to its northern counterparts and Brazil primarily in commodity groups *Crude materials, inedible, except fuels; Minerals fuels, lubricants and related materials* and C*hemicals and related products* (SITCs 2, 3 and 5). However, relative to the SADC-G1 trading partner, South Africa's comparative advantage lies primarily in commodity groups *Chemicals and related products* and *Machinery and transport equipment* (SITCs 5 and 7). Additionally, the country has also shown relative export and competitive advantages in manufactured goods (SITC6) but it is relatively disadvantaged in the other manufactured goods (SITC8). Also, in the most recent year, comparatively in all three case studies of the top 10 RXA, South Africa's RXA products lie in explosives; pyrotechnic products; matches, pyrophoric alloys and certain combustible preparations.

From a policy perspective, the Department of Trade and Industry 'trade policies informed by South Africa's industrial upgrading and employment objectives' are important areas for growth (DTI 2010). However, any policies aimed at improving the competitiveness of South Africa's trade and potential benefit from an FTA should be 'evolutionary in nature to adapt and reflect changes in economic conditions' (Tang 2008). By the same token, to promote efficiency and hence increase competitivenesss, developing countries in Africa need to continuously restructure their economies.

Appendix 1.1 RCA1-RXA (SA-EU)

Commodity description (code)	2000	2001	2002	2003	2004	2005	2006	2007	2008	2009	Mean
Food and live animals (0)	1.73	1.84	2.22	2.05	1.91	**1.95**	**1.63**	**1.47**	**1.50**	**1.94**	**1.824**
Beverages and tobacco (1)	**1.00**	**1.11**	**1.22**	**1.23**	**1.26**	**1.19**	0.96	0.97	0.98	**1.32**	**1.124**
Crude materials, inedible, except fuels (2)	**5.78**	5.57	6.06	4.60	4.05	4.50	4.79	5.16	6.77	7.30	5.458
Mineral fuels, lubricants and related materials (3)	3.00	4.19	4.33	3.22	2.65	2.41	1.90	2.10	1.61	**2.33**	**2.774**
Animal and vegetable oils, fats and waxes (4)	0.54	0.53	0.52	0.36	0.29	0.30	0.25	0.25	0.63	0.70	0.437
Chemicals and related products N.E.S (5)	0.61	0.57	0.62	0.50	0.52	0.57	0.49	0.46	0.53	0.45	0.532
Manufactured goods classified chiefly by material (6)	**2.05**	**2.82**	**2.14**	**2.90**	**3.02**	**2.91**	**2.93**	**2.95**	**2.68**	**2.66**	**2.706**
Machinery and transport equipment (7)	0.39	0.44	0.53	0.48	0.45	0.46	0.50	0.48	0.51	0.50	0.474
Miscellaneous manufactured articles (8)	0.36	0.35	0.43	0.40	0.35	0.31	0.26	0.24	0.23	0.25	0.318
Commodities and transactions not elsewhere classified (9)	**2.25**	0.10	0.03	0.03	0.19	0.01	0.13	0.03	0.07	0.05	0.289

Appendix 1.2 RCA2-RTA-RCPT (SA-EU)

Commodity description (code)	2000	2001	2002	2003	2004	2005	2006	2007	2008	2009	Mean
Food and live animals (0)	0.89	1.15	1.22	1.18	1.06	**1.09**	**0.87**	**0.69**	**0.67**	**0.86**	**0.968**
Beverages and tobacco (1)	**0.03**	**0.19**	**0.23**	**0.13**	**0.05**	-0.01	-0.27	-0.40	-0.48	-0.42	-0.995
Crude materials, inedible, except fuels (2)	**2.09**	2.61	2.08	2.05	1.70	2.18	1.92	2.29	2.18	2.53	2.163
Mineral fuels, lubricants and related materials (3)	1.19	1.49	1.67	1.50	1.18	1.32	0.89	0.91	0.67	**0.86**	**1.168**
Animal and vegetable oils, fats and waxes (4)	-1.48	-1.53	-1.52	-1.84	-2.02	-1.76	-1.84	-2.11	-1.07	-1.00	-1.617
Chemicals and related products N.E.S (5)	-1.03	-1.03	-0.83	-1.02	-0.81	-0.83	-0.81	-0.90	-0.83	-0.93	-0.902
Manufactured goods classified chiefly by material (6)	**0.62**	**1.00**	**0.65**	**0.92**	**1.12**	**1.01**	**1.13**	**1.20**	**1.08**	**0.88**	**0.961**
Machinery and transport equipment (7)	-0.97	-0.93	-0.77	-0.93	-0.96	-0.99	-0.93	-0.98	-0.95	-0.91	-0.932
Miscellaneous manufactured articles (8)	-0.57	-0.53	-0.31	-0.32	-0.54	-0.74	-0.97	-0.90	-0.95	-0.91	-0.674
Commodities and transactions not elsewhere classified (9)	**0.54**	-3.21	-3.69	-4.14	-2.34	-5.71	-2.65	-4.42	-3.14	-2.70	-3.146

Appendix 1.3 RCA1-RXA (SA-SADC-G1)

Commodity description (code)	2000	2001	2002	2003	2004	2005	2006	2007	2008	2009	Mean
Food and live animals (0)	0.18	0.34	0.37	0.55	0.55	0.63	0.56	0.67	0.99	0.63	0.547
Beverages and tobacco (1)	0.73	1.28	0.59	**1.04**	0.71	0.73	0.33	0.69	0.20	0.25	0.655
Crude materials, inedible, except fuels (2)	0.76	**1.85**	**1.93**	**1.23**	**1.33**	**1.25**	**2.01**	**2.17**	**1.94**	**1.73**	**1.62**
Mineral fuels, lubricants and related materials (3)	0.48	**1.41**	0.93	0.75	0.73	0.69	0.65	0.67	0.89	0.64	0.784
Animal and vegetable oils, fats and waxes (4)	0.14	0.14	0.27	0.33	0.17	0.28	0.23	0.19	0.65	0.57	0.297
Chemicals and related products N.E.S (5)	**45.42**	**34.86**	**46.57**	**23.40**	**117.78**	**123.40**	**103.44**	**38.97**	**32.52**	**28.32**	**59.468**
Manufactured goods classified chiefly by material (6)	**1.63**	0.68	0.64	0.68	0.69	0.67	0.69	0.65	0.65	**24.21**	**3.119**
Machinery and transport equip (7)	**7.72**	**9.28**	**6.11**	**4.99**	**5.86**	**6.56**	**6.36**	**5.93**	**5.60**	**2.45**	**6.086**
Miscellaneous manufactured articles (8)	**1.72**	**1.68**	**3.54**	**2.46**	**5.24**	**1.76**	**3.05**	**2.21**	**3.14**	**1.21**	**2.601**
Commodities and transactions not elsewhere classified (9)	**6.88**	0.09	0.05	0.18	**1.26**	**1.40**	0.40	0.14	0.04	0.01	**1.045**

Appendix 1.4 RCA2-RTA-RCPT (SA-SADC-G1)

Commodity description (code)	2000	2001	2002	2003	2004	2005	2006	2007	2008	2009	Mean
Food and live animals (0)	-0.53	**0.26**	**0.07**	**0.60**	**0.70**	**0.91**	**0.71**	**1.08**	**1.08**	**0.58**	**0.546**
Beverages and tobacco (1)	**0.69**	**0.65**	-0.21	**0.06**	-0.41	**0.07**	-0.68	-0.42	-1.52	-2.25	-0.402
Crude materials, inedible, except fuels (2)	-0.76	-0.18	-0.47	-0.23	-0.45	-0.23	-0.10	**0.08**	-0.21	**0.37**	-0.218
Mineral fuels, lubricants and related materials (3)	-0.80	-0.99	-0.35	**0.01**	-0.24	-1.14	-0.52	-0.53	-0.22	-0.78	-0.556
Animal and vegetable oils, fats and waxes (4)	-1.45	-1.60	-1.24	-0.67	-1.18	-0.48	-0.58	-1.11	**0.63**	**0.27**	-0.741
Chemicals and related products N.E.S (5)	**3.23**	**2.80**	**3.18**	**2.67**	**4.46**	**4.27**	**4.33**	**3.24**	**3.25**	**2.95**	**3.438**
Manufactured goods classified chiefly by material (6)	**0.76**	-0.67	-0.50	-0.52	-0.34	-0.41	-0.31	-0.47	-0.39	**3.46**	**0.061**
Machinery and transport equipment (7)	**1.81**	**1.38**	**1.32**	**1.20**	**1.27**	**1.50**	**1.42**	**1.36**	**1.36**	**0.70**	**1.332**
Miscellaneous manufactured articles (8)	**0.25**	**0.44**	**1.05**	**0.51**	**1.80**	**0.24**	**0.58**	**0.31**	**0.70**	-0.27	**0.561**
Commodities and transactions not elsewhere classified (9)	**0.71**	-0.72	-1.88	-0.99	**0.83**	**1.44**	**0.02**	-1.05	-2.22	**3.77**	-0.009

Appendix 1.5 RCPT (SA-Brazil)

Commodity description (code)	2000	2001	2002	2003	2004	2005	2006	2007	2008	2009	Mean
Food and live animals (0)	-0.43	-0.59	-0.40	-0.41	-0.88	-0.89	-1.00	-1.26	-1.21	-1.13	-0.82
Beverages and tobacco (1)	-0.69	-0.60	-0.46	-0.44	-0.64	-0.58	-0.50	-0.83	-1.09	-1.17	-0.7
Crude materials, inedible, except fuels (2)	-0.45	-0.21	-0.49	-0.35	-0.62	-0.15	-0.26	-0.04	-0.36	-0.21	-0.314
Mineral fuels, lubricants and related materials (3)	1.85	1.12	1.10	0.89	0.92	0.80	0.24	0.23	-0.10	-0.14	0.691
Animal and vegetable oils, fats and waxes (4)	-2.22	-3.06	-3.06	-3.80	-4.00	-3.62	-3.55	-3.99	-3.08	-2.42	-3.28
Chemicals and related products N.E.S (5)	0.62	0.67	0.97	0.77	1.07	0.85	0.81	0.59	0.90	0.75	0.8
Manufactured goods classified chiefly by material (6)	0.15	0.60	0.20	0.46	0.66	0.68	0.85	0.88	0.93	0.98	0.639
Machinery and transport equipment (7)	-0.35	-0.14	-0.16	-0.34	-0.27	-0.27	-0.14	-0.28	0.06	0.29	-0.16
Miscellaneous manufactured articles(8)	-0.77	-0.76	-0.36	-0.42	-0.49	-0.54	-0.60	-0.55	-0.36	-0.35	-0.52
Commodities and transactions not elsewhere classified (9)	-2.53	-6.60	-8.55	-9.71	-8.40	-11.60	-7.73	-3.22	-8.62	-6.69	-7.365

References

Andreosso-O'Callaghan, B. 2009. Economic structural complementarity: how viable is the Korea-EU FTA? *Journal of Economic Studies*, 36(2), 147-167.

Balassa, B. 1965. Trade liberalization and revealed comparative advantage, *Manchester School of Economics and Social Studies*, 33, 99-123.

Department of Trade and Industry (DTI). 2010. *RSA trade statistics,* Available at: http://www.thedti.gov.za [accessed: 31 August 2010].

DTI. 2010. *A South African Trade Policy and Strategy Framework*, Sunnyside Pretoria, May 2010.

Ferto, I. and Hubbard, L.J. 2003. Revealed comparative advantage and competitiveness in Hungarian agri-food sectors, *The World Economy*, 26(2), 247-259.

Greenaway, D. and Milner, C. 1993. *Trade and Industrial policy in developing countries: A manual of policy analysis*, London: Macmillan.

Hoen, A.R. and Oosterhaven, J. 2006. On the measurement of comparative advantage, *The Annals of Regional Science*, 40(3), 677-691.

Holden, M. and McMillan, L. 2006. Do free trade agreements create trade for South Africa? *Trade and Industrial Policy Strategies (TIPS) Trade and Industrial Policy Monitor*, 37, 677-691.

Jonsson, G. and Subramanian, A. 2001. Dynamic gains from trade: evidence from South Africa, *IMF Staff Papers*, Number 48, 197-224.

Laursen, K. 1998. Revealed Comparative Advantage and the Alternatives as measures of International specialisation, *Danish Research Unit Industrial Dynamics* Working paper Number 98-30.

Lorde, T., Alleyne, A. and Francis, B. 2010. An assessment of Barbados' Competitiveness within the EU Market 1992-2006, *Global Economy Journal*, 10(2), Article 7.

Tang, V. 2008. Zoning in on South Africa's Industrial Development Zones, *Trade and Industrial Policy Strategies (TIPS)*. Available at: http://www.tips.org.za/publication/zoning-south-africas-industrial-development-zones [accessed: 10 August 2010].

United Nations Conference on Trade and Development (UNCTAD) 2012. Available at: http://unctadstat.unctad.org/TableViewer/ [accessed: 2 January 2013].

Vollrath, T.L. 1991. A theoretical evaluation of alternative trade intensity measures of revealed comparative advantage, Weltwirtschaftliches Archiv, 127(2), 2 65-279.

World Economic Outlook (WEO). 2010. International Monetary Fund world economic outlook April 2010 database. Available at: http://www.imf.org [accessed: 6 September 2010].

Chapter 2
Understanding Regional Integration Policies in Africa

Emmanuel Fanta

Although not a new phenomenon, regional integration has, since the end of the Cold War, evolved both quantitatively and qualitatively. A great variety of dynamics have led regional processes to encompass increasing numbers of tasks while at the same time the number of these regional frameworks has increased exponentially. The African continent has also been fully participating in this trend as some new regional arrangements were set up, old ones were revamped and existing ones saw their mandates being enlarged so as to tackle new issues. The enthusiasm for regional integration has been such in Africa that there is no state in the continent that is not involved in at least one regional process.

However, this apparent enthusiasm by African states in favour of regional integration is not always shared by those that have tried to assess the success of the regional schemes in the continent. Analysts tend to point out that regional organizations in Africa have failed most notably because of their inability to establish themselves as strong institutions that ensure the application of their regional policies. Regional organizations have thus been criticized for their structural weakness that hinders their capacity to contribute to the socio-economic development of the African continent (Elbadawi 1997, Fine and Yeo 1997, Foroutan 1996, Mistry 2000, Onwuka and Sesay 1985, UNECA 2006).

Nevertheless, such assessments of regional integration in Africa suffer from various shortcomings that lead them to give these negative accounts. These analyses tend to be based on a narrow understanding of regional integration and the form it should take. The overbearing European experiment in regional integration has cast a long shadow over the study of other forms of regionalisms as those taking place in Africa (Acharya and Johnson 2007, Gibb 2009, Draper 2010, 2012). In fact, an increasing number of authors are now calling for a more comparative approach that would review the different experiments in integration so as to learn lessons and apply them to other parts of the world, including the EU (Fawcett and Gandois 2010, Söderbaum 2009, Laursen 2010).

Another notable caveat in existing studies of regional integration in Africa is the tendency to overlook the policies of the member states. To understand why and how a regional organization functions and evolves, it is important to take into account the actual aims and intentions of those participating in the process. The aim of this chapter is thus to contribute to the debate about regionalism and regional integration in Africa by adopting a perspective that focuses on the agents of the regional integration process. As such, the regional processes are studied in the light of three driving factors of the foreign policies of African states, these being: i. the strengthening of the state; ii. the reinforcement of the authority of the leaders; and iii. the attempts to overcome the marginality of Africa in the international system (Clapham 1996, Bayart 1986, 2002, Sindjoun 2002, Ayoob 1997, 2002, Englebert 2009).

The New Regionalism approach provides a useful framework through which the regionalization phenomenon in Africa can be apprehended, but it also helps to enlighten some of the peculiarities of the institutional regional arrangements that have developed on the African continent. This is mainly so because of the distancing this approach has taken from viewing the regional process as being solely a statist project and adopting a more critical perspective on regional processes. Similarly, in the case of Africa, it is necessary to look beyond the restrictive traditional and westphalian conceptualization of the 'state' to understand the processes of regionalization. When dealing with international relations in Africa, several authors have already pointed out the necessity to not be blinded by the ideal of 'state' (Dunn and Shaw 2001, Lemke 2003, Brown 2006). The same cautious approach that refuses reifying the 'state' has to be taken when studying African regional integration experiments.

This chapter first attempts to give some explanatory elements regarding the policies of regional integration in Africa, focusing in particular on the incentives that can be found in participating in such regional processes. The following part, on the other hand, explores some of the reasons why there has been some wariness over regional integration and the strategies that have been used to resist a regional integration that is too strong. The last part draws some conclusion on the type of institutional regional integration that is to be found in Africa.

African Policies for Regional Integration

In order to understand the tendency that African states have to become part of regional processes, it is necessary to look into the various incentives offered by these processes. Firstly, in regard to the need for strengthening the state, joining the regional projects offers several advantages to the African state. Various decisions adopted at the regional level have actually served to strengthen the authority and legitimacy of member states. One such case is the OAU's recognition of the intangibility of colonial boundaries, which strengthened African states by preventing them from challenges on their territorial integrity (Sindjoun 2002). In as much as all African states had to abide by this rule, it established a regime of collective security that prevented external military contestation of the state's authority on its territory (Herbst 2007). Another corollary of this decision has been to further legitimize the ideal of statehood and of the African state as a 'national project' (Englebert 2009). In other words, the OAU's adoption of the principle of intangibility of borders has helped African states to reinforce themselves by delegitimizing any secessionist claims. The power of this regional norm and its common upholding by all African states has been such that it has in return been accepted by the international community (Clapham 1996: 45). The force of this norm can still be felt today; for example, in the non-recognition of Somaliland as a rightful independent state.

But regional integration has also been useful for African states by providing them with instruments to boost their national development needs and projects (Shaw 2001: 217). This has been made possible mainly via the Regional Economic Communities (RECs) and other regional economic organizations (such as the Mano River Union) as well as the numerous technical functional organizations that have mushroomed throughout the continent. The economic integration processes aim to overcome the problem of small national markets and increase regional trade, whereas functional organizations have focused on increasing cooperation in various development challenges. The technical regional organizations have been instrumental in being able to respond to problems that cannot simply be solved at the national level but need a regional answer. For example, the Nile Basin Initiative has been set up to offer a common framework for all the riparian states. The importance of this particular type of regional organization should not be dismissed as, through a process of functional spill-over, they can come to cover a very broad range of issues. The Inter-Governmental Authority for Development (IGAD) itself started as such an organization with a mandate limited to tackling issues of drought and desertification in the Horn of Africa, but later evolved so that it nowadays deals with peace and security and even plans to become a regional Free Trade Area.

Participating in the processes of regional integration does not only offer 'statist' advantages. In fact, following from the neo-patrimonial conduct of state affairs, it also allows national elites to reap the profits for their very individual gains (Bayart 1986, 2002, Medard 1990, 1991). Thus, being a member of a regional organization enhances not only the legitimacy of the state but also the legitimacy of African rulers, a much sought-after resource in African politics (Jackson and Rosberg 1982). Söderbaum considers this as being a regime-boosting regionalism for which 'the main concern of involved regimes is with their own survival and status, rather than broader national and societal goals' (2004: 112). A very good example of how a regional organization can come to legitimize a national ruler is offered by the case of Somalia's former President. Abdullahi Yusuf was appointed as President of Somalia mainly through an agreement managed by a regional organization, IGAD, rather than a national legitimization process in Somalia. A similar case could also be made regarding the Democratic Republic of the Congo's joining of SADC in 1997 at a moment when the leadership of Kabila was under threat and when SADC could provide the Congolese President some political (and later on even military) support.

In many ways, it seems that policies and decisions adopted at the regional level provide African heads of state and governments with such advantages that it amounts to a new form of the 'politics of solidarity' (Clapham 1996). Still, in the field of regional security, whether it is the AU, the EAC or IGAD, states themselves are seldom recognized as a potential source of insecurity (Laakso 2005: 501). And rather than openly criticizing the role of ruling regimes in fomenting violence and conflict, the practice is to push for negotiated agreements with the government. It is quite common for the regional organizations to band-wagon behind the head of state and offer him as much support as possible. As observed by Söderbaum, 'security organization can be used in the interests of the ruling regimes, with the overall goal to preserve state and political stability, regardless of whether these are democracies or dictatorships' (2003: 175). It often is much easier to find a consensus to act against rebels or insurgents rather than taking action that would end up in removing official office holders. The AU intervention against Anjouan's renegade leader is an illustration of how anyone violating the principle of juridical statehood can expect to be met with a common African front. In comparison, the AU has been walking on egg-shells when dealing with the conflict in Darfur where an important part of the responsibility for insecurity comes from the actions of the Sudanese government itself. Even in the case of the political crisis that followed the elections in Côte d'Ivoire in 2011, both ECOWAS and the AU were met by the resistance of some of their member states that refused to act against Laurent Gbagbo. Similarly, a feel of 'politics of solidarity' can be found in the support AU provides against 'unconstitutional' change of government (AU Constitutional Act Art.30). While adopting a provision sidelining coup makers, the AU is clearly weighing in favour of incumbent leaders even if their own legitimacy and democratic credentials are dubious. Thus remains the possibility that governments remain in power, not thanks to their internal legitimacy, but because of the support from their fellow African heads of state (Sindjoun 2002: 91). Another consequence of this provision is that a government just needs to label the opposition as attempting an 'unconstitutional' move to legitimate any action to crush it. Such was the strategy used during the elections in Ethiopia and Uganda in 2005.

For a member state, partaking in regional organizations does not only offer advantages at the national level but also at the international one. In this regard, a distinction needs to be made between regional hegemons and the lesser powers that exist in Africa. For African (would-be) regional hegemons, the push for regional integration is also linked to an attempt to have better control over their sub-region. In their cases, participation in regional organizations allows them to have a more legitimate institutional framework through which they can try to advance their agenda. In West Africa, 'Nigeria's military brass hats were determined, at all costs, to make a success of their historical role as the protective "big brother" with special responsibilities in their sub-region' (Adebajo and Landsberg 2005: 190). Similarly, the SADC intervention in Lesotho in 1998 is believed by many to have been driven by South African interests and that SADC offered a regional legitimacy to its action which contradicted to the apartheid era interventions (Söderbaum 2003: 176, Matlosa 2001: 95, Adebajo and Landsberg 2005: 186, Vale 2003: 132). Even in cases where the regional hegemonic status is more disputed and challenged, like Ethiopia in the Horn of Africa, for example, the would-be hegemon can try to move the regional organization closer to its own strategic goals. Moreover, talking about regional hegemons does not necessarily exclude it from having neo-patrimonial characteristics. Coming back to the role of Nigeria in spearheading the deployment of ECOMOG in Liberia, the intervention can also be partly explained by the personal relationship and business interests that tied Ibrahim Babaginda and Samuel Doe (Hutchful 1999: 4, Francis 2006: 154). In fact, 'President Ibrahim Babangida was seen by some as Doe's sub-regional god-father' (Ero 2005). Similarly, the involvement of high-level Zimbabwean officials in exploiting natural resources in the Congo while partaking in the SADC operation is well documented.

This does not mean that African regional organizations are institutions under the sole control of the regional hegemon. To the contrary, these regional organizations may at the same time offer some attractive features to the less powerful states. Regional frameworks can be used by these states to act collectively to deter and resist the influence of the regional hegemon. Adebajo and Landsberg (2005: 172) thus consider that 'Pax Pretoriana has to contend with "bargainers" like Zimbabwe, Namibia, and Angola, while Pax Nigeriana faces "bargainers" like Côte d'Ivoire, Senegal, Liberia, and Burkina Faso. These states have the capacity to increase significantly the cost of the aspiring hegemons' attempts to impose their will on their respective sub-regions'. The ability of states to counteract the power of the regional hegemon is also increased by the institutional structures of African regional organizations which are often based on the principle of state equality and functions following a strict intergovernmental decision process (Clapham 1996: 121, Herbst 2007: 130). Such institutional arrangements therefore prevent any state taking control over the agenda of the organization by itself. There have even been cases where less powerful states made use of the regional organizations *against* the regional hegemon. In fact, 'It would be easier for [Lesotho or Swaziland] to hide behind the cloak of collective action than to unilaterally conduct a foreign policy toward South Africa, especially a confrontational one' (Babarinde 1999:227).

Using regional organizations to defuse the influence of regional hegemons in fact replicates the way that African states (both regional hegemons and the less powerful ones) have used their collective power (including through regional frameworks) to resist against the involvement and pressure by external actors (Ravenhill 1993). The adherence of African states to regional organizations – and in particular, the pan-African one – not only served to ensure some safeguards against their immediate neighbours but also provided them with a framework that could be used when engaging with the rest of the world. In analyzing Southeast Asia's regional architecture, Amitav Acharya (2009: 172) considers that:

> Individual ASEAN members lack structural power, but collectively they acquire (as its founding members would have rationally calculated) enough bargaining clout to command the attention of great powers and even to socialize them

> through its regional institutions. Developing multilateral institutions to engage great powers is part of the game.

A similar framework of analysis can be applied to African regional organizations. African leaders were fully conscious that in order not to be pawns in the hands of external powers, they needed to collaborate and work in unison. This was particularly evident in the late 90s when OAU member states challenged the US, UK and even UN position against Libya and called for the end of sanctions against Tripoli (Matar and Thabit 2004: 95-98). More recently, African states have also sided with the AU in the case of the indictment of President Omar Al-Bashir, and in doing so have acted against some of their obligations as signatories of the ICC. However, such a strategy is not always successful, as was proven by the AU's inability to prevent NATO's campaign in Libya in 2011.

Policies of Non-Integration

Even though there are many elements pushing African states to take part in regional integration processes, there are also several tendencies that drive these same states to limit the depth of the regional integration processes. And just as for the integrational tendencies, the roots of these limits on the integrational projects can be found in the political dimensions of African foreign policy identified earlier.

In regard to the strengthening of the state apparatus, African states are particularly wary of the fact that regional organizations can potentially dilute the little power these states have. According to Haas, integration is a process 'whereby political actors in several distinct national settings are persuaded to shift their loyalties, expectations, and political activities towards a new larger centre, whose institutions possess or demand jurisdiction over the pre-existing state' (1961: 366-367). Such an interpretation of regional integration is relevant for Africa not so much to explain the current state of regional integration but to understand why it has been so much resisted by African states. This wariness of institutions with jurisdiction over the state is in fact rooted in the historical process of African state formation. For African states, the struggle against ('neo-')colonialism was also a struggle to gain their national sovereignty and free the state from external jurisdiction (Nkrumah 1965). As a result, African states have resisted political processes that could impede their national sovereignty. And as such, regional integration has been perceived as a process that hinders their hard-gained sovereignty. In Herbst's words, 'the type of cooperation that is most likely to fail in Africa actually does challenge the sovereignty of countries' (2007: 136). Since sovereignty is viewed as an essential element of a state's claim to power and authority, any loss of sovereignty is believed to lead to a further weakening of state's authority. For both historical reasons and more practical and economic reasons, in Africa there is a strong reluctance to transfer sovereign powers to other levels of governance than the state (whether upward or downward). Therefore, the advantages of being a member is continuously weighed against the opportunity cost of free riding. Another more extreme solution may yet be to leave the regional organization altogether. Despite IGAD's framework being based on strict inter-governmentalism, Eritrea decided to opt-out once it felt that the organization became too constraining and no longer served its own security purposes. The calculation made in this case somewhat resembles the Moroccan withdrawal from the OAU in 1984. It is also interesting to note that the decisions are not only made for questions relating to security but also apply to economic matters. In 2000, Tanzania withdrew from COMESA not only to focus more on its membership to SADC, but also because it did not agree with the plans being drawn up by COMESA to introduce its Free Trade Area (NPafs 1999).

It is not just their sovereignty that African states are afraid of losing to regional organizations. Another important element feared to be undermined by integration processes relates to the control of the border. Because of the artificiality of borders in the African continent, their validity has often been questioned both internally and externally (Clapham 1999). These external contestations of the borders are not so much the result of irredentist claims being made by some states (although they do exist) but rather the repeated calls for the full integration of the continent amounting to the unification of all African states. While it was impossible for them to shy away from the norm of pan-Africanism, African states have found it hard to relinquish their control over their borders (Clapham 1996: 106-107, Herbst 2000, Englebert 2009). Ever since Nkrumah proclaimed that 'Africa must unite', this ideal of African unity has represented a major difficulty for African states who preferred a less radical integration framework. In many ways, this replicates what Barnett and Solingen have found out regarding the Arab League and the ideal of Arabism, where 'Leaders committed to their own domestic political requirements got the weak institutions they wanted: just enough to demonstrate their commitment to Arabism but not so much as to allow Arabism to threaten their individual sovereignties, domestic political alliances, and power base' (2007: 184-185). The fact remains that despite the pan-African unification *telos*, the control of borders – and therefore their maintenance – represents a major source of both political and economic power for the state. '[…] African states depended on extracting resources from external trade, to an extent that made their leaders extremely reluctant to release control over this trade to any supranational body' (Clapham 1996: 119).

Borders are fundamentally important because they define the territorial limits of a state's authority, or more exactly they define the geographical extent to which this authority can apply (Donnan and Wilson 1999). With time, borders have also served to differentiate one state from another and establish the roots for the emergence of a 'nation' (Clapham 1999: 62). However, by erasing these boundaries and the differentiation they have permitted, regional integration processes have the potential to reverse the long – and often still unfinished – process of national construction. This potential threat pushes African states to be cautious of strong regional integration and to prefer much weaker integration frameworks. It is also for their national economic interests that some states may be reluctant to give away the benefits gained from the control of borders and custom duties. 'In states which derived a high proportion of their income from customs duties, and from state manipulation of markets for agricultural produce, control over the boundaries was essential to provide the financial underpinning of the state itself (...)' (Clapham 1999: 55). From certain states' perspective, the advantages of non-integration are greater than the advantages of strong integration. Thus when the COMESA Free Trade Area was launched in 2000, only nine out of the 19 member states of the organization took part in it.

The gains from resisting an integration process that is too strong or advanced are not only found at the state level but also for those occupying positions of power. It is thus possible to identify various dynamics through which a refusal to integrate serves the interests of the small elite which is in control of the state apparatus. Partaking in a strong institutionalized regional integration process can reduce the gain they make from the existing situation through various types of networks. There exists a neo-patrimonial structure at the regional level that replicates the one existing at the national level and whose power and advantages are threatened by strong processes of integration. This regional neo-patrimonialism also includes both elements of rational-legal ideal type represented by the regional treaty agreed by the member states, but also characteristics pertaining to patrimonialism as is demonstrated by the networks extending regionally (Reno 2001: 202-203). The most flagrant examples illustrating this scenario concern the 'networks of plunders' established following military intervention under the guise of regional organizations (MacLean 2004). The case of the ECOMOG plunder of the resources in Liberia is already well documented and explains why the ECOMOG was nicknamed 'Every Commodity and Movable Object Gone' (Klay Kieh 1992, Ofuatey-Kodjoe 1994). A similar case can be made in regard to the SADC intervention alongside Kabila in the DRC during the second Congo war. The official stance was that the DRC, who had just recently joined SADC, had been attacked and thus should benefit from SADC support under the common defence pact (Nathan 2002: 76, Francis 2006: 196). However, the underlying interest of the intervening states was much more directed towards the economic opportunities of the mineral richness the DRC offered and other national security concerns (MacLean 2004, Francis 2006: 197-8). However, in order for these regional neo-patrimonialisms to prosper, African leaders have to ensure that regional organizations do not develop enough power to disrupt their 'network of plunders'. The continuation of neo-patrimonialism itself is also an obstacle to the establishment of strong regional organizations that can promote such things as democracy and respect for human rights (Taylor and Williams 2008).

The foreign interventions in the second Congolese war not only offer one of the best examples of the regionalization of neo-patrimonialism in Africa, but also show many features of what may be called 'shadow regionalism'. The idea behind shadow regionalism follows from the interpretation that characteristics of the conduct of politics in African states increasingly extend beyond their border and apply to the international and regional relations African states entertain (Söderbaum 2004: 103-108). The concept of shadow regionalism brings together the concept of the shadow state coined by William Reno and the intellectual findings of the New Regionalism approach. Therefore, shadow regionalism refers to a situation where two somewhat parallel structures of power exist in regard to the regional integration process. One is the formal process marked by the regional organizations and agreements reached at the regional level, while the second process concerns the informal links that are established among the many actors interacting within the region. 'The concept of shadow regionalism suggests that important state elites and rentier classes actively seek to preserve existing boundary disparities and the continued failure of regional organizations and policy frameworks' (Söderbaum 2004: 105). In such a scenario, African states adopt a dual strategy. One refers to the official stance and is in line with the regional or international regulations. The second one is not officially recognized but still better allows the state leaders to achieve some of their aims (Söderbaum 2004: 99). 'Although the rhetoric and ritual of regional diplomacy serves the goal of the reproduction and legitimization of the state, it can also be a means to create a façade that enables certain regime actors to engage in other more informal modes of regionalism, such as trans-state regionalism or networks of plunder' (Hettne 2005: 555).

A weak regional integration process also offers some advantages in what concerns the possibility for member states to conduct their foreign relations with the rest of the world as independently as possible. While, as shown earlier, partaking in a regional process may boost the bargaining and negotiating capacity of the group, the corollary is also that it can put many more constraints on the member states. This represents a major challenge for African states as they have been strongly attached to their ability to deal independently at the international level, including in their quest for a powerful patron (Clapham 1996: 112-113, Taylor 2010). This is exemplified by the fact that during the Cold War, African states as a whole heartily embraced the ideal of non-alignment while at the same time a large number of them were affiliated to one bloc or the other. 'Insofar as the principle of sovereignty conflicted with that of non-alignment, it was sovereignty – and hence the right of any national government to invite military assistance from any external ally – that prevailed' (Clapham 1996: 113). For most African states, the most important locus of foreign policy is still the relationship with the major powers found outside of the African continent, whether it is the former colonial power, the leaders of one or the other bloc during the Cold War, or more recently China and other emerging powers. 'Even in its early years, the OAU was unable to displace the much more important links between African states and their external protectors' (Clapham 1996: 112). Be it economically or politically – and in several cases, militarily as well – the linkages with these powers outside of Africa in several cases can be stronger than the ties with the states in the immediate regional surrounding. Looking at it from a trade perspective, Baldwin has for example defined the African continent as being characterized by a 'hub-and-spoke' arrangement where 'Europe and North America are the 'hub' and the African nations are the spokes. The key feature of a hub-and-spoke arrangement is that trade between the hub and each spoke is easier than trade among the spokes' (1997: 55). As trade patterns still remain increasingly focused on the outside world rather than the neighbouring countries, it is not so surprising that there is little pressure to liberalize trade and improve regional integration for African states. From a security point of view, the reliance of many African francophone states on the military prowess of France has survived, despite the regular declaration stating the end of 'françafrique'.

Weak Regional Integration in Africa

Overall, African states have persistently tried to retain as much room to manoeuvre as possible, even if it was at the expense of the effectiveness of regional integration. The institutional design of the African regional organizations is also made so that any action, in the end, rests on the willingness of the member states (Haacke and Williams 2008: 215). There are many more provisions giving final responsibilities to the member states rather than transferring them to regional institutions. In 2006, UNECA (2006:73) lamented that:

> In most African countries regional cooperation does not go far beyond signing treaties and protocols. The objectives of the treaties are not integrated at the right time or with the requisite commitment in national development plans or in the sectoral programmes of appropriate substantive ministries. The inability to translate regional economic community goals into budget and national plans could also be attributed to lack of commitment to integration.

There is therefore an evident risk that African integration processes fall into the trap of 'virtual regionalism' as coined by Allison in his assessment of Central Asia where (2008: 185):

> [The regional] bodies outwardly take the form of 'hard regionalism': pan- or sub-regional groups formalized by interstate arrangements and organization that promote different forms of functional cooperation. However, irrespective of the official discourse about these groupings by member states, their cooperative projects usually lack substance and their agreements are mostly only partially or occasionally implemented (…).

Similar dynamics are at play in regard to African regional organizations that are strong formally but are undermined in their effectiveness by the role played by the member states themselves. A UNECA report on regional integration in Africa clearly put it, saying (2006: 78-79):

> [...] when political considerations rather than economic ones drive membership, countries may sign protocols to show their commitment, but not ratify them because they do not benefit from them. So, unless protocols consider the concerns and interests of all parties, integration programmes can be delayed by countries that perceive themselves as potential losers.

Conclusion

The process of regional integration in Africa has to deal with a dilemma as it offers both incentives and disincentives for African states and their leaders. On the one hand, regional institutions provide African states and leaders with a source of legitimacy that also partly ensures their security. Although in different ways, this includes the provision of security against internal threats (for example, by delegitimizing secessionist claims), immediate neighbouring threats (against a regional hegemon) but also threats coming from the rest of the world. The regime-boosting capacity of regionalism is also of great value to African leaders.

On the other hand, there are also several factors that push African states to adopt a more cautious approach towards regional integration. Not only does integration open the door for losing a hard-fought sovereignty to supranational institutions, it also represents a threat against the possibility to accumulate revenues. Not only for states who would have to lower their tariff barriers, but also for the state elites who are engaged in a 'shadow regionalism' that takes advantage of the current situation and would be threatened by a regional institution that is too strong. This dilemma has led African states to design regional institutions with several safeguards that prevent them from becoming too powerful. A middle ground has been found under the form of permanently weak regional organizations.

Despite their weaknesses, these institutions can still offer most of the advantages sought after by leaders of African states while at the same time their structural weakness still hinders their capacity and prevents them from becoming a threat to the power of African heads of states and governments. This is in fact very visible in the form of resources that African states dedicate to the regional organizations to which they belong. Many, if not all, of the African regional organizations suffer from financial problems which are mainly due to payment arrears from several member states (UNECA 2006: 59). Similarly, the staffing of these organizations is not the most adequate and is rarely based on merit or on capacity but is rather driven by political motives (UNECA 2006: 60). It is therefore not so surprising that the regional organizations themselves cannot spearhead the integration processes as, for example, the EU commission has managed to do in Europe.

African states also benefit in this regard from the low level of economic pressure to integrate. While they may be very well aware of the economic advantages of integration (or non-integration for that matter), the regional processes are still very much dominated by political considerations and strategic concerns. A survey conducted by UNECA on regional integration in Africa found that 'Half the countries cited political and strategic reasons as the main determinant for joining regional economic communities. Economic interests rank a distant second, cited by only 35%' (2006: 52). This also helps explain why overlapping memberships to various economic regional organizations such as the RECs are not seen by African states as being so problematic since the economic aspect is not their priority. Meanwhile, as political and strategic considerations, these multiple memberships not only allow some of the benefits provided by participating in the regional integration process to be gained, but also permit some forum shopping to the advantage of the member states.

References

Acharya, A. 1997. Ideas, identity and institution-building: from the "ASEAN way" to "Asia-Pacific way"? *The Pacific Review*, 10(3), 319-46.

Acharya, A. 2009. The strong in the world of the weak: Southeast Asia in Asia's regional architecture, in *Asia's New Multilateralism: Cooperation, Competition, and the Search for Community*, edited by M.J. Green and B. Gill. Columbia: Columbia University Press, 172-90.

Acharya, A. and Johnston, A.I. 2007. Comparing regional institutions: an introduction, in *Crafting Cooperation: Regional International Institutions in Comparative Perspective*, edited by A. Acharya and A.I. Johnston. Cambridge: Cambridge University Press, 1-31.

Adebajo, A. and Landsberg, C. 2005. South Africa and Nigeria as regional hegemons, in *From Cape to Congo: Southern Africa's Evolving Security Challenges*, edited by M. Baregu and C. Landsberg. Boulder: Lynne Rienner, 171-204.

African Union (AU). 2000. *Constitutive Act of the African Union*, Lomé: AU.

Allison, R. 2008. Virtual regionalism, regional structures and regime security in Central Asia, *Central Asian Survey*, 27(2), 185-202.

Ayoob, M. 1997. Defining security: a subaltern realist perspective, in *Critical Security Studies: Concepts and Cases*, edited by K. Krause and M.C. Williams. London: Routledge, 121-46.

Ayoob, M. 1998. Subaltern realism: international relations theory meets the third world, in *International Relations Theory and the Third World*, edited by S.G. Nueman. New York: St. Martin's Press, 31-54.

Babarinde, O.A. 1999. Regionalism and African foreign policies, in *African Foreign Policies*, edited by S. Wright. Boulder: Westview, 215-36.

Baldwin, R.E. 1997. Review of theoretical developments on regional integration, in *Regional Integration and Trade Liberalization in Sub – Saharan Africa, Vol. I*, edited by O.T. Ademola, I. Elbadawi and P. Collier. London: Macmillan, 24-88.

Barnett, M. and Solingen, E. 2007. Designed to fail or failure of design? the sources and institutional effects of the Arab League, in *Crafting Cooperation:*

Regional International Institutions in Comparative Perspective, edited by A. Acharya and A.I. Johnston. Cambridge: Cambridge University Press, 180-220.

Bayart, J.F. 1989. *L'Etat en Afrique – la politique du ventre*, Paris: Fayard.

Bayart, J.F., S. Ellis, and Hibou, B. 1999. *The Criminalization of the State in Africa*, Oxford: James Currey.

Bratton, M. and van de Walle, N. 1997. *Democratic experiments in Africa*, Cambridge: Cambridge University Press.

Brown, W. 2006. Africa and international relations: a comment on IR theory, anarchy and statehood, *Review of International Studies*, 32(1), 119-43.

Clapham, C. 1994. The longue durée of the African state, *African Affairs*, 93(372), 433-9.

Clapham, C. 1996. *Africa and the International system*, Cambridge: Cambridge University Press.

Clapham, C. 1999. Boundaries and states in the new African order, in *Regionalisation in Africa: Integration and Disintegration*, edited by D. Bach. Oxford: James Currey, 53-66.

Donnan, H. and Wilson, T.M. 1999. *Borders: Frontiers of Identity, Nation And State*, Oxford: Berg Publishers.

Draper, P. 2010. Rethinking the (European) Foundations of Sub-Saharan African Regional Economic Integration: A Political Economy Essay, *OECD Development Centre Working Papers*, No. 293.

Draper, P. 2012. Breaking Free from Europe: Why Africa Needs Another Model of Regional Integration, *The International Spectator*, 47(1), 67-82.

Dunn, K.C. 2001a. Introduction: Africa and international relations theory, in *Africa's challenge to International Relations Theory*, edited by K.C. Dunn and T.M. Shaw. Hampshire: Palgrave, 1-8.

Dunn, K.C. 2001b. The (Blank) African state: rethinking the sovereign state in international relations theory, in *Africa's challenge to International Relations Theory*, edited by K.C. Dunn and T.M. Shaw Hampshire: Palgrave, 46-63.

Dunn, K.C. and Shaw, T.M. (eds.) 2001. *Africa's challenge to International Relations Theory*, Hampshire: Palgrave.

Elbadawi, I. 1997. The impact of regional trade and monetary schemes on intra-sub-Saharan African trade, in *Regional Integration and Trade Liberalization in Sub-Saharan Africa*, Vol. 1, edited by O.T. Ademola, I. Elbadawi and P. Collier. London: Macmillan, 210-55.

Englebert, P. 2009. *Africa: Unity, Sovereignty, and Sorrow*, Boulder: Lynne Rienner.

Ero, C. 2005. ECOWAS and the subregional peacekeeping in Liberia, *Journal of Humanitarian Assistance*, [Online] September 2005. Available at: http://jha.ac/articles/a005.htm [accessed 19.10.2009].

Fawcett, L. and Gandois, H. 2010. Regionalism in Africa and the Middle East: Implications for EU Studies, *Journal of European Integration*, 32(6), 617-636.

Fine, J. and Yeo, S. 1997. Regional integration in sub-Saharan Africa: dead end or a fresh start?, in *Regional Integration and Trade Liberalization in Sub-Saharan Africa*, Vol. 1, edited by O.T. Ademola, I. Elbadawi and P. Collier. London: Macmillan, 429-74.

Foroutan, F. 1996. Regional integration in sub-Saharan Africa: past experience and future prospects, in *New dimensions in regional integration*, edited by J. De Melo and A. Panagariya. Cambridge: Cambridge University Press, 234-277.

Francis, D.J. 2006. *Uniting Africa: Building Regional Peace and Security Systems*, Brookfield: Ashgate.

Gibb, R. 2009. Regional Integration and Africa's Development Trajectory: meta-theories, expectations and reality, *Third World Quarterly*, 30(4), 701-721.

Haacke, J. and Williams, P.D. 2008. Conclusions: security culture and transnational challenges - ECOWAS in comparative perspective, *Journal of Contemporary African Studies*, 26(2), 213-22.

Haas, E.B. 1961. International Integration: the European and the universal process, *International Organization*, 15(3), 366-392.

Herbst, J. 2000. *States and Power in Africa: Comparative Lessons in Authority and Control*, Princeton: Princeton University Press.

Herbst, J. 2007. Crafting regional cooperation in Africa, in *Crafting Cooperation: Regional International Institutions in Comparative Perspective*, edited by A. Acharya and A.I. Johnston. Cambridge: Cambridge University Press, 129-44.

Hettne, B. 1999. Globalization and the New Regionalism: the second great transformation, in *Globalism and the New Regionalism, Vol. I*, edited by B. Hettne, A. Inotai and O. Sunkel. London: Macmillan, 1-24.

Hettne, B. 2005. Beyond the "New" Regionalism, *New Political Economy*, 10(4), 543-71.

Hettne, B. and Inotai, A. 1994. The New Regionalism: implications for global development and international security, *Research for Action* 14, Helsinki: UNU-WIDER.

Hutchful, E. 1999. The ECOMOG experience with peacekeeping in West Africa, *ISS Monograph* 36, Pretoria: Institute for Security Studies.

Jackson, R.H. 1993. *Quasi-states: Sovereignty, International Relations, and the Third World*, Cambridge: Cambridge University Press.

Jackson, R.H. and Rosberg, C.G. 1982. Why Africa's weak states persist: the empirical and the juridical in statehood, *World Politics*, 35(1), 1-24.

Klay Kieh, G. Jr. 1992. Combatants, patrons, peacemakers, and the Liberian civil conflict, *Studies in Conflict and Terrorism*, 15(2), 125-43.

Laakso, L. 2005. Beyond the notion of security community: what role for the African regional organization in peace and security? *The Round Table*, 94(381), 489-502.

Laursen, F. (ed.) 2010. *Comparative regional integration: Europe and beyond*, Surrey: Ashgate.

Lemke, D. 2003. Review: African lessons for international relations research, *World Politics*, 56(1), 114-138.

MacLean, S.J. 2004. New Regionalism in conflict in the Democratic Republic of Congo: networks of plunder and networks for peace, in *The New Regionalism in Africa*, edited by A.J. Grant and F. Söderbaum. Aldershot: Ashgate, 110-24.

Matar, K.I. and Thabit, R.W. 2004. *Lockerbie and Libya: A study in International Relations*, Jefferson: MacFarland.

Matlosa, K. 2001. The Dilemma of security in southern Africa: the case of Lesotho, in *Security and Development in Southern Africa*, edited by N. Poku. Westport: Praeger, 83-100.

Médard, J.F. 1982. The underdeveloped state in Africa: political clientelism or neo-patrimonialism? in *Private Patronage and Public Power: Political Clientelism and the Modern State*, edited by C. Clapham. London: Frances Pinter, 162-189.

Médard, J.F. 1990. L'État patrimonialisé, *Politique Africaine*, 39, 25-36.

Médard, J.F. 1991. L'Etat neo-patrimonial en Afrique noire, in *Etats D'Afrique noire: formation, mécanismes et crise*, edited by J.F. Médard. Paris: Karthala.

Migdal, J.S. 1988. *Strong Societies and Weak States. State Relations and State Capabilities in the Third World*, Princeton: Princeton University Press.

Mistry, P.S. 2000. Africa's record of regional co-operation and integration, *Journal of Modern African Studies,* 99(397), 553-573.

Nathan, L. 2002. "Organ Failure": a review of the SADC organ on politics, defence and security, in *Regional Integration for Conflict Prevention and Peace Building in Africa: Europe, SADC and ECOWAS*, edited by L. Laakso. Helsinki: University of Helsinki, 62-102.

NPafs. 1999. Tanzania withdraws from COMESA, New People African Feature Service, 90, September 1999. [Online] Available at: http://ospiti.peacelink.it/npeople/sep99/Pag1sept.html [accessed 7 March 2011].

Nkrumah, K. 1965. *Neo-Colonialism, The Last Stage of Imperialism*, London: Thomas Nelson & Sons.

Ofuatey-Kodjoe W. 1994. Regional organisations and the resolution of internal conflict: the ECOWAS intervention in Liberia, *International Peacekeeping*, 1(3), 261-302.

Onwuka, R.I. and Sesay, A. 1985. *The Future of Regionalism in Africa*, London: Macmillan.

Ravenhill, J. 1993. When weakness is strength: the Lomé IV negotiations, in *Europe and Africa: The New Phase*, edited by W. Zartman. Boulder: Lynne Rienner, 41-61.

Reno, W. 2001. How sovereignty matters: international markets and the political economy of local politics in weak states, in *Intervention and Transnationalism in Africa: Global-Local Networks of Power*, edited by T. Callaghy, R. Kassimir and R. Latham. Cambridge: Cambridge University Press.

Shaw, T.M. 2001. African foreign policy in the new millennium: from coming anarchies to security communities? from new regionalisms to new realisms? in

Africa's challenge to International Relations Theory, edited by K.C. Dunn and T.M. Shaw. Hampshire: Palgrave, 204-219.

Sindjoun, L. 2002. *Sociologie des Relations Internationales Africaines*, Paris: Khartala.

Söderbaum, F. 2003. Whose security? Comparing security regionalism in West and Southern Africa, in *New and Critical Security and Regionalism, Beyond the Nation State*, edited by J.J. Hentz and M. Bøås. London: Ashgate, 167-182.

Söderbaum, F. 2004. *The Political Economy of Regionalism; The Case of Southern Africa*, London: Palgrave-Macmillan.

Söderbaum, F. 2009. Comparative Regional Integration and Regionalism in *SAGE Handbook of Comparative Politics*, edited by T. Landman and N. Robinson. London: Sage.

Taylor, I. 2010. *The International Relations of Sub-Saharan Africa*, New York: Continuum Publishing.

Taylor, I. and Williams, P.D. 2008. Political culture, state elites and regional security in West Africa, *Journal of Contemporary African Studies*, 26(2), 137-149.

United Nations Economic Commission for Africa (UNECA) 2004. *Assessing Regional Integration in Africa,* Addis Ababa: UNECA.

United Nations Economic Commission for Africa (UNECA) 2006. *Assessing Regional Integration in Africa II; Rationalizing Regional Economic Communities*, Addis Ababa: UNECA.

United Nations University – Comparative Regional Integration Studies (UNU-CRIS) 2008. *Capacity Survey: Regional and Other Intergovernmental Organizations in the Maintenance of Peace and Security*, Bruges: UNU-CRIS.

Vale, P. 2003. *Security and Politics in South Africa: The Regional Dimension*, Boulder: Lynne Rienner.

Zartman, W. 1995 *Collapsed States: The Disintegration and Restoration of Legitimate Authority*, Boulder and London: Lynne Rienner.

Chapter 3
UNASUR in the Context of a Changing Regional Environment: Prospects and Challenges

Mark Kirton

The changing global political, economic and social environment has undoubtedly brought new thinking and perspectives on issues related to regional integration and resulted in a new phase of regional integration arrangements being initiated in South America in the recent past. Indeed, there is general consensus that regional integration is of significant value in this current 'globalized' world and while, for decades, integration has been promoted as a means through which economic development and self-sufficiency within a grouping could be attained, the rapid changes that are taking place have caused a reconfiguration in terms of the priority elements in the integration process. This has resulted in the emergence of new issues such as democratic consolidation, security, the environment and physical infrastructural integration, among others, as 'front burner' priority issues. Equally as important, as Shaw *et al.* (2010) suggest, the proliferation of 'new' issues such as civil society, climate change and corporate social responsibility (CSR) has lead to a burgeoning of novel heterogeneous global and hemispheric coalitions. Additionally, it has been observed that regionalism in Latin America has a history unlike any other, and from the onset of independence; various attempts have been made to pursue integration and regionalism as development strategies, from the historical efforts by Simon Bolivar to the most recent efforts seen in initiatives such as the Union of South American States (UNASUR). In the case of the Caribbean, the thinking with respect to regional integration is not a new phenomenon, and since the 1950s, with the establishment of the West Indian Federation, until contemporary times, with the birth of CARICOM and most recently the Association of Caribbean States (ACS), the Caribbean has witnessed significant efforts aimed at uniting the small states of the region. It is not without significance that, in the changing framework of regional integration, two CARICOM member states, Guyana and Suriname, both South American by geography, are active participants in UNASUR and therefore provide an opportunity to enhance the regional process and act as a 'bridge' between CARICOM and South America. It is against this background that this paper sets out to assess the emergence of UNASUR and to examine its major priority issues as well as the prospects and challenges related to its development, especially for its small members, Guyana and Suriname.

Shaw *et al.* (2010) have observed that a regionalized world is not a novelty but an integrated part of human history and in the case of Latin America, as we have observed, the thinking on integration in Latin America is also not recent. Since the 1800s, Simon Bolivar and Francisco de Miranda, among others, have been advocating the unification of Latin America. Additionally, in the post-World War II period, the establishment of The Latin American Free Trade Association in 1960, and its successor, the Latin American Integration Association (LAIA) in 1980, the Central American Common Market in 1958, and the Andean Pact in 1969 were indicators of Latin America's continuing commitment to the efforts to sustain collaboration among the states of the region, while at the same time reducing their dependence on the states of the North. It was, however, the return to democratic rule in Latin America in the 1980s which brought with it a new leadership that saw, as a priority, the need to institutionalize regional collaboration. Indeed, the establishment of the Rio Group in 1986, the revitalization of the Central American Integration System (SICA), the establishment of the Southern Common Market (MERCOSUR) and the Association of Caribbean States (ACS) all pointed towards a new thrust for greater regional collaboration. These trends in regional integration can be seen in the context of 'new regionalism' which according to Caballero (2007) can be described as 'a constructed, multilayered space involving several regionalizing actors'. Additionally, Soderbaum (2003) sees the process of new regionalism as 'fluid, multi-dimensional, multi-actor and multi-level' which according to Hettne (2005) took shape 'in a multi-polar world order'. It is also useful to note that De Lombaerde (2006) concurs with this view and has posited that this new regionalism is 'part of a global structural transformation in which the non-state actors are active participants, found at different levels of the global system'. New regionalism is also seen as a comprehensive process and as Hettne (1999) noted, this process includes 'trade and economic integration, but also the environment, social policy, security and democracy, including the whole issue of accountability and legitimacy'. As Nillson and Gustaffson (2012) also note, the last two global decades have seen a general trend of strengthening relationships between members of the developing world instead of relying completely on old alliances with the northern hemisphere and, as they suggest, Latin America is no exception.

It was against the background of the global and regional reconfigurations in the integration process that UNASUR was born and several factors can be attributed to its establishment. In the first place, the view has been advanced that a new level of self-assertion emerged in the region in the post-Cold War era, and that the creation of a clearly defined regional political and economic space for autonomous development became a priority. It has also been noted that the emergence of UNASUR was part of the 'project' in the development of a post-hegemonic regional order, but according to Riggirozzi (2010), like other emerging regional efforts, UNASUR should not be seen simply as 'an ad hoc sub-regional response to the recurrent crisis of neoliberal governance and the collapse of US-led hemispheric leadership', but as she noted, the new arrangement in South

America should be seen as 'a viable manifestation of the re-politicization of the region, creating foundations for new policies in which citizens, social movements, political parties and government leaders interact and construct new understandings of regional community'.

Of equal importance in the establishment of UNASUR, however, was the influence and leadership of Brazil, and its demonstration of a proactive and assertive foreign policy. By the end of the twentieth century, a priority in Brazilian foreign policy was increased coordination and collaboration with South American states under Brazilian leadership, and as Saraiva (2010) contends, 'integration with its neighbours was seen as the surest route for Brazil to gain international standing, while also helping Brazil realize its potential and form a bloc that was strong enough to have more international clout'. The Brazilian government, under Fernando Henrique Cardoso, presented clear signals that South America would lead the way in reengineering the integration process when, in 2000, it hosted the First Summit of South American Presidents. At the summit meeting in Brasilia it created the platform for sustained regional collaboration, based on Cardoso's vision of a 'South American Union'. At that meeting, the priorities that were established included higher levels of political cooperation and the enhancement of physical infrastructure among the South American states, which were aimed at reigniting the region's development through improved communications and transportation networks. In 2004, Cardoso's successor, President Ignacio 'Lula' Da Silva, sustained the regional agenda of his predecessor and led the effort for the establishment of the South American Community of Nations (SACN). The Cuzco Declaration, signed by the South American heads of state in Peru in 2004, clearly indicated the new priorities. These included political and diplomatic coordination, physical integration through the creation of new transport networks, and increasing the regional states' bargaining power in the international arena, leading to its main goal: the formation of an integrated union among the people of South America. The Constitutive Treaty of UNASUR further presents this objective:

> to build, in a participatory and consensual manner, an integration and union among its peoples in the cultural, social, economic and political fields, prioritizing political dialogue, social policies, education, energy, infrastructure, financing and the environment, among others, with a view to eliminating socioeconomic inequality … to strengthen democracy and reduce asymmetries within the framework of strengthening the sovereignty and independence of the States.

The Cuzco Declaration also indicated the South American leaders' determination to 'develop a politically, socially, economically, environmentally and infrastructurally integrated South American area that will contribute toward strengthening the unique South American identity and, from a sub-regional standpoint and in coordination with other regional integration experiences, that of Latin America and the Caribbean and will give it a greater weight and representativeness in international forums'. It was therefore clear that the advancement and reinforcement of strategic linkages among the states, as well as the inclusion of the Caribbean in the region's increased insertion into the global arena, were among its priorities.

As has been the case in other regional arrangements, there are undoubtedly clear challenges to the success of UNASUR. In the first place, there are those who suggest that adding another institution to the plethora of integration efforts existing in the region could add to the economic and human resource constraints currently being experienced, especially by the small states of the grouping as they confront the pressures of multiple regional and international commitments. Further, there is the concern that Brazil, as the leading player in UNASUR, could seek to flex its muscles especially in relation to its influence on the smaller states in the grouping, and strengthen its role as the 'reluctant hegemon'. It has also been posited that, given the unquestionable supremacy of the Brazilian economy in the region, any slippage or deterioration in Brazil's economic fortunes could negatively impact all the member states. Additionally, the prevalence of low-intensity conflicts and border issues among member states, as exemplified in the Venezuela-Guyana border issue, the Suriname-Guyana boundary dispute, the Colombia-Venezuela disagreements, and the maritime controversy between Peru and Chile, among others, are historically rooted and could constrain efforts at unified approaches to common challenges. It is also noted that South America's record with respect to economic and social equality has not been impressive, and persistent poverty has been a consistent barrier to development in the member states. As these states choose varying economic pathways and political orientations, their divergent approaches can serve to constrain the emergence of a cohesive unit. One must also consider the challenge that faces UNASUR in its attempt to unite, in the economic sphere, two existing large free trade systems, The Andean Community and MERCOSUR, and simultaneously integrate Chile, Suriname and Guyana in this arrangement. It has also been noted (Rodrigues 2011) that in the preparation of the agenda for the development of UNASUR, there has been a preference for 'presidential diplomacy' and the absence of civil society participation in the formulation of its guiding policy framework, and this 'participation deficit' could limit the emergence of a strong unified group.

While these challenges and constraints may seem daunting, there are potential benefits that can accrue to the grouping. With UNASUR's total population of over 370 million people and its large market size, its combined GDP of $2 trillion, its status as one of the world's leading food production and export regions, and the region with more than 25% of the world's remaining fresh water, it can be seen that UNASUR has the capacity, as a region, to influence the global balance of power. Further, it has been seen that the leading country, Brazil, has reached out to the smaller states. As Espinoza (2011) suggests, Brazil has adopted a policy of multilateralism which allows equal participation by small states like Guyana and Suriname, and in the process, avoided the traditional hegemonic practices that could have created early tensions in the grouping. Espinoza further contends that the resistance to political hegemony that could have occurred 'has been transformed to "states' cooperation and active participation".'

As we examine the priority items on UNASUR's agenda, it is clear that the maintenance and consolidation of the democratic process and the promotion of peace are major features in this new regional arrangement. As the Constitutive Treaty states, UNASUR has as one of its main pillars a firm commitment to stability and the rule of law with its aims directed

> towards the strengthening of multilateralism and the rule of law in international relations … a culture of peace in a world free of nuclear weapons and weapons of mass destruction. UNASUR is also based upon the guiding principles of: unlimited respect for sovereignty and territorial integrity and inviolability of States; self-determination of the peoples; solidarity; cooperation; peace; democracy; citizen participation…

Further, one can glean that the objectives and scope of UNASUR place democracy and territorial integrity and the inviolability of borders as paramount and that the organization is committed to upholding these ideals. With this level of commitment from a region which has had a long association with authoritarian rule, the consolidation of the democratic process seems assured. It is also important to note that in order to further reinforce its commitment to democracy, UNASUR, at its summit meeting in 2010 in Guyana, put in place The Additional Protocol to the Constitutive Treaty of UNASUR on Commitment to Democracy, which states that UNASUR is committed to 'the promotion, defence and protection of democratic order, rule of law and its institutions, human rights and fundamental freedoms', and provides mechanisms in cases of 'a breach or the threat of a breach against the democratic order, a violation of the constitutional order or any situation that jeopardises the legitimate exercising of power and the application of the values and principles of democracy'.[1] These institutional arrangements provide increased levels of confidence to the region's citizenry as the remaining fragile democracies in the region seek to sustain the democratic gains made over the last two decades.

Another important issue since the establishment of UNASUR has been the continuation and strengthening of regional infrastructural projects, which were launched in 2000 as the Initiative for The Integration of the Regional Infrastructure in South America (IIRSA). Infrastructure has traditionally served as a key driver in stimulating economic growth by facilitating production and trade, thus generating income and employment. According to the Inter-American Development Bank, (IDB), IIRSA has been established as a forum for coordination of intergovernmental actions, with the aim of promoting the development of transportation, energy and communications infrastructure to strengthen the physical integration of the 12

---

1 Protocol to the Constitutive Treaty of UNASUR on commitment to democracy. http://opnew.op.gov.gy/index.php?option=com_content&view=article&id=1108:additional-protocol-to-the-constitutive-treaty-of-unasur-on-commitment-to-democracy.

It has been noted that UNASUR has also included the issues of economic security in its mandate. The Bank of the South, which was initially proposed by Venezuela and agreed upon in 2007, has as its main goal to 'finance the social and economic development of the region; making use of regional savings, to strengthen regional integration, to reduce asymmetries and to promote an equitable distribution of investments within bank member countries.' This new entity, which will serve as a development bank for the region that will count on US$20 billion for development projects, has been established, and when operational according to Ortiz and Ugarteche (2008) it will seek 'to win autonomy and "policy space" to implement different development policies, new policies supportive of the region's sovereignty and responsive to their citizens'. The bank will provide access to resources to promote trade and support investment in education, health and other social areas, and a unique feature is that unlike other international financial institutions, such as the IMF and the World Bank, each country has one vote and the right to vote is not determined by the level of financial resources invested in the bank. This is an important feature in the new integration arrangement and can add to the confidence level in the process, especially among the small member states like Guyana and Suriname who are seeking to ensure the implementation of the consensus principle as much as possible in the organization.

As described above, UNASUR has prioritized some important issues including the maintenance and consolidation of the democratic process, the integration of the region's physical infrastructure to enhance trade, economic competitiveness and citizen contact, and development cooperation, through the establishment of the Bank of the South and security and defence through the South American Defence Council. The question therefore arises as to the long-term benefits and the potential challenges to its development, especially with regard to the participation of small states like Guyana and Suriname. In the first place, the relatively fast pace of the development of UNASUR, in comparison to the seemingly lethargic condition of contemporary CARICOM processes, along with the potential trade and developmental benefits present the two CARICOM member states, Guyana and Suriname, with an attractive option and the possibility of strong insertion into the South American region. As then-President Jagdeo noted in his address to the Fourth Summit of UNASUR in Guyana in 2010, Guyana has moved towards taking a firm place among South American nations since the new grouping has been established on 'a set of shared, progressive values. The chief of these values is the belief that all peoples, nations and countries should be treated equally – whether large or small, rich or poor, geographically central or of the periphery'.

The commitment to sustained involvement in the South American integration process by Guyana and Suriname is also seen as emerging from the perception that South America has now found a new place in the global political and economic environment. As President Jagdeo posited, 'we can draw satisfaction from South America's place in the world today. We are no longer a continent associated with dictatorships. We are no longer seen as the region that precipitates repeated economic collapse. We are no longer just a commodity producer that powers the industries of the rest of the world. And in the same way as Guyana is no longer part of the periphery of our continent, South America is no longer seen as peripheral to the global economy or major international decisions'.

Additionally, the focus on democratic consolidation implies that there is an emerging consensus among South American nations in relation to democratic governance, and the introduction of the 'Democratic Clause' indicates that the states are prepared to put their full weight behind protecting legitimately elected governments in the event of any extra-constitutional threats to their authority. Especially in the fragile small states of the organization, this must be seen as a reassuring development that demonstrates total intolerance for the breakdown of constitutional order, which can have serious negative implications for the process of democratic consolidation. Of equal significance is the mediating role UNASUR has played in providing conflict transformation mechanisms in issues involving member states. In the light of the experience gained in its interventions in conflicts involving member states, the organization can play a transformative role in the border controversies between Guyana and Suriname and Guyana and Venezuela and advance the process of regional cohesion.

The priority that has been given to the development of the region's physical infrastructure through the IIRSA project is also important to the small states like Guyana and Suriname since it can provide the basis for the emergence of new centres of economic gravity in the region. Additionally, road and bridge networks play an important role in stimulating trade and economic activities and generate job creation and income generation. For small South American states like Guyana and Suriname, this prospect for enhanced connectivity is critical since it can also facilitate the shift from their strong reliance on the coastal regions, currently populated with a majority of the countries' inhabitants and the focus of the major economic activity, to sustained development of the hinterland regions, with the promising prospects for investments in new export-oriented industries, as well as improved access to large South American markets, like Brazil. The surface communication enhancement, as part of the IIRSA process, can also serve to link the 'Guianas' and as a result, create the opportunity for increased trade and investment with France, through French Guiana, which remains an overseas 'department' of France. In addition, the IIRSA project also carries with it the potential for greater tourism levels among the UNASUR states which can also serve to promote greater understanding among the people of the region and reduce the remaining areas of mutual suspicion and mistrust which can limit the success of integration process. The critical importance of the infrastructural linkage has been recognized, and as President Bouterse noted,

> Suriname considers the physical integration of the infrastructure as essential, and the improved connection with the rest of the countries of the continent is qualified as a basic condition for a meaningful and successful integration in South America. (2010)

The thrust towards increased cooperation in security must be of great interest to the small states, especially Guyana and Suriname, which have become important transhipment points for cocaine and other illicit drugs and which have limited capacity to deal with interdiction and border control. Indeed, a clear recognition of the need to collectively confront the security challenges and transnational threats of organized crime, and domestic and interstate conflicts which negatively impact regional stability, has brought positive responses from Guyana and Suriname. Even though, as Flemes and Radseck (2009) suggest, South America's security agenda is so extensive, multi-level and complex that 'it demands simultaneous management of domestic crises, interstate conflicts, and transnational threats', the creation of the region's own security governance structures can provide for the emergence of collective strategies which can serve to reduce crime, and inspire further confidence in the regional effort at providing its citizenry with greater levels of public safety and security.

While there may be lingering concerns about the viability and sustainability of UNASUR, in the light of the varying political and economic pathways, the membership, the establishment of the Community of Latin American and Caribbean States (CELAC), and the Pacific Alliance which includes three UNASUR members (Colombia, Chile and Peru), and their potential for overlap and fragmentation as well as the multiple commitments of other member states in the 'spaghetti bowl' of regional integration arrangements in South America, there are positive signs related to the development of UNASUR. The organization's potential contribution to democratic consolidation and its commitment to the protection of citizens' rights and the constitutional provisions of all member states, in a process that goes beyond trade-led issues, has led to the adoption of the 'Democratic Clause' to UNASUR's Constitutive Treaty and approved by all member states. Already, the organization has mediated in domestic and international disputes and has gained valuable experience in the process. This can be utilized in conflict management and transformation processes in the future, and reduces the need for extra-regional intervention. The commitment to integrate the region's infrastructure has already seen positive results and can serve in the future to promote sustainable development, generate employment and improve the quality of life of the region's citizenry. The influences of new regionalism are evident with the emergence of new space for consultation and collaboration in South America. With the sustained engagement of member states, UNASUR can emerge as a viable model of 21st-century regional integration.

Table 3.1 IIRSA – Developmental Hubs and Country Beneficiaries

HUB	BENEFICIARIES (Countries)
Andean Hub	Venezuela, Colombia, Ecuador, Peru, Bolivia
Southern Andean Hub	Chile, Argentina, Bolivia
Capricorn Hub	Brazil, Argentina, Paraguay, Bolivia, Chile
Paraguay-Parana Waterway Hub	Paraguay, Uruguay
Amazon Hub	Colombia, Ecuador, Peru, Brazil
Southern Hub	Argentina, Chile
Central Inter-oceanic Hub	Bolivia, Brazil, Chile, Paraguay, Peru
MERCOSUR-Chile	Uruguay, Paraguay, Brazil, Chile, Argentina
Peru-Brazil-Bolivia Hub	Peru, Brazil, Bolivia
Guianese Shield Hub	Venezuela, Brazil, Guyana, Suriname

References

Bouterse, D. 2010. *Intervention on the occasion of the MERCOSUR Summit*, Brazil.

Burges, S. 2007. Building a Global Southern Coalition: the Competing approaches of Brazil's Lula and Venezuela's Chavez. *Third World Quarterly*, 28(7), 1343-1358.

Bryan, A. 1990. The Integration Movement in Latin America: Theory, process, trends and options, in *Regionalism: Comparative Experience and prospects*, edited by A.T. Bryan and L. Dembinski. Geneva: Graduate Institute of International Studies.

Caballero, J. 2007. *Problematizing Regional Integration in Latin America: Regional Identity and the enmeshed State – The Central American Case*. [Online.] UNU-CRIS Working Paper 2007/2. Available at http://www.iadb.org/intal/intalcdi/PE/2007/00037.pdf [Accessed on 22.09.2011].

Castaneda, S. 2009. *The Consolidation of U.S. Military Presence in Colombia and Those Who Are Apprehensive Over it*. [Online.] Council of Hemispheric Affairs, 25 September 2009. Available at http://www.coha.org/the-consolidation-of-u-s-military-presence-in-colombia/ [Accessed on 22.09.2011].

Espinoza, R.S. 2011. *Could Brazil become a world power in the 21st Century without an integrated South America?* [Online.] IPSA-ECPR Joint Conference, Sao Paulo, Brazil, 16-19 February 2011. Available at http://www.saopaulo2011.ipsa.org/sites/default/files/papers/paper-1148.pdf [Accessed on 22.09.2011].

Farrell, M., Hettne, B. and Langenhove, L. (eds.) 2005. *Global Politics of Regionalism: Theory and Practice*. London: Pluto Press.

Flemes, D. and Radseck M. 2009. *Creating Multilevel Security Governance in South America.* Hamburg; GIGA Working Paper No 117.

Hettne, B. and Inotai, A. 1994. *The New Regionalism.* Helsinki: UNU World Institute for Development and Economics Research.

Hettne, B., Inotai, A. and Sunkel, O. (eds.) 1999. *Globalism and the New Regionalism.* London: Macmillan Press.

Hurrell, A. 1998. Security in Latin America. *International Affairs.* 74(3), 529-546.

Ishmael, O. 2010. *UNASUR Health Council promotes training and research.* [Online.] Available at http://world-countries.net/archives/20325 [Accessed on 22.09.2011].

Jagdeo, B. 2010. *Address at the Fourth Summit of UNASUR*, Guyana.

Killeen, T. 2007. *A Perfect storm in the Amazon Wilderness: Development and Conservation in the context of the IIRSA.* [Online.] Available at https://www.conservation.org/publications/Documents/AABS.7_Perfect_Storm_English.low.res.pdf [Accessed on 22.09.2011].

Ortiz, I. and Ugarteche, O. 2008. Bank of the South: Progress and Challenge. *Latin American Network on Debt, Development and Rights. (LATINDAD).*

Mace, G., Cooper A.F. and Shaw, T. (eds.) 2010. *Inter-American Cooperation at the Crossroads.* London: Palgrave Macmillan.

Nillson, M. and Gustafsson, J. (eds.) 2012. *Latin American Responses to Globalization in the 21st Century.* London: Palgrave Macmillan.

Phillips, T. 2009. South American Nations Agree on Technical Rules for the Bank of the South. [Online.] *Americas Program Report.* Available at: www.iadb.org/intal/intalcdi/PE/2009/03636.pdf [Accessed on 22.09.2011].

Radu, M. 2005. The Latin American Vortex. *The Journal of International Security Affairs*, 9, 13-18.

Riggirozzi, P. 2010. *Region, Regionness and Regionalism in Latin America: Towards a new Synthesis.* [Online.] Latin American Trade Network. Available at http://www.latn.org.ar/web/wp-content/uploads/2011/03/WP130.pdf [Accessed on 22.09.2011].

Rodrigues, G.M.A. and Rodrigues, T. 2011. La Union de las Naciones Sudamericanas (UNASUR) y los nuevos temas de la agenda regional de paz y secguridad: roles y mecanismos de participacion de sociedad civil. *In De loa ONU al ALBA: Prevencion de conflictos y espacios de participacion ciudadana.* Barcelona: Icaria Editorial.

Sanchez, A. 2008. *The South American Defense Council, UNASUR, the Latin American Military and the Region's Political Process.* [Online.] Available at http://www.coha.org/the-south-american-defense-council-unasur-the-latin-american-military-and-the-region%E2%80%99s-political-process/ [Accessed on 22.09.2011].

Sanchez, A. 2009. *South America and its Likelihood of a Season of Splendid Little Wars: An Analysis of Arms Races and Regional Geopolitics.* [Online.] Council on Hemispheric Affairs. Available at http://www.coha.org/south-america-and-its-likelihood-of-a-season-of-splendid-little-wars-an-analysis-of-arms-races-and-regional-geopolitics/ [Accessed on 22.09.2011].

Saraiva, M.G. 2010. Brazilian Foreign Policy towards South America during the Lula Administration: Caught between South America and MERCOSUR. *Revista Brasileira de Politica Nacional,* 53, 151-168.

Sennes, R. and Onuki, J. 2006. The Brazilian Foreign Policy and the Hemispheric Security. *Revista Fuerzas Armadas Soc.* Vol.1.

Soderbaum, F. 2003. Introduction: Theories of New Regionalism, in *Theories of New Regionalism: A Palgrave Reader*, edited by F. Soderbaum and T. M. Shaw. New York: Palgrave.

Soderbaum, F. and Shaw, T. (eds.) 2003. *Theories of New Regionalism.* London: Palgrave Macmillan.

Stone, M. 2009. Security According To Buzan: A Comprehensive Security Analysis. *Security Discussion Papers Series, 1.* New York: Columbia University.

Union of South American Nations Constitutive Treaty. Available at http://www.brasilemb.org/component/content/article/6-uncategorized/77-south-american-union-of-nations-constitutive-treaty. [Accessed on 22.09.2011].

Van Dijck, P. 2008. Troublesome construction: The rationale and risks of IIRSA in *European Review of Latin American and Caribbean Studies*, 85, 101-120.

Varas, A. 2008. *Brazil in South America: from indifference to Hegemony.* [Online.] FRIDE. Available at www.fride.org/download/COM_Brazil_Sudamerican_ENG.pdf [Accessed on 22.09.2011].

Varas, A. 2010. *Current Trends in Latin America and the Caribbean.* [Online.] Norwegian Peacebuilding Centre, September 2010. Available at http://www.norlarnet.uio.no/pdf/news/noref_current_trends/2010_aug.pdf [Accessed on 22.09.2011].

Chapter 4
Constraints to Regional Integration in Central Africa

Jean Kenfack

The issue of integration in Central Africa cannot be examined without taking into account the context of the African independences, and the debates that shook the continent before and immediately afterwards concerning the correct formula to be adopted in order to establish, in the long-term, the break away from colonial domination and to lay the foundations for the autonomous development of the African continent. This reflection on the appropriate model was fuelled by the fact that Africa was able to take its cue from the other continents where regional integration initiatives were in progress. However, the African process towards embracing this universalist tendency and embarking on the road towards the proliferation of concerted, inter-State action was marked by disorganization, which is why the results in many cases were actually contradictory to the original goals.

After gaining independence, the idea of integrating in such a way as to encompass in one model all of the political and economic aspects was not the primary preoccupation for the majority of African leaders. It was not until the Kinshasa summit in 1967 that the General Secretary of the OAU, Diallo Telli, highlighted the undeniable connectivity between the political domain, the sphere of privileged interest of the Organization, and the economic domain, pushed into the background and left to the United Nations Economic Commission for Africa (UNECA). Telli instigated the process that would continue with the Alger summit in 1968, where the idea of a common market and of sub-regional organizations was launched. The declaration resulting from the Alger summit highlighted the essential nature of economic integration in order to fulfil the goals of the OAU. A resolution in that sense was actually adopted in 1970 by the Conference of Heads of State and Government, unfortunately with no practical effect. However, it did have the advantage of having specified a certain number of principles in the domain of economic development. The Addis-Ababa declaration instigated a significant turning point in this direction by the formulation of recommendations to achieve 'the economic independence and development of the continent through the effective mobilization of its immense human and cultural resources'. However, this Declaration was not met with a different fate than its predecessors, and there were no satisfactory consequences, due, among other things, to the absence of a common political will. Its authors were not discouraged by these difficulties, however, which constitutes one of the paradoxes of economic integration in

Africa. It gives the impression that the repeated failures in the process actually bestow upon it a more substantial legitimacy. As Kamto notes: 'because the economic situation on the continent has continued to deteriorate, integration has kept its appeal. People even see it as a panacea' (1987: 840). The process continued in Addis-Ababa in 1973, then in Libreville in July 1977 with a decision of the Conference concerning the progressive creation of an African Economic Community.[1]

Within this same approach, African experts held a conference in Monrovia in 1979 and laid the foundations for the Monrovia Declaration adopted by the OAU. Its *leitmotiv* was to achieve 'collective self-reliance in social and economic development'. This Declaration is entitled 'Monrovia Declaration of Commitment of the Heads of State and Government, of the Organization of African Unity on Guidelines and Measures for National and Collective Self-Reliance in Social and Economic Development for the Establishment of a New International Economic Order', and it calls for the creation of a common market, as a precursor to an African Economic Community.

Building on the Monrovia process, the Conference of Heads of State and Government of the pan-African organization adopted the Lagos Plan of Action (LPA) in April 1980, confirming Africa's choice for the promotion of collective, independent and endogenous development as well as achieving economic independence (OAU 1982: 230). The African leaders committed themselves to 'establish[ing] national, sub-regional and regional institutions which will facilitate the attainment of objectives of self-reliance and self-sustainment'. The text denounces the injustices and pressures put upon African States, criticizing the constraints and the insidious nature of the international economic system, while at the same time observing the failure of global development strategies.[2] What is more, the LPA decided to undertake the reworking and reorientation of the structures that supported the economic foundations of the continent. While flawed with contradictions, the LAP nonetheless constitutes a noteworthy stage in the history of the OAU. The growing awareness by the African States was further strengthened by the Abuja Treaty of 3 June 1991, which created the African Economic Community (AEC), invested with the power to take binding decisions.

However, even in 1962, the UN Economic Commission for Africa had recommended the creation of common markets in the same mould as the EEC. Furthermore, while concerting with the OAU, the Commission divided up the continent into economic sub-regions: North Africa, East Africa, Southern African, West Africa and Central Africa.[3] The Economic and Social Council of the United

---

1 The decision of the Conference confirms the Kinshasa declaration of the Council of Ministers adopted in December 1976.

2 The LPA designated the year 2000 for the actual establishment of an African Economic Community.

3 See: Resolution CM/RES.464 (XXVI) of the Council of Ministers of the OAU on the Division of Africa into Five Regions.

Nations adopted this initiative as its own during a meeting in Geneva on 13 July 1964, and considered this division to be the basis of the project of sub-regional cooperation and concerted industrial development. The originators of this compartmentalization were convinced that the eventual outcome would be the creation of a common market on the continental level, representing a fundamental step for the establishment of an African Economic Community. This viewpoint was adopted by the OAU in 1973 (Sekou Toure 1980). With this in mind, a Treaty establishing the Economic Community of West African States was adopted on 28 May 1975 in Lagos, uniting 16 States[4] regardless of their different historical and cultural backgrounds, as the organization comprises Anglophone, Francophone and Lusophone countries. A few years later, this model was reproduced in Central Africa by the Treaty of Libreville, on 18 October 1983, creating the Economic Community of Central African States[5] between 11 States. Along these same lines, a 'Memorandum of understanding on the institutionalization of the SADCC'. was adopted in July 1981 in Salisbury. Similarly, a Treaty bringing about the establishment of the Preferential Trade Area (PTA) was signed in Lusaka on 21 December 1981 and entered into force on 30 September 1982. In this way, Africa was able to utilize the impetus of the UN in order to start to build the structures that would enable integration to materialize over the continent. With this in mind, the LPA had planned to cover the whole of the continent in its organization in order to deal with its economic difficulties, both present and future. Unfortunately, soon after the launch, the achievement of its objectives was slowed down considerably by these economic problems along with the Structural Adjustment Plans (SAP) introduced by the World Bank and the IMF, as well as the adoption of a strategy designed to reinforce national economies, which negatively affected the integration process.

The creation of large-scale organizations did not spell the end of smaller organizations based upon colonial solidarity and affinities (Kenfack 2003: 11). In fact, in parallel to the timid integration efforts on the continental level, a sub-regionalist trend has developed; although it is possible to criticize this tendency to create international organizations that reproduce the colonial divides. Already during the colonial period, certain colonizing countries had attempted to favour these groupings (Gonidec 1985:147). We can use as examples the creation of the EACSO (East African Common Services Organization), ECOWAS (Economic Community of West African States) created by the Treaty of Adidjan the 17 April 1973 comprising six ex-French colonies from Western Africa (Ouali 1982), the WAEMU (West African Economic and Monetary Union) through its Treaty of

4 The member States of the ECOWAS are Benin, Burkina Faso, Cape Verde, Côte d'Ivoire, The Gambia, Ghana, Guinea (Conakry), Guinea Bissau, Liberia, Mali, Niger, Nigeria, Senegal, Sierra Leone, and Togo. Mauritania withdrew from the Organization.

5 The member States are Angola, Burundi, Cameroon, Central African Republic, Chad, Congo, Democratic Republic of Congo, Gabon, and São Tome and Principe. Rwanda is in the process of withdrawing.

23 November 1973, the Customs and Economic Union of Central Africa (UDEAC) on 8 December 1964,[6] as well as the Economic Community of the Great Lakes Countries (CEPGL) by a Treaty on 9 September 1977. The same can be said for the attempts to group together the Lusophone countries in the form of international organizations.

We can see therefore that several factors contribute to the multiplication of international integration Organizations and Communities in Africa. This situation reproduces itself over the whole continent, which represents a rather fragmented landscape for the purposes of integration, even if there are noticeable differences.

In Central Africa, this multiplicity of institutions is rife, even if the integrationist position seems to accommodate the official line. Consequently, the salient feature of the region is the existence of a whole spectrum of international organizations oriented towards pursuing the integration process (CEMAC, ECCAS, CEPGL, OHADA, CIMA, the Commission of the Gulf of Guinea…). This wide range of structures is, however, in great contrast to the actual progress made in this domain, given that Central Africa is generally presented as the 'weak link' of African integration, and the region where integration encounters the greatest problems. In this international context with an unprecedented salience of regional issues, we are faced with the need to transform this region into a partner capable of taking on its responsibilities in both the African and international contexts. It is therefore necessary to identify the different constraints that surround the integration process in this geographical area, in order to devise a cure to save Central Africa from its inertia. These obstacles are principally the unfavourable political environment for the purposes of integration (I), and a lack of ownership of the integration process by endogenous actors (II).

An Unfavourable Political Environment for the Purposes of Integration

Heavy obstacles weigh upon the integration process in Central Africa. Not only does this endeavour concern economically frail countries, but at the same time the conflicts that constitute one of the principal characteristics of this part of the continent have a harmful effect on the attempts to form compact groupings of States that would be able to become real decision-making hubs for the region. In fact, Central Africa can be considered on the same level as those regions where peace remains but a mirage for their populations, whether before or just after their independence, or even today. The number of conflicts may be decreasing, but

6 We must underline the fact that the customs and economic relations between Cameroon and the other territories were subject to regulation in 1942, and a customs union was established between Cameroon and French Equatorial Africa by a decree on 27 December 1942, which remained in force until 1948. A convention was also signed on 19 October 1948 and renewed on 17 February 1955 which formed the basis of quotas for the trade between these territories.

the States of this region are by no means free from the causes of instability. The crises that have affected or continue to tear apart this part of the continent can be classified either as conflicts that aim to achieve the right to self-determination, or conflicts concerning legitimacy. In spite of this, Central Africa holds a privileged geopolitical position, seen as the heartland of the African continent due to its importance and centrality. This conflict-ridden situation is understandably preoccupying, given that it annihilates any efforts to accomplish the wellbeing of the populations (Kenfack 2009). Alongside the proliferation of conflict, we must emphasize the issue of the appropriate level for African integration, for which it seems difficult to find a suitable solution. The resulting hesitation has a stifling effect on the regional integration initiatives.

The Proliferation of Conflicts

A quick glance at 'Greater'[7] Central Africa confirms that only two of the member States (Cameroon and Gabon) are in a situation of peace and relative stability. The region is worn down by conflicts of an internal nature as well as with external elements that feed and consequently revive them. This area is therefore renowned for its conflicts, a situation that neutralizes the efforts made towards regional integration and supported by international partners.

In Angola and Brazzaville, the rebel movements were reduced to silence as a result of the military power struggle in favour of the authorities in place, but we are still far from achieving a stable situation. The civil war in Congo culminated in the victory and return to power of the ex-President Sassou Nguessou, whereas in Angola, the death of the UNITA leader Jonas Savimbi during battle brought the movement back to the negotiation table to discuss the pacification of the country. In Congo, a consensus has not yet been found regarding the exact cause of the explosion of the munitions depot in Mpila, Brazzaville where there were more than 200 deaths, 1240 injured and 5000 people left without shelter at the beginning of March 2012. As for Rwanda, Burundi and the DRC, the efforts made to pacify these countries were faced with irredentism of various origins. The Great Lakes Region, in which we find these States, is considered a hotbed of conflict, and there have even been instances in this area where several States have been at war on the territory of another State. This was for example the case for Uganda and Rwanda on the territory of the Democratic Republic of Congo. As for Chad and the Central African Republic, these States are vulnerable to internal factors of instability, multiplied by the neighbouring Sudanese conflict, in this case in Darfur and Uganda. Equatorial Guinea and Sao Tome and Principe are not lacking in this respect, where the fear of destabilizing factors has become practically permanent. It is therefore nothing new when we say that Central Africa is the arena of conflicts *par excellence.* The situation leads the countries to deploy their resources in order

7 This 'Greater' Central Africa comprises 11 states and results from the division used by UN institutions.

to obtain military means rather than seeking the economic and social wellbeing which would be attainable in many ways through regional community building.

Alongside the conflicts that are taking place in the Central African area, the States of this region also suffer the effects of the conflicts ongoing either in the immediate vicinity (such as in Darfur between sedentary farmers and the pastoral populations of Nigeria), or further afield (like conflicts in the Horn of Africa). This situation is also caused by the increase in cases of cross-border criminality, particularly the pillage of natural resources, poaching, or the heedless slaughter of protected species, such as in the Bouba Ndjida National Park where the population of elephants was systematically destroyed by poachers from Sudan in February 2012.

This situation, containing both active and passive elements, resituates Central Africa at the heart of the issue of the threat to international peace and security. The link between peace, security and regional integration has already been established, without which it is difficult to operate the integrated framework of inter-state action constituted by regional integration organizations. The conflict is stoked by the economic potential of the region, seen as one of the largest reserves of natural resources on the planet. This gives rise to greed, and the emergence of a range of interests, which are difficult to reconcile with the purpose of regional integration.

In any case, conflict must be seen as one of the main obstacles to integration in Central Africa. Alongside the proliferation of these conflicts, there are also some political factors, which hinder the emergence and prosperity of integration in the region.

Other Obstacles to Integration on a Political Level

Among the factors that weaken integration in this region, we find the question of the appropriate level of integration, which continues to divide the States and their international partners. We must also add to this the way in which the States value their sovereignty.

The question of the appropriate level of integration

If there is one question to be solved on the political level which would be crucial for the integration process in Central Africa, it is that of the appropriate level of integration. It is well known that the integration organizations present on the ground today are the result of a historical heritage which is rather hard to accept. This is why the principal integration structures that operate in this domain conform to a particular rationality. The immediate consequence of this is a competitive situation that is harming the potential for Central African integration to thrive.

At the time when the ECCAS was created, the terrain on which it was supposed to operate was actually occupied by the UDEAC and the CEPGL. This situation of rivalry forced the community into inactivity for a substantial amount of time. Logically, faced with these circumstances the Central African States showed great creativity by placing this organization in the domain of peace, security and stability.

This reprioritization was the initiative of Cameroon (Njako 2001), who held the Presidency of the organization in 1986. Faced with the lack of activity of this new organization as a result of the competition from UDEAC,[8] Cameroon rallied its peers to the idea that the mission of economic integration of the community was closely linked to attaining a climate of regional peace, security and stability. This mission was presented as being implied by and inherent to the original statutory mission. With this in mind, Cameroon conceived of a project designed to identify the necessary measures for building and consolidating trust, security and development in the region. The proposed programme was submitted to the United Nations General Assembly on 28 November 1986 where it was favourably received. The Resolution A/Res/46/37/3 of 6 December 1991 accentuates therefore the need to work towards peace, security and stability in Central Africa. In order to follow this text up formally, a permanent Advisory Committee for peace and security in Central Africa was set up.[9] This is not a community body, but the ECCAS played an important role in its construction. In February 1988, the United Nations had made available to the ECCAS member States the premises and means of its own regional structure (Regional Centre for Peace and Disarmament in Africa), which works on researching the themes of security, development and promoting trust between the member States of the ECCAS. As an extension of this initiative, a document on measures for trust, security, disarmament and development in the region was adopted during the Yaoundé meeting from 17 to 21 June 1991. Using this document as a basis, the General Assembly decided to enter the theme of 'Regional confidence-building measures' onto the provisional agenda of the 46th session. Admittedly, the ECCAS only has the status of permanent observer to this UN body, but we must bear in mind that it is made up of member States of the Organization, of which the different institutions are widely and generally involved in the preparatory work for Committee meetings. Within this framework, a number of peacekeeping instruments have been produced and made available to the States.[10]

This attempt at specialization demonstrates an operational creativity designed to rationalize the integration process, while awaiting the emergence of a formula that would enable the States to settle on the appropriate level of integration in the region. The foundations have been laid for this rationalization process but there are no conclusive results as yet. The underlying philosophy of this idea is to put into place platforms for coordination, which would lead to a harmonization of policies, and eliminate contradictions. This would be achieved through an in-depth examination of the rules and policies that duplicate one another. The harmonization

8 The Central African Economic and Customs Union (UDEAC), founded on 8 December 1964 by the Brazzaville Treaty.

9 This was announced by the United Nations General Secretary on 28 May 1992.

10 For example, the non-aggression pact of 8 July 1996, the mutual assistance pact between the member states of the ECCAS signed on 25 February 2000 and the protocol on the Council for Peace and Security in Central Africa (COPAX) of 25 June 2000.

approach could even progressively lead to the unification of market regulations, and contribute to the unification of programmes and the management of common and joint sectorial programmes. The formula is currently starting to become operational in the region.[11] At the same time, this rationalization is hampered by the different conceptions of the project and its limited domain.

In any event, the constant trend in Central Africa is that the States have not yet decided upon the appropriate level of integration in the region, given that the texts adopted by the ECCAS are sometimes reused *in extenso* or reproduced in the CEMAC framework.[12] This can be explained by the weakness of regional solidarity but also by the fact that certain States are also members of other communities. This is the case for Angola, the Democratic Republic of Congo and Burundi. As a result of these multiple memberships, the other States can no longer refer to the core of integration that they created, which would enable them to find solutions to their common problems. The consequence of this is a state of inconsistency and hesitation, which is unfavourable to the acceleration of the regional integration process.

The value attached by the States to their sovereignty

Integration is a policy involving substitution and reproduction. It implies the creation of a whole from distinct elements. Once the structure invested with the power to act in the name of its component States is operational, they must respect its legal personality by way of the transfer of competences, which can sometimes affect traditionally sovereign domains. Symptomatic of the disregard for the legal personality of integration organizations and communities in the region is the attitude of the President of the Central African Republic, who in March 2011 bluntly refused the CEMAC Commission President access to the Central African territory, violating all of the obligations incumbent on a State which hosts the seat of an international organization. Community building is based on the progressive introduction of supranationality but the salient feature of the treaties establishing regional integration organizations in Central Africa is the strong dose of intergovernmentalism, especially in the composition of the different bodies and even in the decision-making procedures. Deliberative bodies are essentially intergovernmental. Intergovernmental methods such as unanimity and consensus

---

11 The process involves: the re-launching of the FTA/ECCAS with a capitalization and improvement strategy, and extending the groundwork of the CEMAC; the conclusion of a memorandum of understanding which should culminate in a cooperation agreement on the creation of a cooperation framework CEA/CEMAC/ECCAS; studies and joint meetings; the instigation of the process of harmonization of commercial policy instruments (the Douala Consensus) even if the results remain elusive today; and ongoing initiatives concerning studies of the harmonization of a CET, Customs Code and ICC/ICT.

12 In 2008, the CEMAC States decided on a transfer of competences for security, peacekeeping and stability to the ECCAS. However, the CEMAC has by no means relinquished these issues entirely.

are preferred in the decision-making process, be it in the ECCAS or the CEMAC framework. As a result, institutionalism in the system is insufficient and the immediate impact is the weakening of the integrated bodies which are supposed to represent the centre of gravity of decision making in the integrated legal order.

The preponderance of intergovernmentalism is actually not particularly surprising in this geographical context characterized by presidential political regimes where the personalization and concentration of power are the predominant features. In this context, we cannot expect the States to be open to an effective transfer of their competences to a supranational institution. The value attached to sovereignty by the States helps to explain the minimalist conception of the notion of integration in Central Africa. The treaties establishing the ECCAS and the CEMAC show that integration has developed within the strict limits of a common market and the goal of economic development. In other words, the human being is not at the centre of the process, and human rights are not taken into account during the construction even if there may be beneficial consequences in this domain. There have been some noteworthy evolutions since the beginning of the process of rationalization by the specialization of the ECCAS in the field of peace and security, or even in the institutional reforms that took place in the CEMAC in order to overcome certain conceptual shortcomings and functional distortions.[13]

In any event, the African States' perceptions of their sovereignty do not contribute to the crystallization of a mode of political behaviour which would favour integration and the construction of the community.

In conclusion, the political environment constitutes the possibility for Central Africa to emerge as a bloc, but is harmful to its position as a heavyweight partner in international negotiations. As well as the political environment, the region is weakened by the lack of ownership of the integration process by the endogenous actors.

The Lack of Ownership of the Integration Process by Endogenous Actors

The success of the integration process is heavily dependent on the action of endogenous actors who must take ownership of the initiatives and actions in the pursuit of this goal. This ownership is far from materializing in Central Africa,

13 In the ECCAS, an opening towards the protection of human rights is demonstrated by the pact on non-aggression of 8 July 1996, the pact on mutual assistance between ECCAS member states signed on 25 February 2000 and the Protocol on the Council for Peace and Security in Central Africa (COPAX) of 25 June 2000. In the CEMAC, this opening in shown in the Preamble of the revised Treaty of 25 June 2008 with the words, 'Reaffirming their commitment to the respect of the principles of democracy, Human Rights, the rule of law, good governance, social dialogue and similar issues.' Similarly, the introduction of dispositions relating to the protection of human rights can be found in article 46 of the UEAC convention.

and the endogenous actors, whether States, infra-State authorities, civil society groups or individual populations, have not taken hold of the process in order to become participants themselves. Analysts are often struck by their indifference, which leads to this absence of ownership of the issues and of the processes which should lead to the establishment of a regional common market or the combination of individual State efforts to shelter the region from factors that cause conflict and instability. Of course, there is no shortage of economic burdens and the area is particularly dependent on the exterior, but this situation which leads to the erosion of the integration dynamic is actually linked to the preference of the States for bilateralism, along with judicial and economic actors' mistrust of the law that is produced in the integrated community legal order.

Bilateralism as the Preferred Option of the Central African States

Bilateralism has an erosive effect on the integration process and the construction of the community, and will play a crucial role in depriving the initiative of its substance if action is not taken quickly to limit its effects. A few examples in Central Africa support this argument. In this area of the continent, the existence of the UDEAC-CEMAC as an economic integration organization or community has not impeded the proliferation of bilateral agreements between the member States of this embryonic organization in its field of competence. Even though bilateralism seems to be losing steam recently, the effects of old agreements have not yet been extinguished. The impact of this increase on legal instruments which all govern the same subject matter is likely to cause confusion for the actors who are responsible for applying them effectively. This would suggest that the efficiency of the acts produced in integrative legal orders such as the CEMAC and the ECCAS is compromised, especially since the administrative authorities and the economic operators are not sufficiently discerning to be able to disentangle the maze formed by this constellation of international legal instruments which govern the same area. There are, however, several solutions that could be effective, if only enough interest were shown. It is in fact possible to reconcile the need for bilateral cooperation with the requirements of community building or economic integration. The preference for bilateralism in its current form remains an obstacle to the process of integration.

An obstacle to the integration process

Bilateral cooperation has often presented itself as a stimulating factor for community construction. In this way, within the framework of the UDEAC, the member States developed and adopted a Maritime Code in order to strengthen solidarity between the States, providing for the participation of land-locked States in the administration by way of 'bilateral conventions between the coastal State and the land locked State' of the ports of the State of transit.[14] This is consistent

14 Article 11 of the UDEAC Community Maritime Code.

with the conventional system relating to the administration of maritime areas.[15] In itself this initiative is commendable, as it will reduce the sphere of conflict facing the members of the organization.[16] The project to create an airline called 'Air CEMAC' follows the same idea. Conversely, bilateral cooperation can also greatly harm the pursuit of community objectives. Its adverse effect can be seen in the means used and their way of compromising the effectiveness of the law that is produced in an attempt to fulfil the functional and statutory objectives of the community.

The instruments used

Normatively speaking, bilateralism uses traditional methods of international law. This is shown by the proliferation of agreements and treaties concluded by the Central African States in fields already covered by the Treaties of the Community, either of the CEMAC or the ECCAS. In terms of the institutions, the bilateral joint commissions seem to constitute the best setting for the member States to circumvent their engagements in the community legal order.[17] The idea of these joint commissions is not always easy to apprehend in theory, even if they are recurrent in practice. Some authors therefore consider them to be political and diplomatic bodies.[18] These commissions have a specialized role of the technical administration of particular subjects or the drafting of international treaties. Therefore these bodies have a principally administrative role and are different from a conciliation or arbitration commission which would have a jurisdictional

15 The Montego Bay Convention, and its annexed 1994 and 1995 agreements.

16 We can compare this to the Schengen Accords concluded between member States of the European Community which reflect the same logic, facilitating the concretization of free movement and thereby strengthening the common market. The Franco-German cooperation in Europe which works as a crucible for European integration is a further example.

17 For example, five agreements were concluded between Congo and the Central African Republic, two of which were of a commercial nature (the Memorandum of Understanding, 28 May 1970 and the Agreement on cement supply from the cement industry of Louété, 20 July 1971). The other accords concerned inland waterway transport (Memorandum of Understanding on inland waterway transport, 28 May 1970 and the implementation protocols signed 21 July 1978. As for the bilateral relations between Gabon and the Central African Republic, there are six agreements in the following areas: Labour relations, materialized by the cooperation agreement on labour and the cooperation agreement on the Central African workforce in Gabon, signed 4 October 1976; Transport, with the agreement on air transport.

18 Joint commissions are therefore seen as structures which are established in order to 'develop, for example, navigation and police regulations for rivers which separate or cross several States, to eliminate the barriers which prevent free navigation of these internal waterways' or in order to 'monitor the operations or cessation of territory' or even in order to 'ensure the execution of certain specifications in peace Treaties' (Pradier-Fodéré 1894: 313).

role. The particularity of joint commissions is that they are flexible, and can therefore adapt to any sector that may be covered by an international agreement. It is for this reason that, according to one author, they can be described as a:

> legal-political framework, created by a cooperation agreement, consisting of diplomats and experts from the two countries in order to discuss a range of issues that relate to the cooperation and to propose to their respective governments the best ways in which to extend, improve and rationalise the cooperation. (Tonye 1989: 21)

The advantage of this flexibility meant that these commissions were sought after by States traditionally very attached to their sovereignty, like those in Central Africa, given that they had the possibility to select and re-compose them as they wished, and entrust them with general or technical missions. This approach seems consistent with the subject matter given to joint commissions by Central African States.[19] The commissions are therefore expected to provide specific services, particularly the harmonization and the coordination but also the continuous monitoring of sectoral and general contractual relations between the two States. This monitoring role breathes dynamism into the cooperation. In sum, through these joint commissions, the States hope to maintain a privileged relationship by attempting to increase the 'flow of exchanges, or at least to ensure its continuity, and to diversify their interactions' (Tonye 1989: 59). The problem therefore is not so much the creation of bilateral joint commissions but the way in which they are used to bypass the commitments made in the framework of the Central African integration organizations. In itself, bilateralism is not a bad thing as within other contexts it has been used as the glue for integration, when two member States have used their privileged relationship as a driving force to the benefit of the Community.[20] It is necessary to call into question this Central African practice in order to highlight its harmful effect on integration and the expectations of the population compared to the advantages that it provides.

The destructive effect of State actors could not be as harmful if it were not for the breeding ground of support that is to be found among other partners in the integration process, which leads to the weakening of the project, despite its many assets.

---

19 For example, article 3 of the Statute of the Central Africa-Cameroon joint commission indicates that the commission 'constitutes the setting for the negotiation of bilateral agreements and the peaceful settlement of disputes of any dispute that could arise between the two countries.' Article 3, Statute of the joint commission Cameroon-Central Africa, 23 November 1971. As for the Congo-Cameroon joint Commission, it has a 'scientific, technical, cultural and social mission between the two States' article 3, 28 January 1981 agreement.

20 For example, the France-Germany relationship in Europe.

The Lack of Ownership of the Integration Process by Other Actors

This lack of ownership is shown by the distrust by judicial and economic actors of the legal texts produced in the regional community legal order. What is more, the law of integration, or community law, is not always favourably received by national administrative authorities.

The distrust of judicial actors

By examining Africa in general, and in particular Central Africa, we can detect apathy in the application of the norms produced at the community level when solving legal issues. However, the development of such a community or integration organization depends on the use of the different mechanisms that the model proposes itself to govern its legal order. It is highly regrettable that the subjects of this law are so slow to use this element that would provide legal certainty and predictability. They would probably have been more encouraged to do so if it were not for the lack of involvement of the judges themselves. This nervousness coming from the would-be privileged users of this normative tool means that it has a marginal role in the settlement of disputes. It is therefore essential to find ways to improve the popularity of the community law and to incite a more active commitment from its users. The exclusion of community law in dealing with many cases to which it should really be applied is striking. This observation is all the more a reality in Central Africa where community law often has a marginal role in the national legal orders of the States (Priso Essawe 1997: 294). We can refer here to the attitudes of the national judges and economic operators, for example in the CEMAC where a Court of Justice was created in order to monitor the uniform application of community law through its case law and particularly through the interpretative role that it was given.[21] With this in mind, a cooperation mechanism was set up between the national and community judges. However, until now, this cooperation has been particularly faint-hearted, and the national judges have been especially reluctant to apply the mechanism of the preliminary ruling. This attitude is confirmed by that of the lawyers who rarely use community law as a basis for petitions or in defence. One cannot expect the community legal order to flourish in such circumstances.

The apathy of economic operators

There is a noticeable tendency among these actors to exclude the legal challenges that relate to the defence of their interests from the toolbox provided by community legal acts. The experience of the UDEAC is a prime example of this. In this legal order, economic operators, like elsewhere, group together in national organizations such as the Syndicate of the Manufacturers of Cameroon (Syndustricam), the Organization of Cameroon Employers (GICAM) and the junior economic chamber

---

21 This cooperation mechanism is emphasized in the Treaty of 30 January 2009 on the Court of Justice, after the collapse of the old structure.

in Cameroon, the Gabon Employers' Confederation (CPG), the Unicongo in Brazzaville and the National Union of Central African Employers (UNPC), in order to reinforce the chances of success of their claims. They may even form regional groups, although the defence of their interests seems limited at this level.[22] In practice, we can see that these structures turn very rarely towards the solutions provided by community law when trying to resolve the problems encountered in their intra-community activities. However, these difficulties are often in themselves the result of the failure to respect community regulations, as shown by a memo of Syndustricam (1990). These violations include disguised import bans from Cameroon put in place by Gabon, in the form of prior authorization that can never be obtained in practice. To this curious formality we can add the import licence, which is required of economic operators by Gabon and Congo. Even more seriously, in 1989 Gabon completely banned imports of Cameroonian origin.[23] The same can be said for the closing of borders, as is the case between Cameroon and Equatorial Guinea at Keo-sy, with the effect of preventing the free movement of persons and goods. During March 2012, Equatorial Guinea again repeatedly closed its border and created several incidents constituting a significant hindrance to community building in Central Africa. Double customs taxes and obstacles to the free movement of persons, particularly businessmen, sometimes reinforce these non-tariff barriers. For example, in December 2008, Cameroonian businessmen denounced the refusal to allow a member of their delegation the right of entry in Gabon and thus prevent him and his goods to be exposed at the Libreville trade exposition. In this context, it is clear that the economic operators refer to community law in order to invoke their claims, particularly relating to the elimination of barriers to free movement. On the other hand, it is striking that the means preferred by these actors to achieve their objective of the respect of community law is not to go before the judge, but rather economic diplomacy, through the bilateral contacts discussed previously.

Ultimately, it must be said that integration in Central Africa is faced with huge difficulties. Admittedly, the States of the region have organized themselves in order to overcome these problems with the support of their international partners, but the results are not always conclusive. Consequently, the perceived image today is that of a centre that is gradually losing its status of a natural pole of attraction. Even so, there is no lack of resources. It is therefore necessary to conduct a serious study of the region in order to prescribe an effective remedy, capable of re-launching the hobbled integration process. This process must first be carried forward by endogenous actors in order to succeed. They must find the best formula for cooperation in order to achieve collectively what they can no longer achieve on their own, and for this, the countries must take on leadership in the region.

---

22 It must be noted here that the Federation of Chambers of Commerce has never fully developed.

23 Decision of the Gabon Ministerial Council, 14 April 1989 banning imports of oil, soap, sugar and cement from Cameroon.

References

Gonidec, P.F. 1985. *L'Etat africain*. 2nd Edition, Paris: Librairie Générale de Droit et de Jurisprudence.

Kamto, M. 1987. La Communauté Economique des Etats de l'Afrique Centrale (C.E.E.A.C.), une communauté de plus? *Annuaire Français du Droit International*, 33, 1987, 839-862.

Kenfack, J. 2003. *Les actes juridiques des Communautés et Organisations internationales d'intégration en Afrique Centrale et Occidentale*, Doctoral Thesis in Law, University of Yaoundé II/FSJP, April 2003.

Kenfack, J. 2009. L'action de la CEEAC dans la résolution des conflits et sa contribution pour le maintien de la paix, in J. Coulon (ed.) *Guide du Maintien de la paix 2009*, Montréal: Athénas.

Njako, F. 2001. *La contribution du Cameroun à la construction d'un espace de sécurité en Afrique Centrale*, DESS Thesis, Yaounde: IRIC.

OAU. 1980. *Lagos Plan of Action for the Economic Development of Africa*, mimeo, 2nd edition, Geneva: IHEI.

Ouali, K.S. 1982. *Intégration Africaine, le cas de la C.E.A.O.* Paris: Economica, 1982.

Pradier-Fodere, P. 1894. *Traité de droit international public européen et américain, Vol. 6*. Paris: Pédone.

Priso Essawe, S. 1997. *Intégration économique et droit en Afrique Centrale. Etude de la zone U.D.E.A.C.* Unpublished PhD Thesis, Université de Montpellier.

Sekou Toure, A. 1980. *Des Etats-Unis d'Afrique*. Conakry: Bureau de presse de la Présidence de la République.

Syndustricam, *Concept Note on Exportation problems in the UDEAC*, Douala, 23 July 1990.

Tonye, A.M. 1989. *Les Commissions mixtes dans la diplomatie camerounaise, Contribution à la connaissance de la diplomatie et de la politique étrangère du Cameroun*, Thesis in International Relations, Yaoundé: IRIC.

Chapter 5

Development in the Caribbeans After a Half-century of Independence: Insights from Regional and Transnational Perspectives

Timothy M. Shaw

> '[T]he circulation of commodities is one of the unifying aspects of Caribbean history [...] Globalization has not just happened to the Caribbean, the Caribbean has participated in the making of globalization [...] four things circulate: people, capital, drugs and information.' (Bronfman 2007: 5-6)

> 'What constitutes the Caribbean? [...] Among scholars, "the Caribbean" is a socio-historical category [...] it embraces the islands and parts of the adjoining mainland – and may be extended to include the Caribbean Diaspora overseas. As one scholar observes, there are many Caribbeans...
>
> In short, the definition of the Caribbean might be based on language and identity, geography, history and culture, geopolitics, geoeconomics, or organisation.' (Girvan 2005: 304)

After 50 years of formal independence, this chapter suggests that gains for both analysis and policy may be made by something of a paradigm shift towards a focus on regional and transnational relations This is especially so for the myriad small, particularly island, states which have always been relatively 'open', especially as contemporary governance demands proliferate as indicated in the first section below. A focus on the regional and transnational helps to transcend the old binary of 'vulnerability' versus 'resilience' (Cooper and Shaw 2009). There are many definitions of the Caribbean(s): from more micro to more macro, including diasporas in North America and Europe. This chapter seeks i) to go beyond the 'new regionalisms' of non-state – corporate and civil society – formulations towards recognition of informal, even illegal definitions. The Caribbeans can be conceived as more than either formal and informal economies/ societies/polities, however compatible or otherwise. They can also be treated ii) as transnational diasporas and/or a nexus of drugs/gangs/guns. Hence the focus here on five sets of overlapping but not necessarily compatible 'transnational' relationships (Hale and Held 2011, Khagram and Levitt 2007): governance, transnational families, civil societies, supply chains, and crime networks. To so conceive, several analytic traditions will need to be transcended; not just IR/IPE/IDS but also anthropology, criminology, economics, history, sociology etc. Together, 'new regionalisms' (Shaw, Grant and Cornelissen 2011) and transnational relations/governance will inform the prospects of several alternative future analytic and applied directions for the Caribbeans in their second half-century … and the revised small state discourse can further advance analysis of development … putting established, somewhat romantic notions of Caribbean Dependency Thought (CDT) into perspective if not the shade (Girvan 2006).

This chapter juxtaposes a set of 'transnational' relations – governance, families, civil societies, supply chains, and crime networks – with fluid definitions of 'regionalisms'. Together these seem to fit or resonate in the case of today's Caribbean(s) after its first five decades as both perspectives develop their own genres such as 'transnational studies' (Khagram and Levitt 2007) and new regionalisms (Shaw, Grant and Cornelissen 2011). Both approaches include economic, ecological, social and state relations, both informal and informal. Together they can advance analyses of both the transnational and the regional and suggest a range of possible futures for the Caribbeans before the end of the second decade of the present century, as indicated in the concluding paragraphs.

They can also inform the binary small state debate – vulnerability or resilience? – as such political cultures/economies are increasingly impacted by the regional and transnational (Cooper and Shaw 2009). And in turn they can inform development analysis and policy in the new century such as the notion of citizen (UNDP 2012) rather than human let alone national security.

Such perspectives are particularly fitting as the Caribbeans' first half-century coincided with the continuing global crisis around the turn of the second decade of the new century, one in which the established neo-liberal trans-Atlantic and EU are in difficulty by contrast to many in the global South, especially Africa and Latin America as well as Asia. Global rebalancing or divergence pose further challenges to the development prospects and policies of the Caribbeans; hence the imperative of links with the five BRICS (Brazil, Russia, India, China and now South Africa) along with the relevance of varieties of new regionalisms and transnationalisms. Jan Nederveen Pieterse (2011: 22) has recently captured the potential of such a post-crisis prospect or direction:

> [T]he rise of emerging societies is a major turn in globalization and holds significant emancipatory potential. North-South relations have been dominant for 200 years and now an East-South turn is taking shape. The 2008 economic crisis is part of a global rebalancing process.

Given the contemporary variety of regional visions on offer at the start of the second decade of the 21st century, the adoption of a 'new' regionalisms perspective on today's Caribbean would seem to be quite sensible and compatible with transnational approaches (Shaw, Grant and Cornelissen 2011). Orthodox frameworks cannot capture the diversity and dynamism of current regional connections: not just micro-, meso- or macro-levels or inter-/non-state but also increasingly informal and illegal at all levels and in all sectors. And enquiring into the interconnections among these three or four distinct yet interrelated 'regions' also challenges traditional disciplinary approaches as indicated in f) below.

Furthermore, interregional relations are also of growing salience, however duplicative or competitive rather than compatible or cooperative, reflective of the proliferation of regions at all levels. This is especially so around the European Union (EU) of 27, such as the Asia-Europe Meeting (ASEM) (Gaens 2008), Economic Partnership Agreements (EPAs) (De Lombaerde and Schulz 2009, Laursen 2010), Mediterranean (Zank 2009), pipelines (Aalto 2008) etc, as reflected in analyses by networks on Global Governance, Regionalization and Regulation: role of the EU (GARNET) and then Network for Regional Integration Studies (NETRIS) (www.garnet-eu.org; www.netris-acp.org) as indicated by this reflective volume. And the distinctive, divergent character of regions has intensified as the current 'global' financial crisis has impacted them differently; i.e. Asia has been less affected than either the EU, North American Free Trade Agreement (NAFTA) or the North Atlantic (Shaw 2010a).

Many Regionalisms; Many Caribbeans?

The 'Caribbean' can be more narrowly and broadly defined, from all/some of the heterogeneous islands to islands and mainland Central America – *el gran caribe* – and onto the diasporas. In formal intergovernmental institutional terms, this means progressing from the Organization of Eastern Caribbean States (OECS) through the Caribbean Community (CARICOM) and Caribbean Development and Cooperation Committee (CDCC) to Association of Caribbean States (ACS). But in terms of non-state actor definitions, it means Caribbean Policy Development Centre (CPDC) to CRIES and Caribbean Studies Association (CSA) for civil society and for the private sector from Unilever to Nestle, Republic Bank to RBC or Scotiabank, Caribbean Airlines to Copa, B-Mobile and Flow to Digicel (Shaw 2012). Certainly, spill-over from the current crisis in the form of the demise of CLICO and Stanford corporate empires has had a continuing negative impact (ECLAC 2009). And cutting across such geospatial and economic networks are linguistic communities: anglophone, francophone, Dutch and Spanish along with several creoles. However, while a few analysts have recognized such diversity in the formal political economy extending to the diasporic, few have extended their analysis to the informal and illegal. Thus arguably just two chapters out of the 37 in the encyclopaedic reader on *The Caribbean Economy* by Dennis Pantin (2005) treat levels of interaction/integration (#14 by Norman Girvan) or diasporas/remittances (#29 by Wendell Samuel). This chapter seeks to go beyond such orthodoxies given the spill-over from the informal and illegal, especially in a period of global economic turmoil and divergence.

The new regionalism(s) perspective (Shaw, Grant and Cornelissen 2011) has itself generated a debate about the informal and illegal with earlier and more formal analyses at the end of the last century tending to exclude these even in its framework of new regionalism (singular!) (Hettne and Inotai 1994, Hettne, Inotai and Sunkel 1999). Here, however, I take the informal and illegal to be inseparable from the formal and legal in terms of definitions and implications of Caribbean relations in the second decade of the 21st century (Shaw 2011).

Symbolic of the contrast between the formal and informal, the legal and illegal is the irony of de facto free trade in drugs and guns by contrast to myriad de jure restrictions on trade in legitimate goods. So CARICOM Single Market and Economy (CSME) has been largely stillborn whereas, despite efforts of the uniformed services, organized crime flourishes. Similarly, informal sector traders – ubiquitous 'higglers' – circumvent myriad obstacles even when regular supply chains cannot. And private security companies – both local and global, legal and otherwise – are increasingly substituting for ineffective official police.

The borderline between legal and illegal, formal and informal is of great importance in the Caribbean given the fine line between, say, offshore banking and money laundering (Vlcek 2008), jewellery and property development. Hence the evolution of international efforts at regulation from the Organization for Economic Cooperation and Development (OECD) Harmful Tax to Financial Action Task Force (FATF) (www.fatf-gafi.org) including the Caribbean office established in Trinidad and Tobago (TandT) in the early 1990s (www.cfatf-gafic.org) and on to Tax Information Exchange Agreements (TIEAs). And now the Obama Administration and global financial crisis have led to the establishment of a Global Forum on Transparency and Exchange of Information to monitor/peer review. Moreover, there is a rich variety of island jurisdictions, both independent and otherwise, from Jersey and Mauritius to Barbados, Bermuda, the British and American Virgin Islands, Caymans and Trinidad and Tobago (TandT); hence the imperative of forms of compliance by the end of the first decade of the 21st century.

Non-independent Overseas Territories (OTs), like other SIDS, seek to minimize vulnerability and maximize resilience (Bishop 2013). In parallel to small states in Central Asia and Central Europe, they have continued to proliferate in numbers, most recently on 10-10-10 (10 October 2010) with the Dutch Antilles splitting into three: two 'autonomous countries' in the Netherlands – Curacao and St Maarten – and a trio remaining 'special municipalities' of the Netherlands: Bonaire, Saba and St Eustatius. The diplomatic status of old and new OTs is problematic, but some of them do have associate status in regional or hemispheric networks like the ACS and/or UN Economic Commission for Latin America and the Caribbean (ECLAC) as well as in some Commonwealth institutions like the Commonwealth Parliamentary Association (CPA) and Commonwealth Games.

Some of the diversity of the Caribbean can be captured in several sets of contemporary regional indicators, from GDP per capita and Human Development Index (HDI) to competitiveness and homicide rates. Here I concentrate on the seven Most Developed Countries (MDC) identified by the Caribbean Development and Cooperation Committee (CDCC) of ECLAC (www.eclac.org/portofspain): Bahamas, Barbados, Belize, Guyana, Jamaica, Suriname and TandT; this sub-branch of ECLAC includes nine 'associated states' from amongst the OCTs drawn from the British, Dutch and US islands, several of which play important communications and financial roles, both legal and otherwise.

Per capita PPP incomes in the Caribbean stretch from US$23 507 for TandT to $1 155 for Haiti through Barbados at $17 966, Suriname at $7 813, Cuba at $6 876, DR at $6 706, Jamaica at $6 079 and Guyana at $2 782. The region likewise is mid-rank along the WEF's Global Competitiveness Index (out of 133 countries ranked) (www.weforum.org): PR at #42 and Barbados at #44 lead with Suriname (#102) and Guyana (#104) trailing; in mid-field, TandT is #86, Jamaica #91 and DR #95. The region scores quite well in terms of the UNDP Human Development Index in 2009, being concentrated in the High and Medium HD categories: from Barbados being the only one categorized as Very High at #37 out of 182; otherwise the range is Antigua and Barbuda at #47 to Haiti at #149, with Cuba at #51, TandT #64, Suriname at #97, Jamaica at #100 and Guyana at #114 (http://hdr.undp.org).

In terms of homicide rates, however, the region presents impressive statistics, with Jamaica's 59.5 per 100 000 in 2008 (Harriott 2003) being just below the highest one from Honduras at 60.9, while TandT at 39.7 (UNODC 2010b: 27 and 237) beats out Columbia at 38.8; St. Kitts at 35.32 just trails South Africa's 36.5. Other high rates are reported for Anguilla at 27.6, DR at 21.5 and PR at 20.4, with the lowest levels coming from the Bahamas at 13.7 and Barbados at 8.7; the US rate is 5.2 per 100 000 population (www.unodc.org). Symptomatic of the Caribbean in the North was a major police raid in Toronto in May 2010 by a thousand police officers. leading to the arrest of some 80 alleged members of the Jamaican 'Shower Posse' gang or network ahead of the month-long 'battle' around Tivoli Gardens in West Kingston for the arrest and extradition of Christopher 'Dudus' Coke. He was eventually captured and extradited to the US before the end of June 2010 (see below).

Transnational Governance

> While private authority beyond the state has become a popular theme of academic writing, the role of stakeholders in the Southern hemisphere as objects and subjects of private transnational governance has rarely been addressed in the literature. (Dingwerth 2008: 607)

'Transnational studies' (Khagram and Levitt 2007) have begun to juxtapose or situate several disciplines, genres or strands: capital, civil society, class, consumption, culture, informal sectors including come/drugs/guns, logistics, migration/diasporas/remittances, sports, supply chains etc. A central subfield can be identified as 'transnational governance' (Hale and Held 2011) which can be considered a generic set of responses to novel and proliferating 'global' issues.

Given its characteristic inclusion of non-state actors, it is also referred to as 'private transnational governance' (Dingwerth 2008), 'non-state transnational transfers' (Brown 2009 and 2012) or 'non-state market-driven' governance (Bernstein and Cashore 2008). It is usually 'hybrid' in character, typically involving a changing range of heterogeneous actors, non-state as well as state, acting in partnerships as in the classic International Campaign to Ban Landmines (ICBL) leading to the 'Ottawa Process' on landmines. The rich variety of such alliances, campaigns, certification schemes, codes, commissions, councils, initiatives, networks, partnerships and processes etc are captured in tables in Dingwerth (2008: 628-630) and Bernstein and Cashore (2008: 281-283).

Such transnational or 'global governance' can be treated as an extension or contemporary form of established international law/organization, which remains primarily, even exclusively intergovernmental. These have evolved from Ottawa and Kimberley processes through Forestry and Fisheries Certification Schemes to Ethical Trade (ETI) and Extractive Industry Transparency (EITI) 'Initiatives' (Bernstein and Cashore 2008, Dingwerth 2008). Thus the rather traditional LoS/SIDS/AOSIS at independence in the 1970s have been superseded by myriad Caribbean/global concerns including climate change in the 21st century: onto Forestry and Fisheries Certification Schemes (FSC/MSC) along with EITI in the second decade of the new century.

Although such governance is of particular relevance to both the global South and small states, it has rarely been so treated. Dingwerth (2008: 607) has lamented the inadequate attention to such governance around the South but the small state genre has yet to so extend:

> While private authority beyond the state has become a popular theme of academic writing, the role of stakeholders in the Southern hemisphere as objects and subjects of private transnational governance (PTG) has rarely been addressed in the literature [...] contrary to common assumptions, PTG schemes exert a significant influence on Southern stakeholders.

Dingwerth (2008) highlights a trio of transnational governance initiatives concentrated in the global South which have yet to receive adequate acknowledgement: the World Commission on Dams, the Global Reporting Initiative (GRI) and the Forest Stewardship Council (FSC).

Hale and Held (2011: 25) echo Dingwerth, including referring to the World Commission on Dams, one of the 50 case studies, by noting in the introduction to their Handbook that there is a '"governance gap" between North and South':

> while many of the programmes rely on Southern participation and serve the interests of Southern stakeholders, almost none of the innovations in transnational governance gathered here have been led by Southern actors. Instead, institutional innovation has been led by Northern states, NGOs, corporations and international organizations.

New forms of governance for the several Caribbeans may lead to alternative futures by the end of the current decade. These were anticipated in advocacy by TandT of the International Criminal Court (ICC); note the role of ANR Robinson in advancing this global coalition, which has yet to include the US despite endless advocacy.

Contemporary public or network diplomacy (cf above) has been adopted by SIDS to maximize leverage internationally using non-state partners such as private sector and civil society, media and culture. Thus diasporas can impact both home and host policies; hence their transnational leverage. As already noted, SIDS were very active around independence in LoS negotiations, albeit largely inter-state in character, but then quiet as the bipolar context yielded to multipolarity until the contemporary era of climate change when they again engaged, but this time with non-state allies from INGOs to diasporas (www.acs-aec.org, Shaw 2010a: 96-100).

New governance networks are being developed in service sectors like finance, telecommunications and tourisms. Caribbean Association of Industry and Commerce (CAIC) advances such private innovation (cf Iheduru 2011 on private sector in ECOWAS). But tourisms and other services are also very transnational: varieties include: business, diasporic, ecological, medical, and sports.

Moreover, the Caribbean is also active in inter-regionalisms, often as the 'junior' partner, such as the not uncontroversial CARIFORUM-EPA, but also links with Mercosur, the OAS (Herz 2010) and now UNASUR in the hemisphere (Mace, Cooper and Shaw 2010) and with AU and ASEAN (Gaens 2008) outside the hemisphere (De Lombaerde and Schulz 2009).

Transnational Families

> The creation of Caribbean transnational networks rests on the foundation of a transnational family, in which migrants and their families have multiple home bases with ongoing commitments and loyalties that straddle territorial boundaries. (Wiltshire 2006: 175)

Contemporary historical migration has been very uneven throughout the Caribbean (Reis 2004, Thomas-Hope 2009), with recent outflows being most significant from Guyana and Jamaica to North America and from Suriname to the Netherlands (some 200-250 000 now in the Dutch diaspora versus 450 000 at home). Such transnational communities/cultures are captured in 'Forward Home', a 2011 research-informed film produced by Keith Nurse (www.shridathramphalcentre.org) facilitated by the International Development Research (IDRC) in Canada (www.idrc.ca) and premiered at the Toronto International Film Festival (TIFF) in September 2011. Both nexuses of transnational families/cultures, remittances/crime are relatively novel sets of relationships, which analysts have only recently discovered; hence the dynamic of Caribbean and development studies at the turn of the decade.

There are estimated to be as many Guyanese in the US, especially NYC, and Canada, particularly Scarborough ON, as at home: +/- 700 000 each. Their presence along with technological changes has led to a dramatic rise in communications, such as phone conversations, especially using mobiles and phonecards, and airline flights, with remittances growing from $20m in 2000 to $200m mid-decade. Guyana's reliance on remittances is highest in LAC, even higher than Haiti (IDB 2009: 10): a quarter of GDP. Similarly for Jamaica: some one million abroad and less than three million at home, with remittances totalling $2 billion in the mid-2000s, some 20% of GDP (World Bank 2008). For example, in 2007, per capita remittance flows were highest to Jamaica ($790) and lowest to TandT ($69); Grenada received $524 per person; Guyana $377; and Suriname $305 (UNDP 2009: 160). Thus Western Union, Money Gram and GraceKennedy have become ubiquitous in diasporic communities in the North and capital cities in the South even if remittance flows have been under pressure particularly from the US because of the financial crisis at the turn of the decade.

Remittances to LAC grew throughout almost all of the first decade of the 21st century but peaked in 2006-2008, declining in 2009 back to 2005 levels as a reflection of the knock-on effects of the global financial crisis, particularly in the trans-Atlantic centres of the US and UK. However, when inflation is factored in, remittances in local currencies may have actually increased in 2009. And stabilization in flows was anticipated in 2010 (IDB 2009: 3).

Transnational Caribbean families can be considered as central to the evolution of transnational civil society focused on the region, facilitating the flows of communications, ideas, events, fashions, technologies etc (Scher 2009).

Transnational Civil Society

> The Caribbean is a unique and complex concatenation of virtually every ethnic group in the world.
>
> Far more interesting than the individual contributions of the various groups constituting the contemporary Caribbean is the process whereby their sociopolitical traits have been amalgamated and Eurocentric dominance has been mitigated. The region has truly been a crucible of various cultures. This blending, not only of institutions but also of ethnicity, has produced the uniquely Caribbean Creoles. (Hillman 2009: 11 and 12)

The digital revolution has transformed both the political economy and the social culture of the Caribbean, especially a trio of 'transformative processes: the introduction of cellular telephones, the adoption of the Internet, and the proliferation of offshore gambling sites' (Bronfman 2007: 12); on the latter, see

Andrew Cooper (2011) on *Internet Gambling Offshore* on the rise and fall of Antigua under bilateral US pressure which the WTO has been unable to contain.

Given contemporary communications, especially the mobile phone revolution, diasporas can make powerful demands regarding development and democracy back home: onto a foreign policy impact in North (see below). An aspect of 'double' 'public diplomacy': both inside and about the Caribbean (see also below), symbolized by the last months in office as Governor General in Canada of Michaelle-Jean who was a celebrity diplomat for her native Haiti after its early-2010 earthquake leading to her post-retirement appointment as a UNESCO Ambassador. Note also the proliferation of Home Town Associations, most active when natural disasters hit home, as in diasporic responses to the earthquake in Haiti in early 2010.

Without being too parochial or sentimental, we should recognize even as we debate the centrality of the federal University of the West Indies (UWI) in keeping the foundation of CARICOM intact and reinforced even if increasingly virtually via the Open Campus etc (www.uwi.edu) (Brereton 2010). This is apparent in numerous UWI-CARICOM functional relations symbolized by the CARICOM-UWI project on regional development (Hall and Chuck-A-Sang 2010) which built on established Caribbean intellectual accomplishments and histories (Girvan 2006, Meeks and Girvan 2010). There are also myriad art forms and carnivals over centuries (Mohammed 2009) now circulated through the digital revolution.

Just as transnational Caribbean civil society has well-established historical roots, so too the region's supply chains go back centuries, including the flow of forced as well as free people.

Transnational Supply Chains

> [T]he circulation of commodities is one of the unifying aspects of Caribbean history. All islands are shaped by things that circulate, and more so in the recent past, when aspects of globalization have made it easier for things to circulate at greater quantities and greater speed. (Bronfman 2007: 5)

Supply chains around the region have evolved from barrels to containers and airfreight/couriers using cellphones and tracking devices so each brands' hubs apparent, plus personal postboxes are bought in Miami to be used as offshore addresses; i.e. from banana boats and Cable and Wireless to Flow and B-mobile internet provision, DHL/FedEx/UPS courier services etc.

Regional and global hubs rise and fall around older and newer supply chains (Gibbon, Ponte and Lazaro 2010), impacted by technological, infrastructural as well as security developments (e.g. expansion of the Panama Canal and container ports, of Copa as well as Caribbean Airlines): emerging economies versus emerging powers, including emerging cities.

As Bronfman (2007) and others indicate, the region has 'advanced' from spices to drugs, cutlasses to guns, pirates to gangs, gunpowder to AK47s, depending on supply and demand, regulations and enforcement: onto novel forms of supply chains given the 'other' side of globalization including intellectual property violations via pirated CDs and apps etc (Naim 2006). Conversely, extra-territorial EU and US rules tend to impact goods and services (Gibbon, Ponte and Lazaro 2010), compounded by diasporic demands/expectations in the North.

But the current global crisis has also exposed challenges of economic/corporate governance in the region given pressures of liberalization, competition etc: CLICO, Stanford, TCL etc: new forms of effective transnational governance are needed to restore financial confidence as treated below.

Transnational Crime Networks

> Illicit flows of all kinds have been part of the Caribbean's history. Goods have circulated to the region, from the region, and through the region. (Bronfman 2007: 8)

> Jamaica occupies a unique place in the history of illicit flows because both marijuana and cocaine move in and out of the island. (Bronfman 2007: 12)

As already noted, Caribbean crime has evolved from spices to drugs, cutlasses to guns, gunpowder to AK47s, from pirates to druglords (UNODC 2010b). In turn, it has encouraged the parallel albeit belated development of analysis and policy at the turn of the century (Barley and Walker 1994, Fiorentini and Peltzman 1997, Friman and Andreas 1999, Friman 2009, Madsen 2009). In response, policy discussions have generated intergovernmental institutions like CARICOM Implementation Agency for Crime and Security (CARICOM-IMPACS) (www.caricomimpacs.org) and professional networks like the Association of Caribbean Commissioners of Police (ACCP) (www.accpolice.org) and Caribbean Association of Judicial Officers (CAJO) (www.thecajo.org).

The value of drugs increases the further away they are from production, where their value is low; their value multiplies 200 times between production and retail levels especially when they move from South to North. So although the Caribbean may be of decreasing importance in global supply chains, the value of the global drugs trade is still greater than 90% of the world's national GDPs (UNODC 2010a and b). Hence the spread of narcostates or shadow states into the Caribbean with their distinctive state-economy balances (Friman and Andreas 1999, Naim 2006, Naylor 2005); amongst the region's political economies so identified recently are the Eastern Caribbean, Guyana, Haiti, Jamaica and Puerto Rico. Legal remittances (IBRD 2006, IDB 2009) and illegal money laundering (Naylor 2005) have together attracted G8 and OECD attention, leading to CFATF (UNODC 2010a, Vlcek 2008).

Meanwhile, as confidence in state security organizations declines, the private security sector has expanded and diversified, both national (e.g. Guardsman in Jamaica and Northern Caribbean (www.guardsmangroup.com)) and global (e.g. G4S (www.g4s.com)): but how is it regulated? The early 2011 Montreux Document, which proposes a code of conduct for private security companies, offers one such framework and many agencies have signed up (www.eda.admin.ch/psc).

Interestingly, the UNDP (2009b) has begun to advocate the notion of 'citizen security' to advance freedom from fear in region. This was adopted and developed at the global level by the World Bank (2011) in its annual *World Development Report 2011* on conflict, security and development (www.wdr2011.worldbank.org). And the early-2012 regional HDR on citizen security based on an end of 2010 survey (UNDP 2012) led beyond generic notions of human security/development given threats in the region, especially the Caribbean and Central America: another 'new' regionalism?

Together, these underline the imperative of informed, flexible 'transnational governance' responses to burgeoning transnational relations, formal/legal as well as informal/illegal.

In conclusion, lessons may be derived from the Caribbean for a variety of analytic perspectives along with their policy implications, in addition to new regionalisms such as:

Development studies – proliferation of issues and actors, especially around 'Asian drivers' like China and India;

Environmental studies – especially climate change, ocean rise and species depletion;

Global governance/multilateralisms – varieties of actors and interests, especially in 'soft' law arenas like fisheries and forest certification;

Global studies – going beyond inter- and non-governmental, even the transnational, towards global structures (www.theglobalsite.ac.uk), as reflected increasingly in academic programmes, publications, appointments and associations (www.globalstudiesassociation.org; www.globalstudiesfoundation.org);

Migration/diasporas/remittances nexus – looking beyond the movement of people to diasporic communities and cultures, especially remittance flows and novel forms of communications from phone cards and texting (Bronfman 2007: 86-107) to financial and technological flows and FDI along with drugs and guns;

Regionalisms, old and new – evolving balance between old and new given post-neoliberal world and proliferating micro-, meso- and macro-level responses to uneven globalization etc;

Security studies – threats to national, human and now citizen security from 'old' and 'new' factors such as climate change and gang culture (Bronfman 2007: 63-85); and

Transnational studies – heterogeneous relations between trans- and inter- and intra-national given changes in state-civil society/private sector relations everywhere leading towards innovative forms of transnational, hybrid governance (Shaw 2010b).

The kaleidoscope of Caribbeans, both contemporary and historical, advances and reinforces notions of varieties of capitalisms and civil societies as well as a plurality of regionalisms. It continues to inform debates about the compatibility or competitiveness of such formal and informal, more macro- and more micro-regionalisms: what futures will there be for the Caribbean by the end of this decade? Such sceptical reflections should be contrasted with the ideological claims of at least one state – TandT – that by then it will have become 'developed' as symbolized by its assertion, 'we're next'!

Many Caribbeans? How Many Futures?

> [T]here is a need for an interdisciplinary introduction to the Caribbean region. Academic, business and policy interests require understanding this complex and significant area, especially in the twenty-first century. But the growing numbers of people who wish to learn about the Caribbean are not able to use narrowly focused studies. Comprehending existing theoretical analyses of the region's socioeconomic and political conditions presupposes expertise and experience. (Hillman 2009: 9)

Just as we may identify several Caribbeans, so we may abstract several futures over their second half-century, particularly along the vulnerable and resilient divide (Cooper and Shaw 2009). But this dialectic becomes more problematic or complicated when more informal and illegal transnational relations are incorporated, with diasporas and remittances becoming increasingly salient. Nevertheless, clearly only a minority of political economies are likely to achieve 'developmental' status. And the majority will have their prospects largely determined by a mix of regional and global fortunes, increasingly impacted by climate change.

The place and possible transitions around Cuba in the second decade of the 21st century will be quite pivotal, especially in the Northern Caribbean and for its generations of diasporas in Florida and elsewhere in the US … reinforcing the 'post-neo-liberal' era in the hemisphere (Macdonald and Ruckert 2009) or removing one focus of regional cohesion? What directions will there be, given the demise of the Washington Consensus in the first decade of the new century and the global crisis at start of the second decade, let alone decline in the Floridian and other parts of the US economy?

So, what regional balances will there be among macro-, meso- and/or micro-levels, in part a function of balance between the more formal versus more informal? And will cycles in the global economy, including balances among sectors, be exacerbated by continuing global rebalancing?

Developmental and democratic deficits will persist, moderated by ubiquitous connectivity facilitating continuous transnational communication. And by 2020, if not before, Caribbean relations with the BRICs will come to balance if not exceed those with the North Atlantic rim, accelerated by the current crisis which is advancing divergence. And for much of the Caribbean, such relations will be more formal with China and Russia and more informal/diasporic with Brazil, India and South Africa.

I conclude by echoing Girvan (2005: 315):

> If the Caribbean was an invention of the 20th century, it seems certain to be reinterpreted and perhaps transcended in the 21st. The Caribbean of tomorrow will not be an exclusively Anglophone or Hispanic conception; and it will not be tied exclusively to geographic space or definition. If it survives at all, it will be a community of shared economic, social and political interests and strategies that encompasses different languages and cultures and the Caribbean Diaspora.

References

Aalto, P. (ed.) 2008. *The EU-Russian Energy Dialogue: Europe's future energy security.* Aldershot: Ashgate.

Bagley, B.B. and Walker W.O. (eds.) 1994. *Drug Trafficking in the Americas.* Miami: University of Miami N-S Center.

Bernstein, S. and Cashore B. 2008. The Two-Level Logic of Non-State Market Driven Global Governance, in *Authority in the Global Political Economy* edited by V. Rittberger and M. Nettesheim. London: Palgrave Macmillan. 276-313.

Bishop, M.L. Forthcoming. *The Political Economy of Eastern Caribbean Development.* London: Palgrave Macmillan.

Bishop, M.L. and Payne A. 2010. Caribbean Regional Governance and the Sovereignty/Statehood Problem. *Caribbean Paper #8*. Waterloo: CIGI.

Brereton, B. 2010. *From Imperial College to UWI: a history of the St Augustine campus, TandT.* Kingston: Ian Randle for UWI.

Bronfman, A. 2007. *On the Move: the Caribbean since 1989.* Halifax: Fernwood.

Brown, S.S. *et al.* 2009. Non-State Transnational Transfers: types and characteristics. *International Studies Review*, 11(2), 4102-450.

Brown, S.S. 2012. *Transnational Transfers and Global Development.* London: Palgrave Macmillan.

Cooper, A.F. 2011. *Internet Gambling Offshore: Caribbean struggles over casino capitalism.* London: Palgrave Macmillan.

Cooper, A.F. and Shaw T.M. 2009. The Summitry of Small States: towards the "Caribbean Summit". Policy Brief # 15. Waterloo: CIGI.

Cooper, A.F. and Shaw T.M. (eds.) 2009. *The Diplomacies of Small States: between vulnerability and resilience.* London: Palgrave Macmillan.

De Lombaerde, P. and Schulz M. (eds.) 2009. *The EU and World Regionalism: the makability of regions in the 21st century*. Farnham: Ashgate.

Dingwerth, K. 2008. Private Transnational Governance and the Developing World: a comparative perspective. *International Studies Quarterly*, 52(3), 607-634.

ECLAC. 2009. *Economic Survey of the Caribbean 2008-2009*. Port of Spain: ECLAC.

The Economist. 2010. Nobody's Backyard. The Rise of Latin America. *The Economist* 396(8699), 11 September: 13 and Special Report 1-18.

Farer, T. (ed.) 1999. *Transnational Crime in the Americas*. New York: Routledge for Inter-American Dialogue.

Fiorentini, G and Peltzman S. (eds.) 1997. *The Economics of Organized Crime*. New York: CUP for CEPR.

Friman, H.R. (ed.) 2009. *Crime and the Global Political Economy*. Boulder: LRP.

Friman, H.R. and Andreas P. (eds.) 1999. *The Illicit Global Economy and State Power*. Lanham: Rowman and Littlefield.

Gaens, B. (ed.) 2008. *Europe-Asia Interregional Relations: a decade of ASEM*. Aldershot: Ashgate.

Gibbon, P., Ponte S. and Lazaro E. (eds.) 2010. *Global Agro-Food Trade and Standards: challenges for Africa*. London: Palgrave Macmillan.

GIIDS. 2009. *Small Arms Survey 2009: shadows of war*. Cambridge: CUP for GIIDS.

Girvan, N. 2005. Reinterpreting the Caribbean, in *The Caribbean Economy: a reader*, edited by D. Pantin. Kingston: Ian Randle. 304-318.

Girvan, N. 2006. Caribbean Dependency Thought Revisited. *Canadian Journal of Development Studies*, 27(3): 329-352.

Glenny, M. 2009. *McMafia: a journey through the global criminal underworld*. Toronto: Anansi.

Griffiths, I. (ed.) 2004. *Caribbean Security in the Age of Terror: challenge and change*. Kingston: Ian Randle.

Hale, T. and Held, D. (eds.) 2011. *Handbook of Transnational Governance*. Cambridge: Polity.

Hall, K.O and Chuck-A-Sang, M. 2010. *CARICOM: policy options for international engagement*. Kingston: Ian Randle for UWI-CARICOM Project.

Harriott, A. (ed.) 2003. *Understanding Crime in Jamaica*. Mona: UWI Press.

Herz, M. 2010. *Organization of American States*. Abingdon: Routledge.

Hettne, B. and Inotai A. 1994. *The New Regionalism: implications for global development and international security*. Helsinki: UNU-WIDER.

Hettne, B., Inotai A. and Sunkel O. (eds.) 1999. *Globalism and the New Regionalism*. London: Macmillan.

Hillman, R.S. 2009. Introduction, in *Understanding the Contemporary Caribbean*, edited by R. Hillman and T.J. D'Agostino. Boulder: Lynne Rienner. Second edition. 1-18.

IBRD. 2006. *Global Economic Prospects: economic implications of remittances and migration*. Washington, DC: IBRD.

IDB. 2009. *Remittances in Times of Financial Instability: impact of the financial crisis on remittances to Latin America and the Caribbean.* Washington, DC: IDB.

Iheduru, O.C. 2011. ECOWAS, in *Ashgate Research Companion to Regionalisms,* edited by T.M. Shaw, A. Grant and S. Cornelissen. Aldershot: Ashgate. 213-239.

Khagram, S. and Levitt P. (eds.) 2007. *The Transnational Studies Reader.* New York: Routledge.

Laursen, F. (ed.) 2010. *Comparative Regional Integration: Europe and beyond.* Farnham: Ashgate.

Macdonald, L. and Ruckert A. (eds.) 2009. *Post-Neoliberalism in the Americas.* London: Palgrave Macmillan.

Mace, G., Cooper, A.F. and Shaw, T.M. (ed.) 2010. *Inter-American Cooperation at a Crossroads.* London: Palgrave Macmillan.

Madsen, F. 2009. *Transnational Organized Crime.* Abingdon: Routledge.

Meeks, B. and Girvan, N. (eds.) 2010. *The Thought of New World: the quest for decolonization.* Kingston: Ian Randle.

Mohammed, P. 2009. *Imaging the Caribbean: culture and visual translation.* Oxford: Macmillan Education.

Naim, M. 2006. *Illicit: how smugglers, traffickers and copycats are hijacking the global economy.* New York: Anchor.

Naylor, R.T. 2005. *Wages of Crime: black markets, illegal finance and the underworld economy.* Ithaca: Cornell UP.

OECD. 2011. *Latin American Economic Outlook 2011: middle classes and development.* Paris: OECD.

Pantin, D. 2005. *The Caribbean Economy: a reader.* Kingston: Ian Randle.

Payne, A. and Sutton, P. 2007. Repositioning the Caribbean within Globalization. *Caribbean Paper #1.* Waterloo; CIGI.

Pieterse, J.N. 2011. Global Rebalancing: crisis and the East-South turn. *Development and Change,* 42(1): 22-48.

Reis, M. 2004. Theorizing Diaspora: perspectives on "classical" and "contemporary" Diasporas. *International Migration,* 42(2): 41-60.

Scher, P.W. (ed.) 2009. *Perspectives on the Caribbean: a reader in culture, migration and representation.* Malden: Wiley-Blackwell.

Shaw, T.M 2010a. Commonwealth and Global Development: contributions to private transnational governance? *Commonwealth and Comparative Politics,* 48(1), 91-111.

Shaw, T.M. 2010b. New Regionalisms Post-EPAs: what prospects for sustainable development in Africa and the Caribbean? in *Comparative Regional Integration: Europe and beyond,* edited by F. Laursen. Farnham: Ashgate. 193-211.

Shaw, T.M. 2011. "New Regionalisms": Caribbean Perspectives in *ACS: promoting the sustainable development of the greater Caribbean. Special 10th edition.* Port of Spain: FIRST. 83-85.

Shaw, T.M. 2012. Energy and CSR in Trinidad and Tobago in the Second Decade of the 21st Century, in (eds.) *Governance Ecosystems: CSR in the Latin American mining sector,* edited by J. Sagebien and N. Lindsay. London: Palgrave Macmillan. 245-259.

Shaw, T.M., Grant, J.A. and Cornelissen, S. (eds.) 2011. *Ashgate Research Companion to Regionalisms.* Farnham: Ashgate.

Thomas-Hope, E. (ed.) 2009. *Freedom and Constraint in Caribbean Migration and Diaspora.* Kingston: Ian Randle.

Townsend, D. 2009. No Other Life: gangs, guns and governance in Trinidad and Tobago. *Working Paper #8.* Geneva: SAS.

UNDP. 2009a. *Human Development Report 2009 Overcoming Barriers: human mobility and development.* New York: Palgrave Macmillan.

UNDP. 2009b. *Opening Spaces for Citizen Security and Human Development; HDR for Central America, HDRCA 2009-2010.* Bogota: UNDP.

UNDP. 2012. Caribbean Human Development Report 2012: human development and the shift to better citizen security. Port of Spain: UNDP.

UNODC. 2010a. *Annual Report 2010: promoting health, security and justice.* Vienna: UNODC.

UNODC. 2010b. *World Drug Report 2010.* Vienna: UNODC.

Vlcek, W. 2008. *Offshore Finance and Small States: sovereignty, size and money.* London: Palgrave Macmillan.

Wiltshire, R. 2006. Implications of Transnational Migration for Nationalism: the Caribbean example. *Annals of the NY Academy of Sciences, Volume 645: Towards a Transnational Perspective on Migration.* 175-187.

World Bank. 2008. *Migration and Remittances Factbook 2008.* Washington, DC: World Bank.

World Bank. 2011. *World Development Report 2011: conflict, security and development.* Washington, DC: World Bank.

Zank, W. (ed.) 2009. *Clash or Cooperation of Civilizations? Overlapping integration and identities.* Farnham: Ashgate.

Chapter 6
Regional Integration in the Pacific

Tiru K. Jayaraman

Despite efforts spanning over more than four decades under the banner of the intergovernmental organization, Pacific Island Forum (the Forum), since 1971,[1] regional integration has remained an elusive goal for the 14 independent Pacific island countries (PICs).[2] Progress has been slow, with successes in some areas and setbacks in some others. The emergence of the Eurozone with one common currency in 1999 in the European Union inspired the PICs to renew their resolve by making fresh initiatives, which culminated in the adoption of a Pacific Plan in the Forum Leaders meeting in Papua New Guinea (PNG) in 2005. One of the four pillars of the Pacific Plan is regional integration.

Efforts in terms of regional trade agreements (RTAs), including a PIC Trade Agreement (PICTA) for promoting freer trade amongst PICs in the first instance by 2011 as a stepping stone, and Pacific Agreement on Closer Economic Cooperation (PACER), both signed in 2001, between PICs and the two advanced countries Australia and New Zealand (ANZ), aiming at the creation of a free trade area (FTA) by 2015, came to be overlapped with a simultaneous move toward freer trade with PICs by the European Union (EU). The latter sought to replace the then expiring Cotonou Agreement with an Economic Partnership Agreement (EPA) with PICs on a regional basis by holding talks with the Forum, rather than on an individual country basis.[3] The apparent rivalry between EU and the region's two

1 In 1971, the Forum was established by seven founding nations, namely Australia, Cook Islands, Fiji, Nauru, New Zealand, Tonga and Western Samoa – now Samoa under the original name, South Pacific Bureau of Economic Cooperation (see below).

2 The Forum comprises 14 Pacific island countries: Cook Islands, Fiji, Kiribati, Republic of Marshall Islands, Federated States of Micronesia, Nauru, Niue, Papua New Guinea, Samoa, Solomon Islands, Tonga, Tuvalu, Vanuatu and the region's two developed countries, namely Australia and New Zealand (ANZ). All of the 16 members are referred to as Forum countries. New Caledonia and French Polynesia, previously Forum Observers, were granted Associate Membership in 2006. Current Forum Observers include Tokelau (2005), Wallis and Futuna (2006), the Commonwealth (2006) and the Asia Development Bank (2006), with Timor Leste as Special Observer (2002).

3 The EU has been negotiating with 76 nations across Africa, the Caribbean and the Pacific (the ACP) all at once. Despite a deadline to complete negotiations before the end of 2007, most ACP nations resisted signing any kind of deal with the EU, while others have signed an interim-EPA because if they did not, Europe would have raised tariffs on their

metropolitan powers, who were keen to be the first to get preferential access to PIC markets, was affecting the progress of the negotiations.

The military take-over of an elected government in Fiji in December 2006 began to have a profound adverse effect on the progress of the regional integration process during the next six years. The military coup elicited a strong reaction from ANZ in terms of economic sanctions against Fiji, followed by Fiji's suspension by the Forum in May 2009 and by the Commonwealth in September 2009. All of them soured the relationships between Fiji and ANZ.

The atmosphere continues to be unfavourable for any fruitful negotiations. With the continued isolation of Fiji,[4] the Forum negotiations on EPA, PACER and PICTA have all been stalled. However, adversity brings forth new initiatives. In the Pacific context, it is the increasing recognition of the need for sub-regional cooperation amongst Melanesian Spearhead Group (MSG) Countries, namely Fiji, PNG, Solomon Islands (SI) and Vanuatu, which comprise 90 percent of the total population of about 8 million of 14 PICs. Similar to these developments, the Polynesian island countries (Cook Islands, Niue, Samoa, Tonga and Tuvalu), which are smaller in size and population and natural resources, have also been exploring avenues for sub-regional integration.[5] The remaining PICs, namely Kiribati, Marshall Islands, Federated States of Micronesia (FSM), Nauru and Palau, are categorized as Micronesia.

The PICs are at a crossroads again. Hurt by isolation for the past three years, Fiji has been drumming up support since 2009 by organizing rival meetings with other sympathetic PIC leaders under the banners of *Engaging with the Pacific (EWP)* and *Pacific Small Islands Developing States (PSIDS)* in August each year,[6] during which month the Forum usually holds its traditional annual Forum Leaders meetings. Further, Fiji has been looking North, West and East (China, North Korea, Indonesia, the United Arab Emirates, Russia and Cuba) and has been cultivating new trade and investment relationships (Okeefe 2012). Already,

---

exports to the EU. Fiji and PNG initialled interim-EPAs in late 2007 to avoid tariff hikes on tuna and sugar exports.

4 The week-long 43rd Forum Leaders Meeting in Cook Islands held in August 2012 decided to maintain Fiji's suspension from the group until 2015, by which time a new democratically elected government would be in place.

5 The Polynesian Leaders Group (PLG) who met in Cook Islands during the 43rd Forum Leaders Meeting held in August 2012 were reported to be considering adding three more members, Hawaii (50th state of USA), Rapa Nui and Aotearoa Māori, into its fold of eight members (Samoa, Tonga, Tuvalu, Cook Islands, Niue, American Samoa, French Polynesia and Tokelau). Prime Ministers of Cook Islands and Samoa explained to media at the conclusion of their closed PLG meeting that the group was not established to counter the influence of the MSG but to unite leaders of a geographical cluster of countries facing similar challenges and limitations.

6 The *Third Engaging with the Pacific* Meeting, held in Nadi, Fiji in the week of August 20, 2012 just a week before the 43rd Annual Summit of Forum Leaders on August 27-31, was also attended by representatives from Morocco, Kazakhstan and Kosovo.

China has become a leading donor in the region,[7] much to the discomfort of the traditional donors including ANZ and the United States of America (USA).

This chapter seeks to take a closer look at past developments, some of which have been seriously hurting regionalism, with new emphasis on the directions in which the major member countries in the Forum should now move to get back on track towards the original goal of integration. This chapter is organized along the following lines. The next section gives a brief background of the Pacific region. The third section reviews the efforts towards regional integration. The fourth section deals with the tasks ahead. The final section is a summary and presents some conclusions with policy recommendations.

Background

There are 22 Pacific island entities in all,[8] whose political status ranges from that of an independent sovereign state to that of a UN Trust Territory, or colonial possessions of the superpowers including Britain and France, which are administered as overseas territories. Only 14 independent states out of 22 entities are members of the Forum.

Hugely Diverse

The 14 PICs are spread over the Pacific Ocean about 10,000 kilometres (km) from east to west and 5,000 km from north to south, with a combined exclusive economic zone (EEZ) of ocean area of about 20 million sq. km. The total land area is just over 500,000 sq. km, of which PNG accounts for 88 percent. Population of the PICs is, as of 2011, almost 8 million, of which over 6 million are in PNG. At the other end of the scale is Niue, with a population of less than 2000. Table 6.1 presents the selected key indicators of PICs.

The 14 PICs display a high degree of diversity in natural and human resources. The Melanesian countries have been endowed with a relatively larger land area

7 China's aid and soft loans to PICs during 2007-2011 have been reported to be around US$ 600 million as against the US aid of US$ 20 million per annum during the corresponding period. Samoa's Prime Minister has expressed his appreciation of China's generous assistance to Samoa on a number of occasions, the latest being the 43rd Meeting of the Forum leaders in Cook Islands in August 2012. He praised the 'unique flexibility' of China in its assistance to develop the Pacific island state, apparently with reference to rigid positions taken by ANZ with reference to labour mobility and OCTA and the like (*Samoa Observer* 2012). Professor Bryce Edwards of Otago University told TV NZ: 'We are having a bit of power struggle here because these Pacific Islands do need resources and money quickly and it gives them some independence from ANZ.' (*Fiji Times*, 2012).

8 Populations in each of the 22 Pacific island entities, who are members of the Pacific Community, range from less than a hundred in Pitcairn Island, the last British outpost, to 7 million in PNG.

with greater arable land for agricultural activities and mineral resources. On the other hand, Kiribati and Tuvalu are atoll islands with limited agricultural activities. Since they have larger exclusive economic zones than other PICs, a major part of their gross national incomes is largely derived from exports of fish and license fees by granting fishing licenses to companies to exploit their marine resources. They also depend upon annual remittances from their seafaring labour employed in foreign ships. In the case of Polynesian countries, land area being small, agriculture is confined only to a few staples such as root crops and a few exports, such as banana and coconut products.

Table 6.1 Selected Key Indicators

	Population ('000)	Per Capita GDP (Current Prices) in US$	HD Index Rank	Aid per capita US$	Aid as % of GDP	Average Growth Rate (%)
	2009	2009	2010	2009	2009	2004-09
Cook Islands	23	7,549	NR	491	28.0	2.3
Fiji	834	3,326	86.0	84	2.5	0.7
Fed. States of Micronesia	108	2,476	103.0	1,093	42.0	-0.8
Kiribati	99	1,306	NR	277	15.6	-0.3
Nauru	10	3,500	NR	NA	NA	NA
Niue	2	NA	NR	NA	NA	NA
Palau	20	8,074	NR	1,733	27.9	NA
Papua New Guinea	6,348	1,172	137.0	61	5.3	4.6
Republic of Marshall Islands	54	2,504	NR	963	32.1	1.4
Samoa	183	2,776	NR	433	16.1	2.1
Solomon Islands	539	1,256	123.0	394	42.9	5.5
Tonga	103	2,991	86.0	380	12.4	0.2
Tuvalu	11	3,318	NR	254	45.0	2.2
Vanuatu	239	2,072	NR	431	16.5	5.6

Notes: NA= Not Available; NR= Not Ranked
Sources: World Bank (2011), ADB (2010), Commonwealth Secretariat (2010), UNDP (2010)

Manufacturing Capacity

Except Fiji and PNG, none of the 14 PICs have any significant manufacturing capacity worth mentioning. The manufactured products in Fiji and PNG include sugar and other processed foods, such as biscuits, cooking oil, cigarettes, beer and rum and a host of minor processed goods for domestic consumption, as well as export to other island countries. Other PICs' manufacturing activities are confined to coconut-based products, such as coconut oil, cream, soaps and detergents.

Almost all PICs, with their attractive beaches and tropical climate, are unique tourist destinations. However, only a few among them have been able to take advantage of these endowments for boosting the national income, such as Fiji and Vanuatu with their head start in physical infrastructure in terms of hotels and resort facilities. Due to the great diversity in endowments, skills and human resources, gross national income per capita varies widely among PICs. Palau and the Cook Islands belong to a group of upper middle income countries (UMIC), whereas Fiji, Samoa and Tonga belong to a group of lower middle income countries (LMIC). The group of low income countries includes PNG, Kiribati, SI and Tuvalu.[9]

Constraints to Growth

Constraints to growth and development of PICs stem from their geographical characteristics. One of the former Forum Secretary-Generals (Urwin 2004) succinctly categorized the constraints as below: (i) remoteness and insularity; (ii) susceptibility to natural disasters; (iii) small population size; (iv) limited diversification; and (v) high dependency on trade in goods and services. Economic development in PICs since their independence was characterized by the dominant role played by large public sectors, which were supported by substantial foreign aid. Despite plentiful aid per capita, weak growth in PICs during the 1980s and early 1990s came to be looked upon as a 'Pacific Paradox' (World Bank 1993), attributing it to the poor use of generous aid in comparison to similarly placed island countries in the Caribbean and Indian ocean regions. Critical views have been voiced from time to time.[10]

9 The income groups defined by the OECD for the purpose of disbursement of official development assistance are as follows: LIC per capita gross national income less than US$ 825; LMIC: between US$ 825 and US$ 3,255; and UMIC: between US$ 3,256 and US$ 10,065.

10 These include Senate Committee of Australian Parliament and Centre for Independent Studies, Sydney as well as by Professor Hughes (2003, 2004 and 2010).

Open Economies

The PICs are open economies. In several cases, this is not because they have low trade barriers,[11] but because they are small with substantially large imports. The PICs' trade volumes in commodities (exports and imports of goods) expressed as percentages of gross domestic product are fairly high (Table 6.2).

Table 6.2 Trade Share of GDP

Country	Trade share of GDP (2005-2009)
Cook Islands	74.0
Fiji	82.9
Kiribati	92.3
RMI	59.2
FSM	56.9
Nauru	166.9
Palau	115.7
PNG	79.9
Samoa	58.1
Solomon Islands	55.1
Tonga	53.7
Tuvalu	56.0
Vanuatu	62.0

Source: ADB (2011)

On an average during the last four years (2005-09), trade volume ranged from 167 percent of GDP in Nauru to 54 percent in Tonga. All PICs have to depend upon imports for all commodities, including staples such as rice and wheat. While PNG's major exports are both minerals (gold, petroleum, copper, natural gas) and tree crops (coffee, tea, timber), Fiji's chief exports have been sugar, mineral water, garments and gold. For smaller island countries, which have negligible manufacturing capacity, reliance on primary exports is much greater. Thus, PICs are more competitive than complementary to each other as they seek the same

11 In fact, the governments of PICs, which have limited capacities in domestic revenue, resource mobilization, taxed imports and exports to raise revenues for meeting the growth in public sector expenditures. In the case of Vanuatu, there is no direct taxation of any kind. Hence, the government has been relying on indirect taxation, including taxes on imports and exports.

markets (Browne 2006). With liberalization in ANZ, which are traditional export markets for PIC products, exports including coconut milk and cream and other copra-based products have been finding it difficult to compete with Thailand, Malaysia and other Asian countries.

Exchange Rate Arrangements

Out of 14 PICs, eight are dollarized. They have adopted the national currencies of Australia, New Zealand or the USA: Kiribati, Nauru and Tuvalu (the Australian dollar); the Cook Islands and Niue (the New Zealand dollar); and FSM, RMI and Palau (the US dollar). The other six PICs have independent currencies of their own. While PNG has a floating exchange rate regime, five PICs, namely Fiji, Samoa, SI, Tonga and Vanuatu, have fixed exchange rate regimes. All PICs have been sourcing their imports from ANZ and the USA, who have been targeting inflation, which explains the low inflation in PICs.

Trends in Regional Integration Efforts

Efforts for forging regional cooperation began when five island nations, Cook Islands, Fiji, Nauru, Tonga and Western Samoa (now Samoa), in the South Pacific soon after their decolonization in 1970 joined hands with ANZ to establish in 1971 the South Pacific Bureau of Economic Cooperation. The name change to Forum took place when the northern Pacific states which were US Trust territories became independent and joined the intergovernmental organization in the 1990s. The Forum establishment is largely funded by the two advanced Forum member countries.[12]

Pre-dating the Forum, there was one other organization known as South Pacific Commission, now called Pacific Community (PC) after being enlarged in the mid-1990s to include the northern Pacific island states, RMI, FSM and Palau. The PC was established in 1947 under the Canberra Agreement signed by Australia, France, New Zealand, the Netherlands, the United Kingdom and the USA. The Secretariat of the Pacific Community (SPC) located in Noumea, New Caledonia assists all 22 entities, including 14 PICs, by providing technical advice, training and dissemination of information in social, economic and cultural fields.

The functions of the Forum Secretariat are: servicing the PIC governments; coordinating regional approaches in areas of common economic interest;

12 As of 2011, the Forum Secretariat's budget is funded mostly by Australia and New Zealand (70 percent) with another 15 percent by the European Union and other donors from outside the region with periodical contributions. Thus, the erstwhile colonial masters of the Pacific region have taken the lead, unlike in the Caribbean where integration efforts are purely CARICOM driven (Fairbairn and Worrell 1996).

overseeing areas of functional cooperation and acting as the focal point for a range of associated institutions. Notably absent from the list of functions, as Fairbairn and Worrell (1996) observed in their comparative study on the South Pacific and the Caribbean island economies, are the issues of a single market and a common currency.

Appendix 6.1 presents, in brief, the milestones of the long journey towards economic integration. Fry (2005) divides the 34-year history on regional cooperation and integration into more or less five distinct phases, with some overlapping. They cover the following: (i) 1971-1975: comprehensive regional integration; (ii) 1975-1980: sectoral integration; (iii) 1981-1985: regional security; (iv) 1985-1990: collective diplomacy; (v) 1991-2000: harmonization of national policies; and (vi) 2001 and onwards to the present: new regionalism.

In the early period, comprehensive regional integration was the main focus, which could be justified on the grounds that small-sized economies, if they could not get it alone, cannot realize the economies of scale in manufacturing operations and in purchase of essential items such as fuel and medicines. Further, national shipping lines, a university and a development bank would not be viable.

Attention was turned to sectoral integration in the second half of the 1970s. The setting up of a regional University and creation of Air Pacific were some important achievements. However, there was some disillusionment with Air Pacific, on the grounds that it was Fiji that had gained more from the common airlines. Over a period, Nauru, Samoa, the SI, Tonga and Vanuatu, while retaining shares in Air Pacific, set up their own national airlines to promote tourist arrivals direct from major airports in ANZ and the USA. In regard to the regional University of the South Pacific (USP) located in Fiji, there were some rumblings as well. Fry (2005) refers to the writings of Crocombe and Ueantabo (1976), which reflected the concerns of other island nations that USP was partial to Fiji's interests.

Although USP responded to various concerns by setting up Extension Centres and special campuses in Samoa (Alafua) and Vanuatu (Emalus), the impression of yesteryears could not be easily erased. Samoa went ahead setting up its own National University of Samoa. During the 2000 coup in Fiji, students enrolled at USP had to return to respective island countries and their education was disrupted for a while. The dormant dissatisfaction surfaced again as some island nations such as SI indicated their desire to set up a university of their own.

Sectoral integration did not proceed beyond USP and Pacific Forum Lines, the shipping service. Fry (2005) notes that sectoral integration in other areas required substantial outlays. PICs were not prepared to sacrifice their autonomy and did not prefer them being located in well-off PICs such as Fiji. The differences between Fiji and other PICs quickly revealed a growing rift between PICs. So sectoral integration was replaced by a more practical approach of collective diplomacy in many soft areas of cooperation, where conflicts were less likely.

The Lome negotiations with the European Community in the 1980s, the Law of the Sea negotiations and environmental protection arguments at the Rio Conference were some outstanding examples of success. Along with these achievements, the regional security concerns of ANZ for containing former Soviet influences in many PICs led to new initiatives to meet situations, such as Kiribati granting the Soviet Union access to fishing in Kiribati waters and similar overtures by Vanuatu. This gave rise to resentment in PICs against Australia that while ANZ had kept diplomatic relations with the Soviet Union, foreign policies of PICs were dictated by the metropolitan states. Fry (2005) observes that the late 1980s witnessed a shift in the approach of Australia. Its foreign policy pronouncements of 1988 indicated 'a constructive commitment', emphasizing partnership rather than an agency of western interests or Australian hegemonic aspirations, which represented past Australian diplomatic thrusts. In the 1990s, the MSG countries forged a trading bloc for free trade in selected goods (see below for details). Since there was no common secretariat to oversee implementation of MSG trade, progress was slow as MSG countries took time to prepare a list of agreed items, instead of drawing a negative list, which would have been simpler.

On a wider regional level, the period witnessed efforts towards harmonization of national policies in the 1990s. The emergence of 'neo liberalism' and wider acceptance of the Washington Consensus of fiscal and monetary restraints, financial sector liberalization and public sector reforms paved the way for ANZ to tie them into their bilateral assistance programmes. Disappointment with the poor progress of structural reform implementation led ANZ to reconsider past approaches. The 9/11 terror attack of 2001 in the USA imposed new responsibilities on Australia to make the Pacific safer from the newly emerging risks of terrorism as well as the already known risks of money laundering and gun-running. Additionally, ethnic rife and civil disorder in SI since the late 1990s and the overthrow of an elected government in 2000 in Fiji caused fresh worries to ANZ. Furthermore, a study by Hughes (2002) described some PICs, which could not effectively use the aid funds and undertake reforms with funds obtained from international and bilateral agencies, with possible diversion for personal use amounting to corruption and wastage as 'failed states'.

Taking the cue from Hughes (2003), an Australian Senate Committee (the Committee) held hearings on Australia's Relations with Pacific island States in 2002 and in their Report (Commonwealth of Australia 2003) concluded that a *Pacific Economic and Political Community,* similar to the EU, should be a consideration in the medium to long-term future of the region. The Committee also considered the region adopting a common currency, preferably the Australian dollar, for promoting fiscal and monetary discipline. Following the Senate Committee's observations in July 2003, Australia floated the idea of a single regional currency prior to the Forum Leaders Meeting in Auckland in August 2003. Since the subject was not included in the agenda, it was not formally discussed but it was decided to examine the idea of a single market, by appointing an Eminent Persons Group (EPG) to undertake a comprehensive review of the Forum with a view to exploring areas of regional cooperation.

Already, increased globalization since 2000 has thrown up some new challenges: The phased discontinuance of preferential treatment by EU for the products of PICs and the end of Sugar Protocol for Fiji's sugar exports by 2007 under the Cotonou Agreement required PICs to re-structure their export industries for competing with the rest of the world for access to EU markets. The Cotonou Agreement was to be replaced by a new agreement, known as the Economic Partnership Agreement (EPA), on the condition that PICs should speed up and promote regional integration on the lines of at least MSG. Further, access to Australia under the South Pacific Regional Trade and Economic Cooperation Agreement (SPARTECA) was also becoming less significant (see below for details).

In the face of stiff competition from competitor economies outside the region, PICs had to take quick action in restructuring their economies and increasing their bargaining position. Further, having found themselves unable to attract foreign direct investment (FDI) in the immediate past, they wanted to come together and offer an assured large regional market without custom barriers for products, if produced in any of the PICs through FDI. Necessitated by the EU offer of EPA to be signed only on a regional basis, PICs signed PICTA[13] for ushering in FTA among the 14 PICs by 2010.

However, PICs were nervous at the prospect of any immediate removal of barriers due to concern over the impact on local manufacturing as well as the impact on government finances due to loss of revenue from tariffs (Scollay 2005). Hence they decided to keep ANZ out of PICTA. Persuaded by the arguments of PICs that they looked upon PICTA as a stepping stone for an eventual closer relationship, including free trade in goods and services as well as mobility of labour with ANZ, the latter agreed and in 2001 signed the separate PACER with them. The PACER[14] required PICs to start negotiations with ANZ by April 2011. In case, any PIC in its negotiations with EU on EPA was to give a reciprocal access to EU, and PACER negotiations would have been deemed to be triggered earlier than 2011.[15]

While PICs were confronted with problems of bewildering complexities involved in trade agreements, the EPG submitted their draft Report. The PIC leaders met in Auckland in April 2004 to consider the Report by EPG, on the basis of which they agreed to evolve a Pacific Plan. The EPG reporting back to the Forum Leaders Meeting in April 2004 observed that although a Pacific economic

13 The PICTA aimed at ushering in free trade among developing PICs (Fiji, PNG, Palau, FSM, Samoa, Solomon Islands, Tonga, Vanuatu) by 2010 and amongst all PICs, including the remaining ones known as small and least developed PICs (Cook Islands, Kiribati, Niue, Nauru, RMI, Tuvalu) by 2012. After obtaining the legally required minimum number of ratifications by the respective legislatures, PICTA became effective on April 13, 2003.

14 After obtaining the legally required minimum number of ratifications by the respective legislatures, PACER entered into force on October 3, 2002.

15 PACER was expanded in late 2008 to include trade in services, capital flows and investment as well as capacity building and promoting labour mobility in identified areas. Appropriately renamed as PACER Plus, it was approved in 2009 by the Forum Leaders in their 40th Annual Meeting held in Cairns.

union was one of the earliest goals of the Forum, the vision 'remains incomplete, though still a relevant objective' (Pacific Islands Forum Secretariat 2004: 27). The EPG's vision was a community of states engaged in deeper integration and greater cooperation in areas such as transport, information technology, quarantine, customs, security, judicial and public administration and regional law enforcement.

Pacific Plan

A Draft Pacific Plan was prepared in 2004 and adopted by the Forum Leaders in their meeting in 2005 held in PNG. The Pacific Plan spells out in clear terms the goals termed as four pillars[16]: (i) economic growth; (ii) sustainable development; (iii) good governance; and (iv) security (Pacific Islands Forum Secretariat 2005). The integration efforts of the kind envisaged by the Pacific Plan did not go beyond trade in goods and services and capital and labour mobility. The goal of a single, common currency along the lines of the euro is not a specific part of the Pacific Plan. The EPG Report, endorsed by PICs, made it clear that the time was not ripe for a Pacific Union similar to the European Union.

However, the military coup in Fiji in 2006, the fourth in the series since 1987, halted the implementation of the Pacific Plan.[17] ANZ immediately imposed economic sanctions against Fiji, which was followed by suspension from the Forum and the Commonwealth in mid-2009. Australia excluded Fiji from the PACER Plus talks in late 2009, creating further tensions in late 2009. The PICs are now divided into three groups: one agreeing with two rich members of the Forum, Australia and New Zealand; the second supporting Fiji's road map to democracy with elections scheduled in 2014; and the third not sure where they should stand. The region is aware that in the past, three military coups in Fiji (two in 1987 and one in 2000) resulted in some setbacks, but the effects were only temporary. The PIC leaders believe the current uncertainties would also eventually pass, as Fiji has assured other PICs that its long-term vision of a well-integrated region remains the same.

16 Specifically in regard to economic growth, the Pacific Plan seeks to integrate trade in services including the temporary movement of labour in PICTA/PACER negotiations and create bulk purchasing capacity for essential items such as fuel and medicines. The second item of bulk purchase has been on the agenda since 1971 without any progress, whereas the inclusion of trade in services indicates the willingness of PICs to consider deeper integration, of course for 'a price': liberalized immigration laws. Thus, the ball has been thrown in the court of advanced Forum member countries to consider relaxation in immigration. The other three pillars are familiar ones. They are now part of heavy involvement of Australia and New Zealand in the region: (i) provision of experts in financial management, public sector reforms and strengthening legal machinery, all contributing to better governance and sustainable development; and (ii) provision of Regional Assistance Mission to Solomon Islands (RAMSI) to improve law and order in the ethnically divided nation.

17 The Pacific Plan is scheduled for a review in 2013.

'infant industries' on the basis until such time they could grow and compete with goods from trading partners.

Amongst the RTAs, MSG FTA appears to have emerged in recent years to be more acceptable in Melanesia, mainly because of the dragging of PACER Plus negotiations and isolation of a fellow MSG country, Fiji. As a Pacific Institute of Public Policy study (2008) notes, support for the MSG FTA empowers Melanesian governments to shift towards trade liberalization and resistance to protectionist pressures at a time when discussion of other (non-regional) agreements tends to stimulate anti-trade sentiment.

In addition to trade in goods, MSG leaders have taken yet another initiative. This is in regard to greater mobility of skilled personnel between MSG countries. If the Skills Movement Scheme is implemented, as planned from September 2012, about 450 trained teachers and nurses from Fiji would move to work in Vanuatu, meeting the current shortages in these two critical areas. However, the reception has been hostile. The Vanuatu Chamber of Commerce disapproved the scheme on the grounds that it will be a disincentive for Vanuatu youth to specialize in these areas and will lead to greater unemployment.

The economic space offered by MSG countries is small for facilitating intra-island mobility of skilled and unskilled labour. The PICs with no manufacturing base would like to move around and work in farms of bigger countries which have real shortages of agricultural labour. It is obvious that integration beyond MSG countries, preferably with ANZ, would be more beneficial, if labour mobility is encouraged. This is true not only for MSG countries but also for smaller PICs like Kiribati and Tuvalu.

Labour Mobility

Since only a few PICs would stand to gain from free trade arrangements in goods, a normal FTA is not uniformly attractive to all PICs. In fact, that was one of the reasons behind the lukewarm reception on the part of smaller PICs including Kiribati and Tuvalu to sign PICTA and PACER. The only comparative advantage which PICs enjoy is the 'export of labour' to work on foreign ships and on horticulture farms for fruit picking and other unskilled employment. The idea of importing labour has remained an attractive incentive for ANZ employers to meet shortages in the farm sector. It was estimated that up to 50,000 seasonal workers across New Zealand would be required at harvest time. In April 2007, New Zealand introduced the Recognized Seasonal Employer (RSE) programme, under which New Zealand employers are allowed to recruit overseas workers from the Pacific and South East Asia for seasonal work in horticulture and viticulture.

The RSE programme began in April 2007. By April 2008, after a year of operation, 92 companies had been approved as RSE employers and 4,070 workers from the Pacific and South East Asia had RSE visa applications approved (Macllelan 2008). Data shows that mean gross seasonal earnings are around NZ$12,700 per worker, most of whom spend between three and seven months working in New

Zealand. A survey of RSE employers conducted in 2011 found that most have enjoyed better quality, more productive workers and a more stable workforce (Guy 2011) and that RSE workers have helped their businesses to expand. From PICs' point of view, the survey results indicated that it was providing valuable income, skills and experience that workers can take back to their home countries.[19]

Australia introduced a pilot scheme, known as Pacific Seasonal Worker Pilot Scheme (PSWPS), in 2009 and three countries were chosen: Kiribati, Tonga and Vanuatu, each one representing Micronesia, Polynesia and Melanesia. Later on, PNG was added. In 2010, Nauru, Samoa, SI and Tuvalu were added to the list. Under this pilot scheme, Pacific Islanders were allowed to work in Australia as fruit and vegetable-pickers for periods of up to six months. About 2,500 Pacific islanders were expected to benefit. However, the number was low. By March 2012, only 1,100 workers were taken, which was far below the 7,000 Pacific workers under New Zealand's RSE scheme (Howes and Hay 2012). Although the programme has been made permanent from 2012, problems relating to red tape and lack of information[20] would render the programme less attractive to employers themselves (Curtain 2012).

PACER Plus

PACER Plus is an extension of PACER, which came out of concerns felt by ANZ subsequent to its signing in 2001 in regard to poor progress recorded by PICs towards achieving the targeted Millennium Development Goals by 2015. It was also influenced by perceived poor governance in PICs, which manifested in the coup of 2006 in Fiji, continuing ethnic tensions in SI and anti-monarchy protests in Tonga. The new approach was towards developing durable partnerships with a view to (i) improving governance; (ii) increasing investment in infrastructure and employment for recording greater economic growth and (iii) achieving better outcomes in health. Further, it was visualized that similar to Doha Development Agenda's for generating development gains to the world's poor, a comprehensive trade pact not only in trade but also services would be necessary in the Pacific region (Crean 2009).

---

19 Vanuatu, which is one of the Melanesian countries with minimal migration experience to Australia and New Zealand, is now benefitting more from remittances received from migrant workers than ever before. In 2007, 36 workers from Vanuatu went to New Zealand. The number increased to 1,855 in 2008, 2,024 in 2009, 2,049 in 2010, 2,521 in 2011 and over 3,000 are expected be sent in 2012.

20 Curtain (2012) writes: 'The Australian seasonal worker program is heavily managed with four federal government departments or agencies involved in administering or monitoring it. This together with its range of requirements and compliance monitoring will discourage employers from taking on seasonal workers under this program, compared with the options of using backpackers or illegal workers. Although some reporting requirements have been reduced (monthly reporting is no longer required), some processes seem to have been made more complex.'

In the Meeting held in Niue in 2008, Forum Leaders agreed to establish genuine regional economic integration of the type already enjoyed bilaterally by Australia and New Zealand and decided to commence negotiations in 2009. The proposed PACER Plus was to comprise a package of trade capacity and trade development assistance by Australia with New Zealand, the Asian Development Bank and the World Bank, which were aimed at securing new opportunities for PICs and cushioning any short-term costs of adapting to the challenges of globalization.

PACER Plus is expected to address a number of issues common to the whole region, which would include (i) how to comply with the quarantine requirements into Australia and New Zealand; (ii) developing consistent rules of origin within the region; (iii) the importance of improving aviation links to encourage greater tourism;[21] and (iv) liberalization of the telecommunications industry (Crean 2009). PACER Plus is also to encompass: (i) Pacific Regional Infrastructure Fund for underwriting critically needed investment; (ii) labour mobility with introduction of a three-year Pacific Seasonal Worker Pilot Scheme, which would help Australian horticultural industry employers who are unable to source local labour, providing employment experience, remittances and training opportunities in the region; and (iii) training of public servants.

A research study indicates that there could be a significant increase up to 30 percent in trade volumes, from the elimination of regional trade barriers and improved efficiencies, although that effect will be due to the aggregate impact of PACER Plus and all the existing RTAs (Institute of International Trade 2008). In addition to benefits of free trade under PACER Plus, which would be complemented by other cooperation on trade facilitation and direct technical assistance to PICs, the aforementioned study highlights the liberalization of the temporary movement of skilled and unskilled labour within the region, as it would enjoy strong support from the Pacific community.

Challenges

There are challenges as well. Aside from the varying sizes and vulnerability of their economies to natural disasters, there is chronic inadequacy of capacity to fully realize the potential gains from trade. While Vanuatu in particular feared loss of revenue as a result of reduced import tariffs, since it depended only on indirect taxes in the absence of direct taxation, smaller PICs that do not have any significant manufacturing base, except for meeting local needs such as copra-based soap, detergents, and bread and biscuits, were worried that they would be swamped by ANZ goods and services to the detriment of local businesses and local employment (Institute of International Trade 2008).

21 The World Bank, which invested US $125 million in the aviation industry across six countries in the Pacific, looks to aviation to help expand economic development in the region.

It is therefore necessary to increase the supply side competitive capacity of PICs; for example, through training the Pacific workforce, assistance to meet Australia's stringent quarantine requirements, a more flexible application of rules of origin or the harmonization of regulatory requirements, that wherever possible are consistent with those required by other developed nations such as the EU or the US. They also raised the complex problem of 'fine tuning' the balance between attracting foreign investment while retaining or possibly introducing subsidies and other direct assistance to support local industries and sectors, particularly those with future export potential (Institute of International Trade 2008).

Considering the capacity limits of PICs to plan, negotiate and implement a fully fledged free trade agreement, Australia decided to provide technical and financial assistance to PICs for raising their ability to commission their own PACER Plus research and training for Forum Island trade officials to prepare for negotiations. Accordingly, an amount of Aus$500,000 a year, for three years, by Australia and Aus$650,000 by New Zealand, in all Aus$1.5 million, was set aside to fund the Office of the Chief Trade Advisor (OCTA), to provide independent support and advice to PICs Forum Countries over the course of negotiation.

OCTA, based in Port Vila, Vanuatu, started operation in March 2010. However, the first incumbent did not complete a three-year term. Due to differences between him and ANZ, he chose to resign from his position in September 2011. A replacement was made in February 2012. Being already engaged in negotiations with EU for EPA, PICs who do not have sufficient capabilities in their trade and law ministries wanted OCTA to assist them in their negotiations with the EU as well. It was a difficult compromise to accomplish, as ANZ felt that OCTA funded by them was primarily meant for PACER Plus.

The Way Ahead

There are increasing concerns about the future of PACER Plus negotiations. Further, there were confused signals since the change in government in Australia in 2011. A new international trade policy announced in April 2011 did not make any reference to PACER Plus. Furthermore, the Australian government's report to the World Trade Organization in March 2011, as part of its Sixth Trade Policy Review, failed to mention PACER Plus (Morgan 2012).

As of August 2012, the PICs' concerns are continuing. So far there is nothing beyond generalities, since meetings of the Ministers in October 2009 and April 2010 did not deal with details.[22] The objective, structure and contents of PACER

22 The negotiations are expected to be based on a few general statements made by Forum Trade Ministers during their meetings in 2009 and 2010. These statements recognized the capacity constraints faced by PICs when undertaking negotiations, and the need for national consultations with all stakeholders; the importance of deepening regional trade integration affirmed that PACER Plus provides the Pacific region with a significant

Plus are yet to be concretized for a negotiation text. As Noonan (2011) pointed out, absence of a document for negotiations is a serious deficiency. These suspicions and fears would be eliminated only if Australia places on the table some tangible proposals. The latter will have to include firmer schemes beyond *ad-hoc* measures. Only concrete proposals for greater intakes under seasonal employment would convince PICs of the intentions of the two advanced Forum member countries which go beyond 'unorthodox trade and development' (Morgan 2012).

Additionally, the decision of the Forum Leaders to keep Fiji away from PACER Plus talks seems to cast doubts on the future of the talks. Although Fiji was a signatory to the original PACER agreement signed in 2001, Australia's argument that PACER Plus of 2010 is different from PACER is based more on political grounds than on logical reasoning, when the thrusts of the two agreements are economic and not different.

To sum up, regional integration in the Pacific would continue to be an elusive goal. There are regional rivalries, not only among the sub-groups within the region but also among ANZ on one hand and the EU. The negotiations between the EU and PICs were initiated in 2004 and are still in limbo. It is understood that if countries do not close negotiations by the end of December 2013, those not classified as Least Developed Countries will lose duty-free and quota-free access to EU markets.

The PICs need OCTA's help in their negotiations with the EU, which is denied on the grounds that OCTA has been created primarily for PACER Plus talks. Further, the continuing isolation of Fiji,[23] which is the second most important country after PNG, and lack of progress towards concretizing the objectives of PACER Plus into a negotiating document are serious issues to be resolved, if PACER Plus, the mother of all RTAs in the Pacific, should take off.

---

opportunity to develop a truly innovative trade and economic agreement that takes account of the different stages of development of each nation.

23 There were high expectations that a week-long 43rd Pacific Island Forum Leaders Meeting in Cook Islands, held in late August 2012, a highlight of which was US Secretary Hillary Clinton's presence, would consider Fiji's re-admission to the Forum by considering ongoing efforts for enacting a new Constitution by 2013 and conducting elections in 2014. The Forum decided against re-admission and preferred to wait until the elections when the new democratically elected government would be in place.

Appendix 6.1 History of Regional Economic Integration in the Pacific

Years/Period	Events
1947	Establishment of South Pacific Commission (SPC) by six countries: Australia, France, New Zealand, Netherlands, the United Kingdom and the United States. SPC was providing technical, consultative and advisory assistance in social, cultural and economic activities. In 1998, with the inclusion of the Micronesian countries and northern Pacific States, which were former US Trust Territories, the name was changed to Pacific Community. The initialism SPC is still retained. However, it stands for Secretariat of Pacific Community. There are 27 members. The programmes of SPC consist of three sectors: land resources, marine resources and socio-economic sectors. The functions are provision of technical assistance, education and training and information/communication. SPC is located in Noumea, New Caledonia.
1968	The University of the South Pacific was established to provide higher education and training that reflects the aspirations and needs of PICs. The main campus is in Suva, Fiji, and there are two campuses, one in Samoa, which hosts the School of Tropical Agriculture and one in Vanuatu, which hosts the Law Unit and Language Unit. There are University Extension Centres in other island states.
1971	Establishment of South Pacific Islands Forum by seven founding members (Australia, Cook Islands, Fiji, Nauru, New Zealand, Tonga, and Samoa). Expanded later to include all 16 States, covering the northern Pacific region. The name was changed to Pacific Islands Forum (PIF). It is popularly referred to as the Forum, which serves as the premier regional policy-making body of the self-governing states. The Secretariat is known as the Forum Secretariat and its objective is to service the Heads of Government meetings; to foster and promote regional economic cooperation, particularly on political, economic and trade issues.
1972	Establishment of the South Pacific Applied Geo-Science Commission (SOPAC). Started as a UN Project for mineral prospecting in offshore areas, it assists member countries in identifying, assessing, and developing mineral and non-living resource potential of extensive marine resources.
1974	Establishment of South Pacific Regional Environment Programme (SPREP). SPREP aims to provide assistance to the member states in the areas of protecting and improving the environment and ensuring sustainable development for the present and future generations.
1977	The Pacific Forum Line was founded for regional cooperation in shipping. It is a private company wholly owned by nine members of the Forum. The share-holding members are: Cook Islands, Fiji, Kiribati, Nauru, New Zealand, Papua New Guinea, Solomon Islands, Tonga and Samoa.

Years/Period	Events
1979	Establishment of the Forum Fisheries Agency (FFA). It provides technical assistance in the development of fisheries management policies and in negotiations on the issue of licenses. Collection of fees, and surveillance of zones; collecting and dissemination of information on prices; shipping, processing and marketing of fish and fish products; focusing on management procedures, legislation, and agreements within and outside the region. FFA is based in Honiara, the Solomon Islands.
1979	Establishment of South Pacific Trade Commission (SPTC) in Sydney to promote trade and development and encourage Australian investment in island countries, through joint ventures; the SPTC holds exhibitions.
1980	Establishment of Pacific Island Development Program (PIDP) in Honolulu under the East West Center. Membership covers all island countries regardless of political status. PIDP conducts research on topics identified by Pacific island leaders.
1980-1989	Period of Collective Diplomacy. Successful negotiations with European Community on Lome Conventions. Negotiations on Law of the Sea. Anti-nuclear dumping campaign against Japan's proposal to dump radioactive wastes in the Marianas Trench, demonstrating collective action. Anti-drift netting campaign against Japan and other environmental initiatives. Institutionalization of understandings: South Pacific Nuclear Free Zone Treaty (1985) The Convention for the Protection of the Natural Resources and Environment of the South Pacific Region (1986) The Convention for the Prohibition of Fishing with long driftnets in the South Pacific (1989).
1990-1999	Period of harmonization of policies. Structural reforms. Policy dialogues. Donor-led reform programmes funded by Asian Development Bank. Melanesia spearhead Group Trade Agreement between four Melanesian countries: Fiji, Papua New Guinea, Solomon Islands and Vanuatu for freer trade.
2001	Pacific Island Countries Trade Agreement (PICTA) for free trade among the Pacific Island Countries by 2010. PICTA was signed in 2001. Pacific Agreement on Closer Economic Cooperation (PACER) for forging greater cooperation and negotiations by Pacific island countries with Australia and New Zealand to start in 2011. PICTA was signed in 2001.
2003	Australian Senate Committee recommendation for a Pacific Political and Economic Community with a single currency.

Years/Period	Events
2004	Forum Leaders decided to have a Pacific Plan for integrating PICs Preparation of Working Draft on Pacific Plan by Task Force.
2005	Approval of Pacific Plan: Four pillars: of (i) economic growth; (ii) sustainable development; (iii) good governance and (iv) security.
2007	European Union's efforts to bring about regional integration: insistence on signing an Economic Partnership Agreement (EPA) with EU only on a collective basis with PICs. EPA is to replace Cotonou Agreement which is lapsing in 2020.
2008	Deadline for signing EPA with PICS: December 2009.
2009	No collective EPA. PICs were not ready. Fiji and PNG signed interim EPA on individual basis with EU. Australia and New Zealand announced PACER Plus for replacing PACER. PACER Plus is designed to cover beyond trade in goods. It is designed to cover services, investment, capacity enhancement, trade facilitation and mobility of labour.
2010	Provision of assistance to PICs for helping them in their negotiations with Aus/NZ for PACER Plus. Office of Chief Trade Advisor is opened in Vanuatu and is fully funded by Australia and New Zealand.
2011	PACER Plus negotiations are scheduled to commence in 2011.
2012	PICs request assistance of OCTA in their negotiations on EPA with EU Differences with Australia and New Zealand, which leads to resignation of Chief Trade Advisor. The position of Chief Trade Advisor is filled from Feb 2012. No decision on PICs' request for OCTA's assistance for EPA negotiations with EU. Continued isolation of Fiji from OCTA and Forum.

Source: Jayaraman (2007), Fry (2005), Fairbairn and Worrell (1995)

References

Asian Development Bank. 2011. *Key Indicators* of *Asia Pacific Developing Countries 2011.* Manila: Asian Development Bank.

Browne, C. 2006. Overview of Regional Economic Performance and Prospects, in *Pacific Island Economies,* edited by C. Browne. Washington D.C.: International Monetary Fund.

Commonwealth of Australia. 2003. *A Pacific Engaged: Australia's Relations with Papua New Guinea and the Island States of the Southwest Pacific, Senate Foreign Affairs, Defence and Trade References Committee.* Canberra: Commonwealth of Australia.

Crean, S. 2009. Our Pacific Agenda: The Opportunity of PACER Plus, *Address at the opening of the Lowy Institute's "Pacific Islands in the World" Conference,* 2 August 2009, Brisbane: Lowy Institute, Brisbane.

Crocombe, R. and Meleisea, M. 1988. Achievements, Problems and Prospects: The Future of University Education in the South Pacific, in *Pacific Universities, Achievements, Problems and Prospects*, edited by R. Crocombe and M. Meleisea Suva; Institute of Pacific Studies.

Crocombe R. and Ueantabo N. 1983. Options in University Education for the Pacific Islands, *Pacific Perspective*, 12(1), 5-17.

Curtain, R. 2012. What future for the seasonal worker program? A conference report on: Australian Government's Seasonal Worker Program: Sydney on 1-3 August, 2012, *Development Policy Blog*. [Online]. Available at: http://devpolicy.org/what-future-for-the-seasonal-worker-program-a-conference-report/?utm_source=Devpolicy&utm_campaign=42cb445c24-Devpolicy_Blog_Digest_June7_1_2012&utm_medium=email [Accessed on 3 September 2012].

Fairbairn T. I. J. and Worrell D. 1996. *South Pacific and Caribbean Island Economies: A Comparative Study*. Brisbane and Suva: Foundation for Development Corporation and South Pacific Forum Secretariat.

Fiji Times. 2012. Pacific Struggle. *Fiji Times*, 4 September 2012, 16.

Fry, G. 2005. *Pooled Regional Governance in the Island-Pacific: Lessons from History*. Paper presented at the Workshop on Regional Integration in the Pacific, Research School of Government and Pacific Studies, Australian National University, Canberra, June 2005.

Guy, N. 2011. *Research shows benefits of overseas worker scheme*, [Online]. Available at: http://www.beehive.govt.nz/release/research-shows-benefits-overseas-worker-scheme [Accessed on 24 August 2012].

Howes, S. and Hay, D. 2012. Australia's Pacific Seasonal Worker Pilot Scheme: why has take-up been so low? *Development Policy Blog*. [Online]. Available at: http://devpolicy.org/australia%E2%80%99s-pacific-seasonal-worker-pilot-scheme-why-has-take-up-been-so-low/ [Accessed on 18 August 2012].

Hughes, H. 2003. Aid has Failed in the Pacific, *Issue Analysis No. 33*. Sydney: The Centre for Independent Studies.

Hughes, H. 2004. *Pacific is Viable!*, Sydney: Centre for Independent Studies.

Hughes H. 2010. Aid has Failed the Pacific: Pacific 2010: Revisited. *Pacific Economic Bulletin*, 25(3), 232-234.

Institute of International Trade. 2008. *Research Study on the Benefits, Challenges, and Ways Forward for PACER Plus*. Adelaide: University of Adelaide.

Macllelan, N. 2008. *Workers for all Seasons: Issues of New Zealand's Recognized Seasonal Employer program*. Hawthorn, Australia: Institute for Social Research, Swinburne University of Technology.

Morgan, W. 2012. New rules to expand Pacific exports? Only if action is taken fast, [Online]. Available at: http://devpolicy.org/new-rules-to-expand-pacific-exports-only-if-action-is-taken-fast/ [Accessed on 22 August 2012].

Noonan, C. 2011. PACER Plus progress and promise: Regional integration challenges and opportunities in the Pacific, *Trade Negotiations Insights*, 10(9).

Pacific Institute of Public Policy (PIPP). 2008. MSG: Trading on Political Capital and Melanesian Solidarity, *Discussion Paper, No. 8.* Port Vila: PIPP.

Pacific Islands Forum Secretariat. 2004. *Working Draft: The Pacific Plan for Strengthening Regional Cooperation and Integration.* Suva: Forum Secretariat.

Pacific Islands Forum Secretariat. 2005. *Pacific Plan.* Suva: Forum Secretariat.

Pacific Islands Forum Secretariat. 2007. Pacific Regional Trade and Economic Cooperation Joint Baseline and Gap Analysis. *Report to the Pacific Islands Forum Secretariat.* Suva: Forum Secretariat.

Samoa Observer. 2012. PM praises China, *Sunday Samoan*, 1 September 2012.

Scollay R. 2005. *Deeper Integration with Australia and New Zealand? Potential Gains for Pacific Islands,* Paper presented at the International Workshop on Pacific Integration and Regional Governance, Asia Pacific School of Economics and Government, Australian National University, Canberra, June 2005.

United Nations Economic and Social Commission for Asia and the Pacific (UNESCAP). 2011. *Economic and Social Survey 2011.* UNESCAP, Bangkok.

Urwin G. 2004. *Economic Development of Pacific Island Economies and Regional Cooperation.* Suva: Pacific Islands Forum Secretariat.

World Bank. 1993. *Pacific Island Economies: Volume 1; Overview.* Washington, D.C.: World Bank.

Chapter 7
Regional Aid for Trade in Africa: Time to Walk the Talk

Melissa Dalleau and Kathleen van Hove[1]

Introduction

From the perspective of African countries, regional integration is a declared ambition, a political aim, an economic necessity, as well as a tool to foster development. As a result, efforts to reinforce regional, sub-regional and continental ties and cooperation are a high-level priority for African countries. For proof, one just has to look at the discussions held during the 18th session of the African Union Summit, held in January 2012, which focused specifically on ways to boost intra-African trade.

However, despite considerable advancements in some areas, progress so far towards the achievement of regional integration ambitions has been disappointingly slow and the capacity of regional organizations to accelerate growth and intra-regional trade among African countries has often been judged unsatisfactory. The facts speak for themselves: more than 20 years after the adoption of the Abuja Treaty, calling for the establishment of an African common market and further economic and political integration in Africa, progress in 'defragmenting Africa' remains limited (World Bank, 2012) and the level of intra-African trade considerably lower than what has been achieved in other parts of the world, representing only 10% of total African trade (African Union, 2011).

Widely documented elsewhere, the reasons for these limited achievements are numerous. Among others, one could cite for instance the underdevelopment of Africa's infrastructure assets and high costs of services provisions (Brixiova *et al.* 2011, AU-UNECA 2006); the numerous regulatory, non-tariff barriers and trade facilitation constraints which continue to impede trade across the continent (BenBarka 2012; World Bank, 2012; African Union, 2011); the limited translation/transposition at the national level of the commitments taken at the regional level as well as the lack of political will to sometimes do so; the limited (technical and absorptive) capacities of regional organizations, the short-term opportunity

1 This chapter builds on the collective work of ECDPM on Aid for Trade (www.ecdpm.org/trade). The authors would therefore like to thank San Bilal, Dan Lui, Jeske van Seters, James Mackie, Isabelle Ramdoo, Quentin de Roquefeuil and Bruce Buyiers for their inputs.

costs for African countries of engaging in projects with long-term benefits, notably in view of inadequate compensation mechanisms (Oyejide and Bankol 2010, McCarthy 1996); and the overlapping membership of African countries in different regional economic communities and blocs that bear the risk of duplicating efforts and spreading thin available financial resources (AU-UNECA2006).

Overcoming those challenges would require tremendous efforts from African countries and regional organizations to successfully implement and lead the political institutional and economic reforms needed to bring the integration agenda forward and lift the continuous barriers to trade within the continent. In this respect, whilst it cannot be regarded as a substitute to the adoption of appropriate trade policies and related measures by developing countries themselves, financial and technical support from donors in this area may prove critical in helping Africa achieve its regional integration objectives, and *a fortiori* its overall development goals, thereby providing a window of opportunity for the *Aid for Trade* (AfT) agenda (Oyejide and Bankol 2010:2).

Initiated in the framework of the World Trade Organization (WTO), the AfT initiative aims to support developing countries in undertaking appropriate trade and regulatory reforms, improving their supply-side capacity and trade-related infrastructure and adopting the necessary adjustment measures to be able to benefit from international trade opportunities (Higgins and Prowse 2010). In this respect, AfT could be critical in supporting regional integration processes in Africa, as pooling resources and opportunities through the creation of effective regional markets can be decisive in stimulating production capacities and trade and investment flows when embedded in a broader development strategy. In the current context marked by the aftermath of the global financial and economic crisis which continues to hit hard in many developed and developing economies, building competitiveness, tapping trade and investment opportunities for economic recovery, and unleashing the potential of (sub-)regional integration to increase shock resilience in Africa (OECD-WTO 2011) has become an even more pressing necessity (African Union 2011). By helping developing countries build supply-side capacity, economic infrastructure and competitiveness, AfT, not least in support of regional programmes and projects, could help make a difference.

Against this background: How can African countries and Regional Economic Communities (RECs) make the most out of the potential benefits of AfT? Under which conditions can the AfT agenda help African countries and regions fulfil their regional integration ambitions? These are some of the questions this chapter tries to answer, notably drawing from examples across both the West African and the Eastern and Southern African regions. Given the complexity and the scope of the issue at stake, this chapter does not intend to be comprehensive, rather to provide a broad picture of what has been achieved so far in the area of Regional Aid for Trade (RAfT), what the major challenges are and what more can be done to improve the effectiveness of RAfT in Africa.

Understanding the Regional Dimension of Aid for Trade – A Complex Matter

Aid for Trade: An Overview

The idea that trade liberalization, through increased market access, reduced prices of imports and associated competitive effects, could foster economic growth and hence development seems to have made its way since Raul Prebish coined the 'trade gap' concept (UNCTAD 2008:1). However, it is also now increasingly recognized that in absence of supporting measures, many developing countries may not be able to put trade at the service of development. It is in this context that the current Aid for Trade (AfT) initiative was developed in the framework of the Doha Development Agenda (DDA) at the WTO, in particular with the 2005 Hong Kong Ministerial Declaration (WTO 2005).

Aimed at 'help[ing] developing countries, especially LDCs, build the supply-side capacity and trade-related infrastructure that they need to assist them to implement and benefit from WTO agreements and more broadly to expand their trade' (WTO, 2005, also quoted in Higgins and Prowse (2010)), the AfT agenda was not necessarily based on new thinking, but it marked an important milestone in the international community by formally recognizing the need for trade-related development assistance to help developing countries reap the potential benefits of trade reforms (UNCTAD 2008: 1, Bilal 2012).

Following the work done by the WTO task force on Aid for Trade, AfT is usually defined around the five following categories: (i) technical assistance for trade policy and regulations, (ii) trade-related infrastructure, (iii) productive capacity building (including trade development), (iv) trade-related adjustment and (v) other trade-related needs.

Beyond formal definitions, however, the concept of AfT is certainly a complex one that is not always understood by all in the same terms. For a start, as can be inferred from the five categories mentioned above, the definition of AfT is relatively broad, subsuming more than 30% of all concessional development assistance (Cadot and Newfarmer, 2011). Therefore, what should be considered as AfT and what is other official development assistance (ODA) is not always an easy distinction (Bilal, 2012). Moreover, African countries, and developing countries in general, are engaged in a number of trade liberalization processes (WTO, regional integration processes, preferential trade agreements such as the Economic Partnership Agreements (EPAs) negotiated between the EU and African, Caribbean and Pacific countries…), creating a certain degree of confusion on the side of stakeholders on how the different dimensions of AfT and support and assistance provided in the context of these different liberalization agendas all fit with one another. This confusion may partly result from the different perceptions some stakeholders may have about what AfT is all about. While some adopt a 'positive' definition, seeing AfT as a means to build productivity and competitiveness to benefit from trade liberalization, others have tended to focus only on the 'compensation' aspects of the initiative, seeing in trade-related support a necessary financial assistance to meet the cost of liberalization in the context of the WTO (ILEAP 2007:6). The ambiguity around the nature of EPA development support and its link with AfT is in this respect a good illustration of this complexity surrounding the definition of AfT.

The Regional Dimension

Because AfT relates to international trade, the concept inherently bears a regional/cross-border dimension that has been recognized right from the very outset of the initiative. As highlighted by the WTO Task Force on Aid for Trade:

> Some of the constraints facing developing countries are regional, sub-regional or cross-border in nature. These needs should be identified and properly addressed. Regional organizations, including regional banks, regional integration organizations and regional economic communities, may play a role in assisting countries to identify such needs. (WTO, 2006)

Moreover, as multilateral trade negotiations under the WTO became increasingly sluggish, one has seen over the years a surge in regionalism (Albertin 2008). It is therefore not surprising that, with the impasse in the DDA, the demand for regional trade-related assistance in the context of the AfT initiative has swollen: in recent years, over half of bilateral donors reported an increase in demand for trade-related support at regional level (OECD-WTO 2011: 41).

The different dimensions of AfT can in a sense hardly be disconnected from one another. The regional/global link is implicitly recognized in the concept: by boosting their productivity and improving their capacity to export, RAfT projects may not only help African countries and regions increase the level of intra-regional trade, but also result in turn into a higher degree of integration in the global economy. Similarly, the regional and national dimensions of AfT should not be looked at independently, not only because, even in the case of regional or cross-border projects, AfT is often programmed and channelled through partner countries, but also because consequently, the greatest 'value added' of the AfT initiative lies perhaps in that it provides the opportunity for countries to integrate trade priorities and concerns more closely into national and regional development strategies, in terms of a prioritized and sequenced approach to improve the quality of available aid.

Against this background, this chapter will consider as Regional AfT, 'Aid for Trade being either *implemented* at a level involving more than one country and/or Aid for Trade *coordinated* at the regional level', notably by the Economic Communities (RECs) (ILEAP 2007:6).

Despite the formal recognition, right from the start of the initiative, the importance of the regional dimension of AfT has been relatively neglected in the early years following the Hong Kong ministerial (ILEAP 2007:5). Most of the attention, notably on the side of donors, has been for a long time very much focused on the commitment of resources for the implementation of *national* AfT programmes and projects and on how best to monitor flows and measure impact at the country level (ILEAP 2007:6). Similarly, it took some time for RECs to be partly charged with the dossier, notably on the coordination aspects. Admittedly, however, a great deal of progress seems to have been made in recognizing the importance of addressing regional AfT needs alongside national ones. The next section looks at the progress made in regional AfT, focusing on recent trends.

Recent Trends in Regional Aid for Trade Flows Across Regions: A Seemingly Positive Picture

Methodological Limitations and Other Shortcomings: The Need for Caution in Interpreting Data[2]

Before going into the issue at stake here, it is important to underline a few methodological issues that need to be kept in mind when observing AfT trends.

When looking at AfT data, OECD DAC statistics remain the primary source of reference to account for the volume, origins and type of flows. While those are used as useful proxies to assess the progress made in quantitative and qualitative commitments and pledges from donors, these figures and the practical accounting exercise behind their generation bear some inherent limitations one should not neglect when interpreting figures.

First and foremost, it is important to keep in mind that since the start of the WTO AfT initiative in 2005, donors have made active efforts to better monitor and report on their financial contributions, in order to track the progress made on their AfT commitments (OECD-WTO 2011, ILEAP 2007, Bilal 2012). Reporting on aid destined for regional programmes has also substantially improved. Whilst therefore there may undoubtedly have been an increase in activity on the part of donors to allocate more AfT resources to developing countries, not least for the purpose of regional programmes, this growth may well be inflated by a better tagging by donors of ODA to trade-related projects and programmes, some improved reporting mechanisms on commitments/disbursement flows, and an increased transparency around the results of these reporting exercises (Bilal, 2012).

Moreover, the methodology for reporting has not always been the OECD's Creditor Reporting System (CRS) on Aid Activities. Prior to 2007, indeed, data reported to the Joint WTO/OECD Doha Development Agenda Trade Capacity Building Database (TCBDB) were being used as a reference when dealing with trade-related assistance (ECDPM 2006). Whilst this is a positive improvement

2 For more information in this respect, please see Bilal (2012) on which this sub-section is based and which proposes a summary of the methodological and practical challenges in reporting AfT.

for systematic reporting and comparability between donors and ensures a better integration of AfT reporting into general ODA reporting systems, it renders comparison between pre- and post-2007 data difficult given that trade-related assistance in the CRS is less well defined than the more specifically tailored TCBDB (Bilal, 2012).

Additional challenges also come from OECD DAC statistics themselves. First, those cover mainly OECD DAC donors and international organizations. Non-DAC donors only report on a voluntary basis, rendering the coverage of non-DAC donors very limited, notably neglecting substantial provider of Aid (for Trade) such as Gulf Countries, China and India, whose assistance to developing countries is therefore not counted in the total of AfT flows provided. For non-DAC countries who do report, statistics are at best unreliable over the years. This means that reporting to the OECD/DAC on AfT categories underestimates the volume of assistance available in overall terms. At the same time, however, it is worth noting that AfT data from the CRS, which are considered as proxies, consider the full amount of an AfT project rather than that portion which relates to trade. In this respect, volumes may be overestimated.

Besides, OECD data are based on reporting by those donors themselves, and as a result interpretation matters. Ultimatel,y what donors report as Aid for Trade is likely to be counted as such. Moreover, ways of reporting may vary from donor to donor, which makes it difficult to have a homogenous picture of who is giving what in the area of AfT.

These considerations and limitations are of course exacerbated when taken at the regional level. What is understood, and in turn reported, as 'regional AfT' may vary greatly depending on the donor considered: while some development partners may report all types of AfT delivered for the purpose of regional or cross-border projects, including when this aid is programmed and channelled through partner countries, others may adopt a different definition.

The Broad Picture

Looking at the most recent figures on AfT flows as recorded in the OECD's Creditor Reporting System (CRS) and compiled in the most recent *Aid for Trade at a Glance Report* 2011, the 'quantitative' picture seems rather positive, with a rising trend in the overall availability of AfTin recent years.

As illustrated in Figure 7.1, aggregate levels of AfT commitment flows to developing countries have grown substantially from approximately US$26bn at the start of the initiative in 2005 to almost US$40bn in 2009 – an increase of almost 60% from the 2002-05 baseline (OECD-WTO 2011: 47). Although these figures bear a number of inherent limitations calling for caution in the interpretation of data, as described above, the picture is clearly one of a rising trend in AfT commitments over the years, with an average annual real growth rate of 15% since 2006 (Lammersen 2011). Actual AfT disbursements seem to have followed

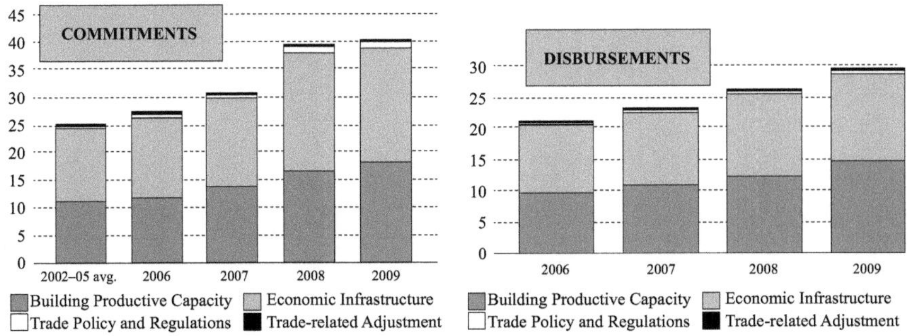

Figure 7.1 Commitments and Disbursements of Total Aid for Trade 2002-2005, US$bn (2009 constant)

Source: OECD-WTO, 2011

through (with an expected and unsurprising time lag), reaching US$29bn in 2009, up 40% (*i.e.* an annual growth rate of 11-12%) since 2006 (OECD-WTO 2011:47).

As emphasized in the latest *Aid for Trade at a Glance* 2011, Africa has become over the years the largest recipient of AfT, with commitments to the continent reaching approximately $16bn in 2009, *i.e.* 41% of total Aid for Trade flows, surpassing Asia – the second largest recipient with 38% of total flows (OECD-WTO 2011: 50-51; Bilal, 2012).

Looking more specifically at the flows of AfT committed to serve the purpose of regional integration, the picture seems as positive, if not more so. Although figures here may be exaggerated as *reporting* on aid destined for regional programmes may have improved recently (Lui and van Seters 2012: 5), overall and as compared to the 2002-05 baseline, regional AfT seems to have increased significantly in all five continents, as shown in Figure 7.2. Admittedly, growth rates vary greatly across regions and from one year to the next,[3] but the general trend is definitely an upward one in all regions of the world, showing therefore an increasing attention paid to the regional dimension of AfT across the board.

As is the case for total AfT flows, the vast majority of RAfT has gone to Africa, as illustrated by both Figures 7.2 and 7.3. Yet these figures also reveal interestingly that RAfT remains more marginal in Asia (which is the second main recipient of total AfT, as indicated above).

Zooming in on Africa

Figures 7.2 and 7.3 show that in just three years, RAfT in Africa has more than tripled as a share of total AfT delivered, representing in 2009 more than 10.1% of

3 Figure 7.2 shows some important fluctuations from one year to the next – fluctuations that are, however, difficult to interpret given the nature of programming cycles.

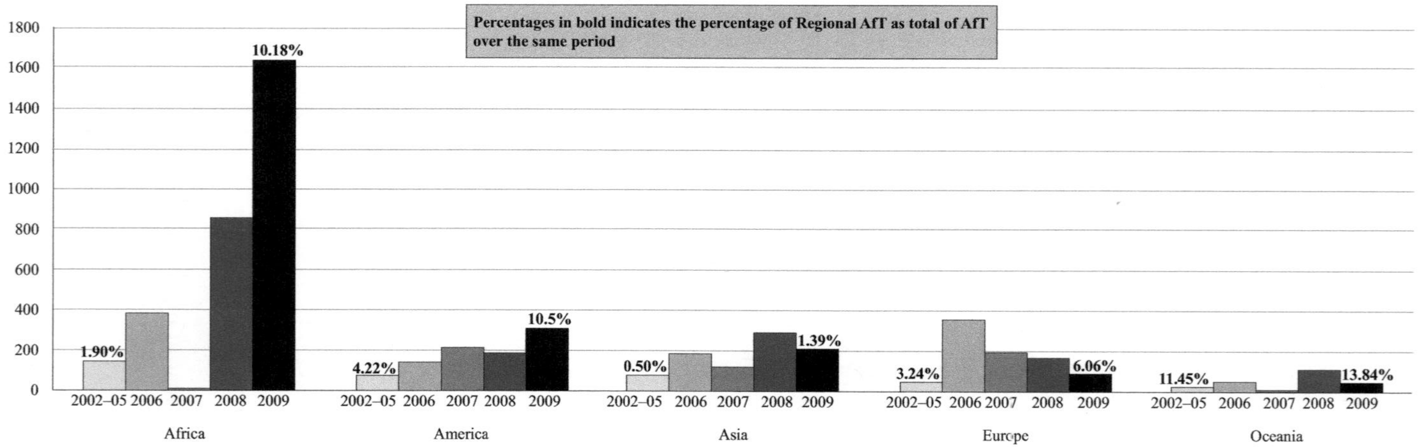

Figure 7.2 Regional AfT: A Comparative Perspective 2002/05-2009, US$ Millions (2009 constant)

Source: OECD/DACAid Activity Database (CRS)

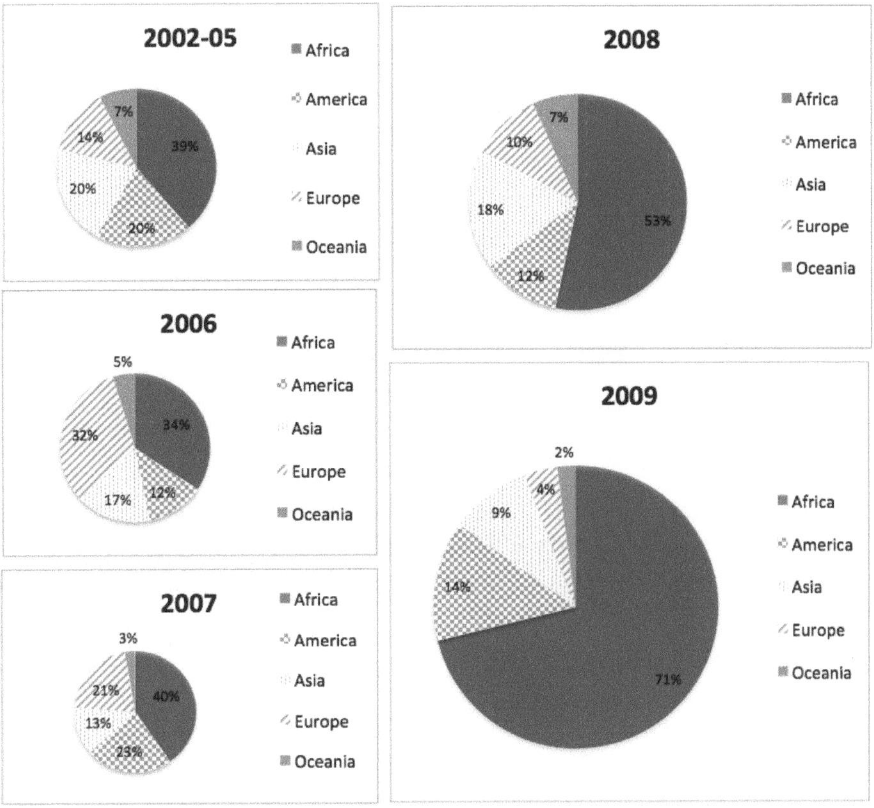

Figure 7.3 Distribution of Regional AfT by Regions
Source: OECD/DAC Aid Activity Database (CRS)

total AfT delivered regionally, as opposed to only 3% in 2007 (also noted by Lui and van Seters 2012).

Based on the OECD DAC statistics, several bilateral donors, such as Japan, Canada and Norway, can be said to have been particularly active in supporting regional integration projects/programmes in Africa, with EU DAC donors taking the lead, as shown in Figure 7.4.

In 2009, AfT commitments were reported to come from both bilateral and multilateral channels. With regard to the latter, however, 97% of the flows were committed by the African Development Fund, the concessional window of the African Development Bank (AfDB), in what seems to be moreover a very recent trend. Judging from these data, commitments from other multilateral donors seem to have been historically limited. Given the methodological concerns, this should of course not be taken to mean that multilateral donors do not support trade-related regional integration programmes and projects: International Finance Institutions

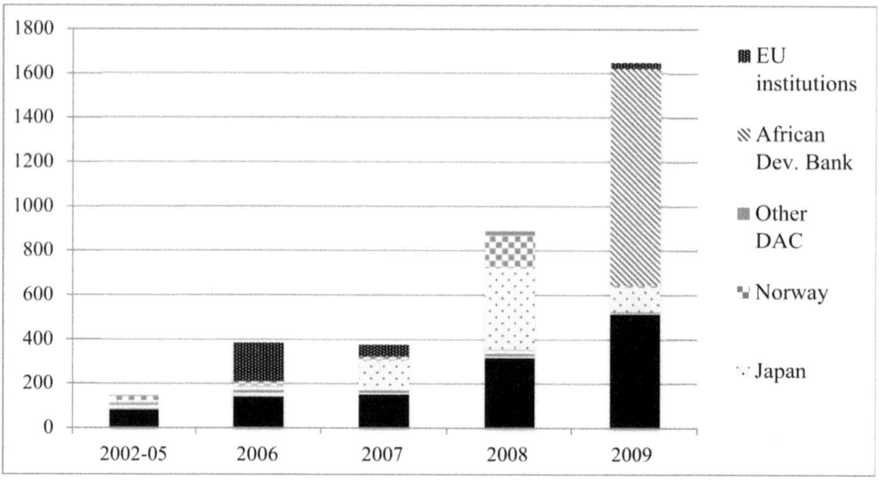

Figure 7.4 Regional AfT Flows to Africa by Donors, 2002-2009 (Commitments, in US$ Millions, constant prices, 2010)
Source: OECD/DAC Database

(IFIs) and other multilateral donors may be active in the area of RAfT, without this involvement necessarily being reflected in these statistics. Most multilateral partners, primarily the World Bank and regional development banks, have indeed been strong supporters of regional approaches to AfT as can be inferred from their respective regional integration assistance strategies (Mackie *et al.* 2010, WTO-OECD 2011: 34). This said, while IFIs, notably the World Bank, have funding available for regional issues, it is also worth noting that multi-country programmes have for a long time constituted only a small proportion of their portfolio (ILEAP 2007: 9, IMF-World Bank 2006: 22). Moreover, it should also be stressed here that even in the case of regional or cross-border projects, aid from multilateral donors (and also to some extent bilateral donors alike) continue to be predominantly programmed and channelled through partner countries, not least due to technical constraints. Indeed, the lack of regional *grant* facilities allowing multilateral development partners to deliver and channel AfT resources to regional bodies on the one hand, and on the other hand the limitations affecting the feasibility of lending for regional AfT projects given the difficulties to find appropriate guarantees to back up multi-country loans, as well as the difficulties of regional organizations to borrow even on concessional terms, are issues that may indeed have limited RAfT/multi-country projects being easily financed in the past (IMF-World Bank 2006). Admittedly, some progress has been made on this front in recent years[4] (IMF-World Bank 2006). Yet, the need to improve the availability

4 By way of illustration, it is worth noting that until the 2009 IDA Mid-Term Evaluation, the World Bank was not able to supply RECs with grants. This posed great

of instruments to address cross-border/regional projects might still be a relevant issue to be granted consideration (for both multilateral and bilateral donors).

Going back to the distribution of RAfT flows by donors, Europe seems to be the most active partner at the regional level. This is hardly surprising in view of the fact that the EU has been one of the most ardent supporters of regional integration notably in ACP countries, inspired by its own regional integration experience over the past 50 years (Bilal 2012).

Figure 7.5 shows that EU commitments to RAfT have been significantly growing since the 2002-05 baseline. In 2009, more than US$541 million had been committed by EU institutions and member states for Regional AfT programmes and projects, as compared to less than US$ 208.5 million in 2007.

Reflecting the overall trend of RAfT to Africa, EU RAfT as a percentage of total AfT given to the region also seems to have tremendously increased, representing more than 10% in 2009, as compared to less than 2% for the 2002-05 baseline (but for which data were not reported in the same thorough manner).

Although these figures have to be interpreted with caution, they fit in with a perceived increase in emphasis and activity on the part of all donors to allocate resources to regional programmes. As reported in the third Global AfT Review (OECD-WTO, 2011), demand for regional integration programmes has been steeply rising in recent years, with over half of bilateral donors reporting an increase in demand across the five categories of AfT, leading many (bilateral and multilateral) donors to change their strategies to better address the regional dimension. Replying to the OECD/WTO questionnaire aimed at monitoring and accounting for AfT, nine out of 10 (responding) bilateral donors considered regional integration as an important change to take into consideration in their respective strategies – a trend that is also echoed in the multilateral donor community where 100% of the respondents cited regional integration as an important change, if not the most important one (OECD-WTO 2011). Overall, multilateral and bilateral donors, the EU most particularly, agree that regional integration, along with economic growth and poverty reduction, represents one of the most important issues in Aid for Trade (OECD-WTO 2011). As highlighted for instance in the Joint EU Aid for Trade Strategy of 2007, one of the stated objectives of the EU is to improve not only the quantity but also the quality of Aid for Trade that is provided at the *regional* level, 'with specific programmes, notably on trade facilitation and connectivity' (EC 2007).

The challenge in the years to come, however, will certainly be to translate these commitments and objectives into actions. The stakes are enormous, given the advantages that regional approaches to Aid for Trade may bring. Those are

challenges to RECs that could not borrow from the IDA as they had no revenue-raising power and were therefore seen as too high risk for lending. Member States were usually not willing to borrow for a regional rather than a national programme. Introduction of recent instruments in this regard to address this situation may help turn the table around.

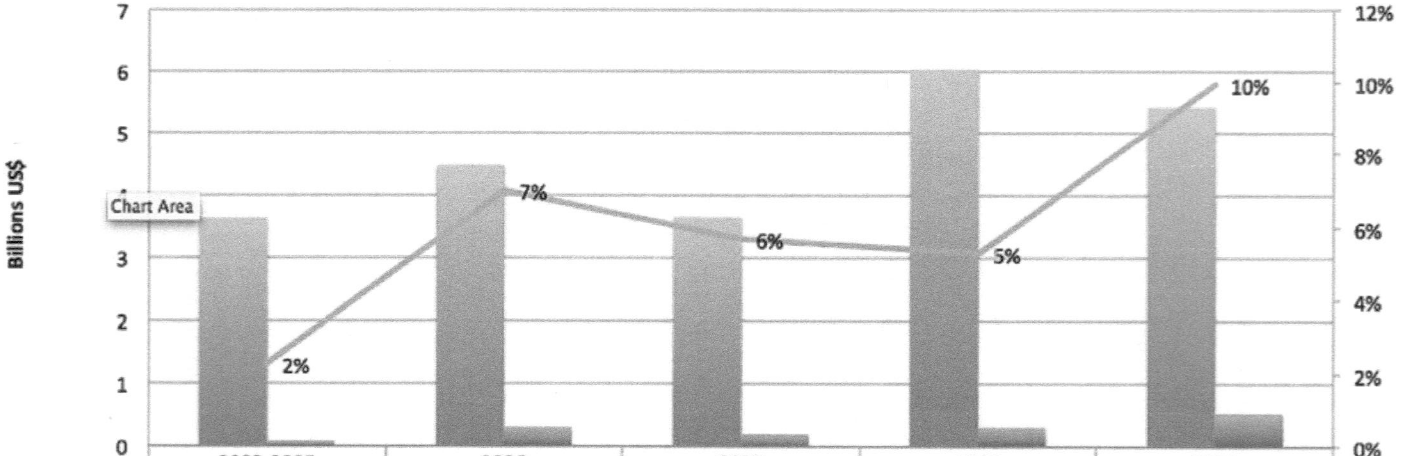

	2002-2005	2006	2007	2008	2009
Total AfT	3.6436	4.4830	3.6626	6.0486	5.4351
RAfT	0.0825	0.3146	0.2085	0.3196	0.5414
% RAfT/AfT	2%	7%	6%	5%	10%

Figure 7.5 EU Total and Regional Aid for Trade in Africa (Commitments, 2002/05-2009, US$Millions, constant prices, 2010)

Source: OECD DAC database

Note: Data reported in this figure include commitments from both EU DAC donors and EU institutions highlighted in the next section. The challenges to reap those benefits may, however, be as great, as will be explored later.

The Potential Benefits of Regional Aid for Trade

The definition by the regions themselves of regional AfT approaches, which could be enshrined in specific regional AfT strategies, could prove particularly useful in helping African countries fulfil their regional integration ambitions, and ultimately their development goals. There are a number of advantages in adopting a regional approach to AfT.

Formulation of the Region's Priorities and Mobilization of Resources

First, the definition of a regional AfT strategy can help a region focus the attention on identifying its trade-related needs and priorities in a comprehensive manner and mobilize resources accordingly. RAfT strategies can help identify cross-border needs; for instance, in the area of transport corridors, regional physical infrastructure, border/customs reforms, harmonization of technical and sanitary and phyto-sanitary standards. RAfT strategies could thereby help formulate and finance accompanying measures for those projects and/or programmes (Farahat 2010) and adopt a holistic/comprehensive approach to trade constraints, so as to promote integrated regional solutions.

Taking for instance the case of the Common Market for Eastern and Southern Africa (COMESA) region, it would appear that a great deal of progress has been made over the last year on moving towards more coherent and integrated approaches to tackling the problems of the high costs of trade in the COMESA region and beyond. Substantial advancements have for instance been made over the last years on developing the North-South Corridor (NSC) AfT pilot programme.

A flagship multi-country project of the EAC-COMESA-SADC Tripartite, the NSC currently links the copper belts in Zambia and the Democratic Republic of Congo, via Botswana, Zimbabwe and Malawi, with the ports in Mozambique, Tanzania and South Africa. Based on a two-pronged approach, the NSC seeks to achieve both physical infrastructure improvements in roads, railways and energy supply as well as the streamlining and harmonization of the regulatory environment through trade facilitation measures at the various borders (ODI 2009).

The conclusion to launch the NSC is based on decisions taken at the Tripartite Summit in Kampala in 2008, as well as on decisions taken at various international forums for Aid for Trade. In April 2009, the Tripartite organized a NSC High Level Conference in which multilateral and bilateral donors pledged US$1.2 billion that is channelled through the national and regional AfT programmes (COMESA, EAC, SADC. 2009). During the conference, the NSC countries were urged to outline the national funding gaps and major infrastructure requirements, which later on led to the identification and approval of 19 prioritized road sections (Lui and van Seters 2012).

Moreover, the Tripartite, the UK's Department for International Development (DfID) and the Development Bank of Southern Africa (DBSA) decided to establish a Tripartite Trust Account with the objective of leveraging funds from commercial and quasi-commercial sources. The DBSA established the fund in 2010 and serves as the fund's management while the DfID so far has granted €67 million. As can be inferred, significant efforts have therefore been made to secure political backing and donor financing for NSC projects and establish mechanisms such as the Tripartite Trust Fund which would play a role in overseeing and channelling resources to projects prepared by the region. Finally, as emphasized by Lui and van Seters (2012: 7) the focus of current work has been to prepare projects to a level that ensures they are sufficiently 'bankable' to be approved by a financier and then go through various tender processes (Lui and van Seters 2012).

So far, the NSC project has achieved some significant results, and the overall transportation costs and time-consuming bottlenecks have been reduced. Approximately 8,599 km of NSC roads have been refurbished or are planned to be renewed within the foreseeable future and the quality and conditions of the routes along the NSC are now surveyed and presented online for interested stakeholders. Likewise, a Non-Trade Barriers Reporting, Monitoring and Elimination Mechanism has been digitalized and is now available online (Lui and van Seters 2012). By 2009, as a part of the NSC, the first Sub-Saharan One-Stop-Border Post (OSBP) was established in Chirundu and despite some major initial challenges, the OSBP is overall considered to have substantially reduced transit time and is now replicated elsewhere along the NSC route (TradeMark Southern Africa. 2011a, 2011b). Admittedly, challenges remain, particularly in the areas of procurement, information flows and the alteration of the financing responsibilities of the road sectors. To a large extent, these challenges relate to coherence and coordination issues that are due to the fact that many decisions and actions still remain at the national level (see below), while the NSC mandate is regional. Furthermore, weak technical capacities amongst the stakeholders often result in sub-optimal project designs and implementation delays (Lui and van Seters 2012).

Yet, these challenges notwithstanding, this project is often cited as a successful example of a holistic approach to trade constraints in a region, which could be replicated elsewhere (e.g. in the context of Northern Corridors, Indian Ocean Commission (IOC) maritime trade corridors...) (Lui and van Seters 2012: 27). In this respect, the NSC project holds a number of lessons for other regions, and ultimately highlights the added value of regional AfT for the promotion of integrated regional solutions and for linking national and regional priorities (Lui and van Seters 2012).

Improved National/Regional Coordination

Second, RAfT should spell out a common regional vision shared by all stakeholders at both the national and the regional level. Such a consolidated regional approach can offer a solid framework to ensure coherence and complementarities between national and regional policies through processes and instruments that mainstream trade as a tool for development. Two examples could be given in this respect.

On the one hand, this is for instance the case of the EPA Development Programme (EPADP) in West Africa.[5] The EPADP was developed in the context of the EPA negotiations as an attempt by the West African region to assess in detail the challenges and opportunities of an EPA. It proposes a positive donor support agenda for dealing with the challenges and maximizing the opportunities of the EPA. Composed of a general regional framework, describing the goals, objectives, and priority axes for intervention, the EPADP is concretized in National Operational Plans (NOP) that further the needs at the project/country level, and a 'Regional Operational Plan' (ROP) presenting regional projects based on the subsidiary principle (Dalleau and van Seters 2011: 3).

By linking the national and regional levels together in a single framework, the EPADP therefore has the potential to help better synchronize and coordinate regional and national initiatives.

The EPADP consists of five axes, described in Table 7.1. The linkages with the AfT categories are also made explicit.

Table 7.1 EPADP Axes and their Concordance with AfT Categories

Structure of PAPED	WTO Aid for Trade Categories
Axis 1: Diversification and increase of production capacities	(4) Building Productive Capacity (2) Trade Development
Axis 2: Intra-regional trade development and trade facilitation to international markets	(1) Trade Policy and Regulations (2) Trade Development
Axis 3: Improvement and reinforcement of trade-related infrastructure	(3) Trade-related Infrastructure
Axis 4: Adjustments costs and other trade-related needs	(5) Trade-related Adjustments (6) Other Trade-related Needs
Axis 5: Implementation, monitoring and evaluation of the EPA	(1) Trade Policy and Regulations

Source: European Commission Work (also quoted in ECDPM, 2010)

5 This example is based on research conducted in Dalleau and van Seters (2011).

These five axes are further broken down into different components describing areas for programmatic support. The total amount of support required for this programme for the first five-year period, running from 2010 to 2015, was initially estimated by the region at €9.54bn, then re-evaluated to €15bn. In terms of EU's commitment to support this programme, the Council Conclusions of 10 May 2010 highlight the availability of at least €6.5bn from the EU for EPADP-related activities for this period. However, this highlights that the total of AfT from all donors might exceed, according to (conservative!) predictions, US$12bn over the same period (Council of the European Union 2010, ECDPM, 2010).

The EPADP was formulated based on a broad participatory approach led by the ECOWAS and UEMOA Commissions and involving regional and national actors (governments, private sector and civil society) (ECDPM 2010). The EPADP has since achieved important political endorsement within the region, and ongoing work to elaborate the EPADP further with national input can ensure greater national ownership as well as coherence with national policies. In this sense, it represents a litmus test of a comprehensive regional package of trade-related assistance that was owned by the region and which could potentially be instrumental in improving aid effectiveness by contributing to a more coherent and coordinated approach to addressing trade-related needs in the context of an EPA (ECDPM, 2010; Dalleau and van Seters, 2011).

Similarly, one could cite as another example the case of the COMESA AfT Strategy. One of the main motivations behind the adoption of the COMESA AfT Strategy, formally endorsed at the COMESA Council meeting of June 2009, was to improve coordination between the national and the regional level. Based on a number of key principles, including being results-oriented and focused on specific, achievable interventions where a regional approach can add value to national efforts (subsidiarity), the Strategy details specific objectives and a set of expected results for each of those, as highlighted in Table 7.2 (Lui and van Seters 2012:1).

Going one step further, when relevant, regional AfT approaches and strategies may also help lift some of the bottlenecks that continue to hamper regional integration processes in Africa. If tailored accordingly, they could for instance help in the transposition of regional commitments at the national level, as illustrated by the case of the Adjustment Facility of the COMESA Fund (CAF). Although the latter facility has until now very much focused its efforts on providing financial support to member states to minimize the fiscal and socio-economic impact of regional integration processes, future support from the Adjustment Facility will go beyond revenue losses, providing broader support for the implementation of regional commitments at the national level. For this purpose, revised CAF operational regulations were adopted by the COMESA Fund Ministerial meeting of June 2010 and a rider to the Regional Integration Support Mechanism was developed, through which the EU is currently supporting the facility (Lui and van Seters 2012:11-12). These state that allocation and disbursement of CAF resources are to be effected against the implementation of well-defined regional integration indicators detailed in a

Table 7.2 Summary Table of the COMESA AfT Strategy Objectives and Expected Results Frameworks

Overall Objective:	Within the overall framework of the COMESA-EAC-SADC Tripartite, to contribute to the impact, efficiency and effectiveness of COMESA member states' trade reforms and regional integration initiatives so that they can fully benefit from regional and international trade opportunities to reduce poverty and to achieve their (MDG) development objectives
Specific Objective 1: The private sector of the COMESA member states reduces regional costs of doing business with and within the COMESA region through coherent packages of inter-related (i) investments in trade-related infrastructures, (ii) trade development and trade facilitation instruments, and (iii) trade regulatory measures	**Result 1.1:** Processes and instruments are operational for coherence and complementarity between national and regional policies that mainstream trade as a tool for development
	Result 1.2: COMESA trade facilitation and trade regulatory instruments are enhanced and harmonized with SADC and EAC to more benefit private sector stakeholders
	Result 1.3: Processes and instruments are operational for strategic and long-term linkages between public sector and private sector, donors and investors in identifying, planning and costing packages of well-defined COMESA AfT projects and programmes along selected Trade Corridors
	Result 1.4: Regionally owned instruments are operational to mobilize and implement support for the 'software' components of holistic projects and programmes along selected trade corridors: trade facilitation and regulatory measures
	Result 1.5: Regionally owned instruments are operational to mobilize and implement support for the hardware components of holistic projects and programmes along selected trade corridors: infrastructure projects (transport, energy, telecoms)
Specific Objective 2: COMESA member states have access to mechanisms to address social and economic costs of trade and integration-related adjustments	**Result 2.1:** Frameworks and capacities exist to assess the impact of trade and integration policies and the resulting adjustment needs
	Result 2.2: Regionally and nationally owned instruments are operational to mobilize and deliver predictable, additional and accessible adjustment resources

Source: Lui and van Seters (2012)

Regional Integration Programme (RIIP), which will outline how a country plans to implement adopted regional integration commitments. Countries will receive a fixed tranche against approved RIIP, followed by annual tranches, based on the achievements of specific indicators defined in the RIIP, with the first payments expected to start in 2012 (Lui and van Seters 2012: 11-12).

Ownership, Horizontal Coherence and Harmonization at the Regional Level

Adopting a regional approach to AfT and detailing such an approach in a related policy document, be it a regional AfT strategy or an equivalent, could be a good way to inform and guide the RECs and their Secretariat to the regional priorities, and ensure the mainstreaming of trade-related priorities across sectors and various departments within the relevant regional economic organizations.

Conceived as an internal document to feed into and guide the more general work of the COMESA Secretariat on regional integration and increase collaboration between various internal departments, the COMESA AfT Strategy may for instance prove instrumental in ensuring that AfT is recognized within the organization as a cross-cutting issue that requires the attention of all within the Secretariat. While the Strategy is more a guiding framework than an implementable plan, it should be recognized that important efforts were made by the dedicated Unit of the COMESA Secretariat in charge of coordinating AfT activities at the regional level (the COMAid unit) to streamline AfT ideas and concepts into the broader work of the COMESA Secretariat and in particular into the region's second Medium Term Strategic Plan (MSTP), where it is included as a broad, cross-cutting issue (Lui and van Seters, 2012). The aim of these efforts was to ensure ownership of AfT across the COMESA Secretariat as well as reinforce the idea that responsibility for implementation lies with its different divisions. To some extent, the mainstreaming of such ideas, notably the Tripartite process and integrated trade and transport corridors (such as the NSC), seem to have been relatively well conducted within the Secretariat and regionally endorsed framework such as the MTSP (Lui and van Seters 2012).

In the same vein, regional AfT Strategies and/or comprehensive regional trade-related development support programmes may also provide the opportunity of ensuring some degree of harmonization and horizontal coherence at the level of a region, notably in the context of overlapping membership. By way of illustration, one could cite the case of the EPADP, which seems to have ensured, at least on paper, a good level of coherence between the priorities defined in the context of the EPADP and those *already* defined in the other existing strategic development and regional integration frameworks of the region as a whole (UEMOA and ECOWAS). A case in point in this respect concerns the linkages between the EPADP and the UEMOA's Regional Economic Programme (2006-2010), which indicate that at the time of its elaboration phase, the former has coherently built upon the latter. The two frameworks very much echo each other, with numerous overlaps of objectives, priorities and components, notably when it comes to the diversification and increase of production capacity, intra-regional trade development and improving infrastructure. Some stakeholders in the region have notably argued that good collaboration between the two regional Commissions, ECOWAS and UEMOA, and, to a certain extent, between the different departments (and/or officials) within these regional organizations, has been critical to ensure the good level of coherence between the priorities defined in the context of the EPADP.

This may hold a number of lessons for the COMESA-EAC-SADC Tripartite, should these regions decide to harmonize and develop a common AfT Strategy, notably at a time where the SADC is understood to be developing its own AfT Strategy. Given that the COMESA Strategy has already existed for some time, the COMESA Secretariat should be able to play an important role in ensuring coherence between the different sub-regions.

Delivering More 'Effective' Aid to the Region

Because they hold the potential to ensure greater coherence and coordination, between and across various levels and within the regions themselves, regional approaches to Aid for Trade constitute an invitation for all donors to engage in a more effective and coherent approach to addressing the trade-related needs of African regions.

On one level, indeed, by providing an overarching mechanism to guide and support the development of AfT packages, they could help facilitate the programming and planning of available resources according to the regions' needs, thereby making aid decisions from donors more efficient and 'aligned' to the regions' own priorities, and pinpointing areas where programming of aid may be adjusted.

In the context of the EPADP, the West African region and the EU have for instance undertaken a comprehensive stocktaking exercise aimed at identifying EPADP-related activities to determine respectively the trade-related needs deriving from the EPA (and beyond), and the funding available from EU institutions and member states to finance those activities. As the EPADP has been/can be a useful mechanism to identify EPA-related needs, including beyond projects for which financing has already been secured, it could be a critical framework to pinpoint 'aid anomalies' that should be corrected. It could not only guide a re-adjustment of aid across countries when necessary, thereby ensuring against the emergence of 'aid for trade orphans', *i.e.* countries whose AfT needs are neglected; it could also ensuring a rebalancing of aid across sectors, when there is an obvious mismatch between resources committed by donors and the needs estimated and presented by the region in the EPADP regional strategic framework (ECDPM 2010; Dalleau and van Seters 2011).

On another level, beyond improving the planning of available resources and making aid decisions more efficient, such approaches may also serve to improve the delivery modalities through which AfT is channelled, providing donors with a common framework to better coordinate their support of African regions within such a framework. For donors, therefore, RAfT Strategies or EPADP-type of development support programmes could be exploited to enhance joint programming/delivery.

For donors, and the EU and its member states in particular, such regional frameworks represent an opportunity to demonstrate they can deliver on their commitments to strengthen aid coordination, as reflected, as far as the EU is

later reformulated to be a COMESA Strategy only, which yet reflects its origins and approach within efforts to build the Tripartite process, as explained in previous sections (Lui and van Seters 2012). However, while previous efforts to develop a tripartite AfT Strategy failed, increased commitment and political ownership of the Tripartite process seem to make it more feasible and desirable in the current context. In this respect, the current efforts, notably on the side of the SADC, to define its own AfT strategy might to some extent build upon what has already been achieved in the context of the COMESA AfT Strategy, as the development of AfT strategies and future regional plans by SADC and EAC (as well as COMESA itself) represent a chance to continually strengthen coherence between the three communities. In Central Africa, similar developments are also worth reporting, as the region has produced various working documents and roadmaps aimed at elaborating a Regional Aid For Trade strategy, with some notable efforts already made in the course of 2011 to list all AfT-related programmes and projects already existing in the region at both regional and national levels.

However, right from the outset, it is important to recognize that in most regions these strategies sit alongside other important trade-related strategies and frameworks, with similar regional integration and development objectives; most notably, EPA-related development support programmes (such as the EPADP in West Africa or the 'Programme regional d'accompagnement du développement dans le cadre de l'APE' (PRADA) in Central Africa), but also various sectoral programmes. This raises the question of how these different frameworks fit with one another in support of the short, medium and long-term priorities of the regions (horizontal coherence).

Taking West Africa as an example, it is worth nothing that the AfT Strategy which is currently being finalized sits alongside the EPADP described before, but also other strategic policy documents, such as the Community Development Programme (CDP) of ECOWAS, as well as sectoral strategies (for instance, in the area of agriculture). And this is not to mention UEMOA's strategy policy documents.

The overlapping membership of RECs/regional groupings in Africa also complicates matters, as it potentially leads to inconsistencies in policy formulation and implementation, to duplications of efforts, and bears the risk of generating a costly competition for resources and reduces in many instances the ability of RECs to design and pursue coherent integration programmes.

Beyond horizontal coherence between the different existing frameworks at the regional level, vertical coherence, *i.e.* between the national and regional levels, is another major challenge. While regional AfT has the potential added value of vertical coherence, ensuring this is by no means a straightforward exercise. Regional programmes often lack well-defined policy objectives that are sufficiently aligned with country interests. Stakeholders often feel that regional frameworks are not building on country strategies enough or that country strategies are sufficiently developed within the regional frameworks (Mackie *et al.* 2010). Moreover, and despite some efforts on the side of African stakeholders to address this problem, there is often a gap between the commitments taken at the regional level when it comes to regional integration and the translation of these commitments into action at the national level. This lack of transposition can be explained by capacity and budgetary constraints, but also by a lack of political support for regional programmes and strategies, which are often not considered national priorities (AU-UNECA 2006).

In view of the difficulty to ensure vertical coherence, the question of subsidiarity and complementarity is one of critical importance. As a rule, regional AfT programmes and projects should be defined when the goals and objectives they are trying to achieve can be best fulfilled at the regional level. Without such subsidiarity, one may risk encouraging an unhealthy competition over resources, vertical incoherencies, and duplication of efforts.

Ensuring that AfT strategies and/or EPA development support programmes are articulated and implemented in coherence with other strategies which partially share the same objectives is of critical importance, whether funds to be provided in the context of those various strategies are to be additional or not. It is only indeed if the 3Cs of coherence, coordination and complementarity are ensured that regional approaches to AfT can serve as useful technical tool and an invitation for all donors to engage in a more effective and coherent approach to addressing the trade-related needs of African regions. Ensuring the 3Cs requires strong communication between various stakeholders and across different levels. Such communication, between national and regional stakeholders, but also between stakeholders involved in different sectors, is therefore critical to ensure and invest in.

The Issue of Capacity

Another common problem that may explain some of the difficulties African countries and regions face when trying to reap the potential benefits of RAfT lies in what has often been identified as the limited financial, institutional and technical capacities of the RECs.

Because they often involve countries that are at a different level of development and that often have different types of institutional arrangements, regional AfT projects and programmes can to some extent be considered a riskier endeavour than purely national projects. As compared to national AfT programmes/projects, RAfT involve more actors, each with their specific set of incentives and interests, and more complex accountability relationships. The additional layer of complexity that RAfT adds to (arguably more simple) country-level projects may therefore require extra effort and time from the part of both African governments and regional organizations and donors alike to prepare and implement projects and programmes (Lui *et al.* 2012). So far, however, inadequate and unpredictable funding dedicated to RECs has often limited the capacity of the RECs and their Secretariat to play a leading role in successful regional cooperation and integration. Indeed, beyond external financing from development partners that may be increasingly difficult to mobilize in the current context marked by the impact of the recent global economic and financial crisis, direct budgetary contributions from member states to RECs have also proven to be relatively unpredictable (AU-UNECA 2006). Regional integration remains a complex reality that often involves trade-offs, conflicts of interest and hence power struggles. The lack of guarantees about the benefits individual member states may draw from regional integration processes often seems to weaken the appetite to contribute financially to regional integration, with an important accumulation of arrears in member states' contributions to the financing of regional bodies. For their part, development partners often seem better structured and equipped to deal with national partners than regional ones. While RECs can receive grants from donors, the latter's financial instruments do not always allow them to give loans to RECs as previously emphasized. Moreover, where development partners feel under pressure to disburse, the perception that supporting regional project is slower and more cumbersome due to complicated procedures can be a disincentive (Mackie *et al.* 2010).

Those capacity constraints on the side of the RECs are clearly a huge impediment for effective RAfT. Indeed, even if RECs are not necessarily in the driving seat when it comes to 'implementing' AfT projects/programmes, capacity constraints might not only prevent them to demonstrate clear and strong leadership and develop bankable projects, but might also limit their ability to address the above-mentioned challenges of coherence, coordination and complementarity. By way of illustration, although COMESA had established the ComAid Unit, the latter has never been given the capacities to fulfil its broad coordination mandate (Lui and van Seters 2012). At the same time, the COMESA Secretariat, together with SADC and EAC, recognized that there was a lack of capacity to conduct many of the technical functions necessary to implement the North-South Corridor initiative and prepare projects sufficiently to bring them to a 'bankable' stage, leading to the establishment (supported with funding from DfID) of TradeMark Southern Africa (TMSA) as a technical support unit for the Tripartite process. Although it is important to recognize that the work of TMSA is highly valued by the region and the COMESA Secretariat and is generally considered to be an efficient support mechanism with which they have established a good working relationship, TMSA only has a limited lifespan. Moreover, the involvement of multiple stakeholders – and the tendency for much of the technical work for Tripartite activities to be 'outsourced' by the RECs – has raised questions in the region about the political ownership and drive for the Tripartite process – both in terms of the development of the vision and accountability for achieving it (Lui and van Seters 2012).

The Limitations of the 'Aid Effectiveness' Agenda at the Regional Level

Finally, whilst donors have taken important commitments to improve the quality and efficiency of Aid, and *a fortiori* Aid for Trade, as stated in the Paris Declaration and Accra Agenda for Action, the principles defined in these agendas have proven more difficult to apply at the regional than at the national level in Africa.

By way of illustration, programming in the context of AfT remains mainly a donor-driven exercise. Some countries even appear to have changed their AfT priorities to match donors' interest. The OECD-WTO's Aid for Trade at a Glance report (2011: 32) notes for instance that Kenya has recently prioritized infrastructure in its demands for AfT 'because OECD countries want to give more aid to infrastructure'. Supply-driven programmes that live outside national and regional strategies may lead to complex and multiple procedures, leading in turn to high demand of staff, lack of control and ownership and a weak integration of the financial instrument into the Government's budget of developing countries. Moreover, whilst general budget support for a region could enhance a donor's alignment, this is still an unusual practice at the regional level, except for a few notable examples such as the EC's contribution agreement with COMESA (Mackie *et al.* 2010).

Although RAfT provide a great opportunity for donors to increase aid coordination, the little progress so far achieved in this area shows that opportunities remain to be seized. In practice, programming continues to be predominantly the result of unilateral decisions and progress in joint programming and delivery of support continues to be limited, despite a few achievements such as the EU-Africa Infrastructure Trust Fund.

Lessons from success stories of joint programming at the national level suggest that for RAfT strategies to be instrumental at both the regional and national levels and act as joint programming tools, African states and regional bodies need to bring them to the fore when agreeing (joint) donor strategies and interventions for the coming period. This would require using appropriate country-donor coordination forums. In many cases, donors can only respond to partner government requests. It might be critical therefore for national and regional stakeholders in African regions to ensure a genuine awareness across departments and ministries about the existence of those priorities and programmes, and a political will to bring them forward during roundtables of donors.

On the donor side, both headquarters and country representations need to be informed about the different frameworks for support containing the priorities of the region considered, which is unfortunately not always the case. Taking the EPADP as an illustration, it is recognized by donors themselves that while the officials attending the Regional Preparatory Task Force (RPTF) meetings in charge of discussing development cooperation issues in the context of the West Africa-EU EPA may be well informed on the EPADP, this is not necessarily the case of other officials at headquarters or those based in West Africa. Yet, for the EPADP to be used as a framework for joint programming, it is crucial for staff directly involved in programming, most often based in the region, to be familiar with the programme, requiring therefore some increased efforts on the side of those officials attending RPTF meetings to inform their respective ministry in charge of cooperation and/or the representations/agencies in charge of cooperation on the field (Dalleau and van Seters 2011).

Moving forward, it is important to recognize that whilst there are a number of technical challenges that will have to be tackled, should donors be serious about the implementation of the Accra/Paris Agenda, operationalizing these concepts is primarily a *political* issue and research shows that this may be inherently more difficult at the regional level. Moreover, it would also seem that regional organizations still have to be fully convinced that aid effectiveness and the Paris/Accra Agenda is not only a donor's affair but a mutual concern. Overcoming those challenges to ensure these Agendas are translated into action to the benefit of African countries and regions will require serious efforts on the side of all stakeholders involved (Mackie *et al.* 2010). Positively, the need to address those challenges was recently recognized by all stakeholders during the Fourth High Level Forum on Aid Effectiveness that was held in Busan from 29 November to 1 December 2011, which called on providers of development assistance to 'reduce fragmentation and curb the proliferation of aid channels', whilst maintaining the volume and quality of resources 'through greater use of country-led co-ordination arrangements, including division of labour, as well as programme-based approaches, joint programming and delegated co-operation' and an improved delegation of authority to field staff (Busan Declaration). Interestingly, it is worth noting that the Busan Declaration also recognized the special role of regional organizations that 'can and should play [...] in supporting implementation [of the commitments taken in Busan] at the country level, and in linking country priorities with global efforts'.

Conclusion

A great deal of progress seems to have been made in recent years in recognizing the importance of addressing RAfT needs alongside national ones. The *quantitative* improvements, however, need to be matched with qualitative ones if AfT is to deliver on the high expectations that have been raised. This chapter has argued that in order to increase the effectiveness of RAfT, it needs to be driven by the principles of the Paris Declaration/Accra Agenda for Action as well as address the following **5Cs: Coherence, Coordination, Complementarity, Communication and Capacity**. It will require genuine political will from all stakeholders involved to address these 5Cs for RAfT not to fall into the traditional 'implementation gap'. Assisting regional integration processes is now featuring higher on the AfT agenda. In this respect, the recognition by G20 Leaders in Seoul of the 'potential for faster growth in Africa, which could be unlocked by African plans for deeper regional economic integration' and the commitments taken in this context to 'support the regional integration efforts of African leaders, including by helping to realize their vision of a free trade area through the promotion of trade facilitation and regional infrastructure'[8] is worth highlighting. Yet, whilst regional integration and RAfT do figure high on the agenda, it is time to walk the talk.

Addressing the bottlenecks that continue to prevent African RECs successfully delivering on RAfT programmes is critical if the long-term viability and credibility of regional integration processes is to be strengthened/supported through AfT. Despite well-sounding declarations in support of regional integration, some donors' priorities, and in particular the EU's priorities, risk being shifted away from supporting regional organizations, precisely in view of the poor results of these RECs to achieve their stated ambitions. This is a worrying evolution for many African RECs that continue to rely extensively on extra-budgetary resources from development partners, and notably the EU, to finance their activities.

Arguably, improving the technical and managerial capacity of RECs to deliver on their regional integration objectives could positively improve their capacity to secure funding from traditional sources of financing. But this may not be sufficient in view of the sheer volume of resources required to finance regional integration ambitions. By way of illustration, in the area of infrastructure – an area of tremendous importance to foster regional integration – the flagship Africa Infrastructure Country Diagnostic study (AICD) estimated that the total requirement for infrastructure financing in Sub-Saharan Africa amounted to almost US$93bn a year in 2008 (Foster and Briceño-Garmendia 2010, Gantsho 2010, Leigland 2010). Given the level of resources required to meet African infrastructural and other development needs, there is a clear sense of urgency to tap new sources of financing for realizing the regional integration and development ambitions; ODA, and *a fortiori* Aid for Trade, alone may clearly not be sufficient, nor sustainable.

The recurrent global financial and economic crises continue to hit many developed countries hard, and to affect the economic prospects of developing countries through various trade and investment channels. The major industrialized countries have difficulties finding fresh money to support their global commitments and/or to justify such commitments to their constituencies at a time of spending cuts at home. Developing countries on the other hand are eager to increase their policy space and distance themselves from the vagaries of external finance. This has led stakeholders on both sides to think outside the box with regards to international relations, development strategies and modes of cooperation, including regional aid for trade.

There are different areas where innovation in financing for development and regional integration may be possible and those have been widely documented elsewhere (Brixiova *et al.* 2011). One such promising area is in the combination of AfT with international capital flows. As argued by Gavas *et al.* (2011), 'if developing countries want to attract significant resources for Aid for Trade, e.g. to cover their infrastructure needs, they need to think outside the box and consider how grants can leverage in other resources (e.g. loans or private finance) and

---

8 G20. 2010. The Seoul Summit Document. http://www.mofa.go.jp/policy/economy/g20_summit/2010-2/document.pdf.

provide a bundle of blended Aid for Trade finance'. Whilst it will be critical to avoid some of the pitfalls in this area, there are important opportunities to develop innovative mechanisms and models that have the potential to use aid to trigger concrete reforms to the trade and investment environment, to finance private sector development or to improve efficiency over traditional aid models by creating better linkages between aid investments and private sector-oriented results.

Similarly, case stories conducted in the context of the Third Global Review on Aid for Trade have revealed across the board that among the several factors that were critical for the AfT initiative to deliver on its long-term trade and development objectives, leveraging partnerships, including with providers of South-South cooperation, could be critical (Lammersen 2011). How the increasing presence of new players in Africa, such as China, India and Brazil, can best help support African-owned regional integration priorities is also a question that will need to be addressed, moving forward.

References

Accra Agenda for Action. 2008. 3rd High Level Forum, 2-4 September 2008, Accra, Ghana.

Ademola Oyejide, T. and Bankole, A.S. 2010. *Aid for Trade and Regional Integration in West Africa,* Trade Policy Research and Training Programme (TPRTP), Department of Economics, University of Ibadan, Nigeria.

African Union. 2011. *Action Plan for Boosting Intra-African Trade.* Draft Zero, Addis Ababa, Ethiopia.

African Union and United Nation Economic Commission for Africa (AU-UNECA). 2006. *Assessing Regional Integration in Africa II. Rationalizing Economic Communities.* Addis Ababa: UNECA.

Albertin, G. 2008.*Regionalism or Multilateralism? A Political Economy Choice, IMF Working Paper No 65,* Washington DC: IMF.

Barker, D. 2011. Third Global Review of Aid for Trade: a snapshot of the outcome, *Trade Negotiations Insights,* 10(7). Maastricht: ECDPM and ICTSD.

Ben Barka, H. 2012.*Border Posts, Checkpoints, and Intra-African Trade: Challenges and Solutions,* Tunis: African Development Bank.

Bilal. S. 2012. *Aid for Trade and beyond. Development Perspectives.* Paper written for European Parliament Workshop on Trade and investment for development, Directorate-General for External Policies, Policy Department, Brussels, 29 March 2012.

Bird, K. *et al.* 2009. *A Regional Approach to Aid for Trade: The Regional Facilitation Programme (RTFP).* London: Overseas Development Institute.

Braun-Munzinger, 2009. *Regionally Owned Funds Mechanisms for delivery of EU Aid for Trade in ACP regions? ECDPM Discussion Paper 90.* Maastricht: ECDPM.

Brixiova, Z., Mutambatsere, E., Ambert, C., and Etienne, D. 2011. Closing Africa's Infrastructure Gap: Innovative Financing and Risks. *Africa Economic Brief*, 2(1).

Busan Declaration. 2011. Busan Partnership for effective development cooperation. *Fourth High Level Forum on Aid Effectiveness*, Busan, Republic of Korea, 29 November-1 December 2011.

Cadot, O. and Newfarmer, R. 2011. Does it work?: Aid for Trade through the evaluation prism. *Trade Negotiations Insights*, 10(7). ECDPM and ICTSD.

COMESA, EAC, SADC. 2009. *North South Corridor Pilot Aid for Trade Conference- Outcomes, Conclusions and Way Forward*, Lusaka, 7 April 2009.

Council of the European Union. 2008.*Conclusions of the Council and the Representatives of the Governments of the Member States meeting within the Council on Economic Partnership Agreements (EPAs)*, 9629/08, Brussels, 27 May 2008.

Council of the European Union. 2010. *Council Conclusions: EPA Development Programme (PAPED)*, 9634/10, 10 May 2010.

Dalleau, M. and van Seters, J. 2011.*Operationalising the West African EPA Development Programme: Moving beyond the paperwork, ECDPM Discussion Paper No 121*, Maastricht: ECDPM.

Davies, P. 2011. *The Role of the Private Sector in the Context of Aid Effectiveness. Consultative Findings Document, Final Report*. Paris: OECD.

European Commission (EC). 2007. *EU Strategy on Aid for Trade: Enhancing EU support for trade-related needs in developing countries.* The General Affairs and External Relations Council of 29 October 2007 [not published in the Official Journal].

European Commission (EC). 2011a. *Increasing the impact of EU Development Policy: an Agenda for Change, Communication from the Commission to the European Parliament, the Council, the European Economic and Social Committee and the Committee of the Regions*, COM(2011) 637 final, Brussels, 13 October 2011. Available at: http://ec.europa.eu/europeaid/news/agenda_for_change_en.htm.

European Commission (EC). 2011b. *Aid for Trade Monitoring Report* 2011, *Annex 6 of the Commission Staff Working Document EU Accountability Report 2011 on Financing for Development Review of progress of the EU and its Member States, volume IV*, SEC(2011) 503 final, 19.4.2011, Brussels, 19 April 2011: The European Commission.

ECDPM. 2006. *EPA Development Support: Consequences of GAERC conclusions for EPAs. ECDPM In Brief 16A*. Maastricht: ECDPM.

ECDPM. 2010. *The EU Commitment to Deliver Aid for Trade in West Africa and Support the EPA Development Programme (PAPED). Discussion Paper No 96.* Maastricht: ECDPM.

Farahat, M. 2010. *How RECs can harness A4T for Regional Integration,* paper presented at Expert Group Meeting and Workshop on Aid for Trade and

Africa's Trading Capacity: Supply, Demand and Performance, 31 May-2 June 2010, UNCC, Geneva.

Foster, V. and Briceño-Garmendia, C. (eds.) 2010. *Africa's Infrastructure: A Time for Transformation.* Washington, DC: World Bank.

Gantsho, M. 2010. *The Role and Pitfalls of Private Sector Involvement in Infrastructure.* Paper presented at Sixth Annual CABRI Seminar: Open Budgets and Good Governance, Pretoria, 19 May 2010.

Gavas, M., Geddes, M. Massa, I. and te Velde, D. 2011. *Aid for Trade and Blended Finance.* London: ODI/OECD Aid for Trade Case Study.

Higgins, K., and Prowse S. 2010.*Trade Growth and poverty: Making Aid for Trade Work for inclusive growth and poverty reduction. Overseas Development Institute. Working Paper 313.* London: ODI.

ILEAP (2007) *Regional Aid for Trade. Negotiation Advisory Brief No 12.* January 2007, Toronto: ILEAP.

International Monetary Fund and World Bank (IMF-World Bank). 2006. Doha Development Agenda and Aid for Trade. Prepared by the Staffs of the IMF and the World Bank: 9 August 2006.

Itaye, S. 2011. Aid for Trade: Success stories and lessons. *Trade Negotiations Insights*, 10(7). ECDPM and ICTSD.

Lammersen, F. 2011. Aid for Trade: Showing Results. *Trade Negotiations Insights*, 10(7).

Leigland, J. and Roberts, A. 2007. The African Project Preparation Gap. *Gridlines: Public-Private Infrastructure Advisory Facility*, 18, 1-4.

Lui, D. 2008. *The Aid for Trade Agenda and accompanying measures for EPAs: Current state of affairs. ECDPM Discussion Paper No. 86.* Maastricht: ECDPM.

Lui, D., Buyiers, B., van Seters, J. 2012. *Rethinking Aid for Trade in the context of Innovative Financing. ECDPM Discussion Paper No. 127.* Maastricht: ECDPM.

Lui, D. and van Seters, J. 2012.*Review of the COMESA Aid for Trade Strategy. ECDPM Discussion Paper No. 130.* Maastricht: ECDPM.

McCarthy, C. 1996. Regional Integration: Part of the Solution or Part of the Problem, in *Africa Now*, edited by S. Ellis. London and Portsmouth (N.H.): James Currey and Heinemann.

Mackie, J., Bilal, S., Ramdoo, I., Hohmeister, H. and Luckho, T. 2010. *Joining up African Support to Regional Integration. Discussion Paper No 99.* Maastricht: ECDPM.

ODI. 2009. *A regional approach to Aid for Trade: The Regional Trade Facilitation Programme (RTFP)*, Overseas Development Institute, London.

OECD and World Trade Organisation (OECD-WTO). 2011. *Aid for Trade at a Glance 2011: Showing Results*, Paris: OECD Publishing.

Oyejide and Bankol. 2010. Aid for Trade and Regional Integration in West Africa. A Paper prepared for discussions at the ECA Experts Forum, Addis Ababa, 31 May-2 June 2010.

Paris Declaration on Aid Effectiveness. 2005. High Level Forum, Paris, 28 February-2 March 2005.

Ponty. N. 2009. *Feuille de Route et priorité a moyen terme de la Commission de l'UEMOA*. Preliminary version of the report. Bordeaux, 2009.

TradeMark Southern Africa. 2011a. *North-South Corridor Roads,* TMSA Case Study Series. Pretoria, March 2011.

TradeMark Southern Africa. 2011b. *Chirundu Border Post,* TMSA Case Study Series. Pretoria, March 2011.

UNCTAD. 2008. *Aid for Trade and development: Global and Regional Perspectives*, New York and Geneva: United Nations.

UNECA and AUC (2012) *Financing for Infrastructure Development in Africa (PIDA*), Report of the Committee of Experts to the 5th Joint Annual Meeting of the AU Conference of Ministers of Economic and Finance and ECA Conference of African ministers of Finance, 22-25 March 2012, Addis Ababa, Ethiopia, E/ECA/CM/45/5/Rev.1.

World Bank. 2009. *IDA 15 Mid Term Review Implementation Report.* International Development Association Resource Mobilization Department. Washington DC: World Bank.

World Bank. 2012. Defragmenting Africa. Deepening Regional Trade integration in Goods and Services. Edited by Paul Brenton and Gozde Isik. The World Bank: Washington DC.

WTO. 2005. *Hong Kong Ministerial Declaration*, DOHA Work Programme, Hong Kong, 22 December 2005.

WTO. 2006. *Recommendations of the Task Force on Aid for Trade*, WT/AFT/1, 27 July 2006, WTO.

Chapter 8

Food Security in ECOWAS

Richard Simson and Vanessa T. Tang[1]

Introduction

Two and a half decades after the 1996 Rome World Food Summit (WFS), the established goal of halving the number of undernourished people by 2015 for Africa remains elusive. According to a Food and Agriculture Organization (FAO) estimate, 925 million people worldwide were still undernourished in 2010, of which 239 million are in Sub-Saharan Africa (SSA) and 37 million in East and North Africa (ENA). However, the recently revised FAO undernourishment estimates from 2010 to 2012 reveal global improvements and distinct progress in South and South East Asia. The vast majority of the world's undernourished people live in Sub-Saharan Africa (27 per cent), the Caribbean (18 per cent) and Asia (14 per cent). Food security is a major concern for the Global South. For Africa, there has been little progress made towards the World Food Summit (WFS) goal.

Food security is the supply of food and a person's demand for the same. Being food secure implies that a person is not permanently hungry and does not face starvation. According to the FAO (2008), to be food secure means that 'all people, at all times, have physical and economic access to sufficient safe and nutritious food that meets their dietary needs and food preferences for an active and healthy life'. By this definition, food security is a broad concept. There is no single determinant of food insecurity. However, there is a general consensus that being food insecure is inextricably linked to poverty. Poor people not only lack the income to purchase enough food but are also forced to obtain cheaper and less nutritious staple foods.

The recent upheavals in global food prices have raised serious concerns about the plight of the poor and have heightened the food insecurity situation in the Global South. According to the Word Bank's *Food Price Watch* (2011), since June 2010, rising food prices may have driven an additional 44 million people in low- and middle-income countries into extreme poverty. At this juncture, it is pertinent to highlight that global food prices have already exceeded their 2008 peak.

The changing food price is a double-edged sword. While high prices are detrimental to consumers, if prices are too low, food producers are less inclined to produce and may look for other profitable opportunities. The FAO publications of 2010 and 2012 have pointed out this dilemma. This is especially true of Africa,

1 UKZN School of Accounting, Economics and Finance. Email: Tangv@ukzn.ac.za.

and points towards African farmers' and poor households' already weak coping mechanisms.

In accepting the proposition that the underlying problem of food security is related to poverty, the resulting question is: How does one address the problem of poverty? The one approach adopted by many countries and regions is the idea of 'development', but this concept implies the need for structural reforms. One way forward is for countries to link their economies to strengthen their development and growth. It is not surprising, therefore, that a large number of African countries have opted to belong to more than one regional integration arrangement. Whilst the idea of regional economic integration is of value, the overlapping membership and fragmented nature of African regional organizations have slowed down African countries' developmental progress, and, additionally, the Economic Partnership Agreement (EPA) negotiations with the European Union have highlighted particular challenges facing African regional economic integration (Tavares and Tang 2011). Alongside this, there is the challenging issue of global governance of food standards. Agro-food standards have undergone fundamental changes: numbers of standards are increasing, standards' content is more demanding, inter-relations between standards have become more competitive and the ownership structure more diverse (Gibbon and Lazaro 2010).

Nevertheless, despite such challenges confronting African countries, producers and exporters, efforts to ensure economic and social development, and attempts to combat poverty and food insecurity, are slowly gaining ground at all levels: national, regional and continental. Recently, African countries have committed to a 'made-in Africa' shared vision and a consensus for agricultural reform via the Comprehensive Africa Agriculture Development Programme (CAADP) and endorsed by the African Union (AU) in July 2003.

In West Africa, the Economic Community of West African States (ECOWAS) comprising 15 countries: Benin, Burkina Faso, Cape Verde, the Côte d'Ivoire, Gambia, Ghana, Guinea, Guinea-Bissau, Liberia, Mali, Niger, Nigeria, Senegal, Sierra Leone, and Togo is fully committed to such developmental programmes. ECOWAS has taken the initiative to commit to positive agricultural changes via ECOWAP. All countries in ECOWAS have experienced food insecurity in various forms and degrees (FAO 2012) and their food insecurity situations have been compounded by the 'unfortunate effects' of climate change, the growing number of agro-food standards and governmental vagaries in the trade policy environment.

Against this background, this chapter is structured as follows. Section 2 discusses the theoretical links that underpin food security with a focus on how, in a race for 'freer' trade, food security can be altered. Section 3 presents an overview of the food security developments in ECOWAS. Section 4 highlights the challenges facing ECOWAS countries in political and economic environments and Section 5 concludes.

Theoretical Links in a Trade and Market Framework

If recent developments on the African continent concerning an enthusiastic call for more free trade between countries in Africa are part of a wider acceptance of the power of a market-orientated approach to policy, it is important to have some market analysis and ultimately a simple but insightful framework to examine food security issues. Food security in the past has been an issue even for rich countries, especially in times of conflict. Recent development in the Sahel region, which straddles the ECOWAS countries of Senegal, Mali, Burkina Faso, Niger and Nigeria, has seen climatic effects worsen food security. And ongoing conflict in parts of the Sahel does not make addressing the food situation easier.

In this context, we revisit the analyses of Samuelson (1972) and Waugh (1944), which continue to be relevant to understanding food security, markets and possible policy responses. In times of conflict and an opposition to the idea that a market-based approach can solve the delivery of food to consumers, many alternatives to a market-based approach have been put forward. Waugh's apparent insight is that consumers might be harmed by stable prices and he argues that a varying price scheme might bring benefits to consumers. Samuelson argues that this is incorrect, as it is tantamount to buying at a high price and selling at a low price. Let us examine this idea, and extract some conclusions for food security. We present in some detail the discussion of the benefits, or otherwise, of price variability based on the careful analysis in Samuelson (1972: 480). We do this first to show how price support schemes are flawed, but mainly to give us a framework within which to deal with food security, as a more market-based approach seems to be where Africa is headed under the guidance of policy-makers at the African Union and NEPAD.

Building a framework based on Samuelson (1972) means that we should be clear about the assumptions he uses. Once these are established, we can move to an analysis as to why price support and other schemes do not work. No model is free of assumptions, and the assumptions of this model are fairly innocuous, with one exception. The analysis uses cardinal utility and this means the benefit or need satisfaction one obtains from choice can be measured, which is problematic. But using ordinal methods is more difficult and it is not clear that there are additional insights anyway. The other assumptions are straightforward. Consumers care about the benefit of their next meal and this extra (marginal) benefit is independent of the choices of others. The model has three 'goods'. A food item is available in two time periods (Q_1 and Q_2) and as they are consumed in two different time periods, say this week and next week, they are seen as two separate items. The third good is the representative input required to produce Q_1 and Q_2, namely labour, although this can be any input. In the two time periods, clearly price is going to be determined by the wage paid to the input as producers must cover their costs. But this popular and familiar analysis in economics can provide a useful benchmark for thinking about food security in a 'market-dominated' policy future for Africa, especially in ECOWAS, as greater trade links are forged between countries in Africa.

There are some issues we need to cover. First, when utility of any of the two (one for each time period) consumer items are measured in terms of labour needed to produce them, the marginal utility curve (in each time period) is the demand curve for the food product in question. Samuelson (1972) points out that this means that the area under this demand curve measures the total utility for say Q_1. This is useful as it can capture the effect on a consumer if they lose access to the food product.

Each Q is produced with a separate allocation of labour, and over two time periods we produce a total amount of the good by adding Q_1 and Q_2 together and this total amount is fixed for now. As a loss of access to food can happen over an extended time period, it is useful to have the one food item, Q, delivered (or not if there is a crisis) in two time periods.

In Figure 8.1 above are the two time periods indicated by either a '1' or a '2' at the top of the diagram for each market. On the horizontal axes are the quantities Q_1 and Q_2 and each Q is produced at a constant cost of 'w' which serves as the initial common price. Income determines the position of the demand curve shown in bold in Figure 8.1. Now Waugh (1944) proposes that a stable price is worse than variable prices. We can use Figure 8.1, based on Samuelson, to examine the validity of this statement, and this analysis can then become a useful framework for those interested in discussing food security in Africa and ECOWAS. This is because policy is now shifting to focus on the market as a solution as the 'within Africa' (and beyond) growth from trade vision, embodied in a recent United

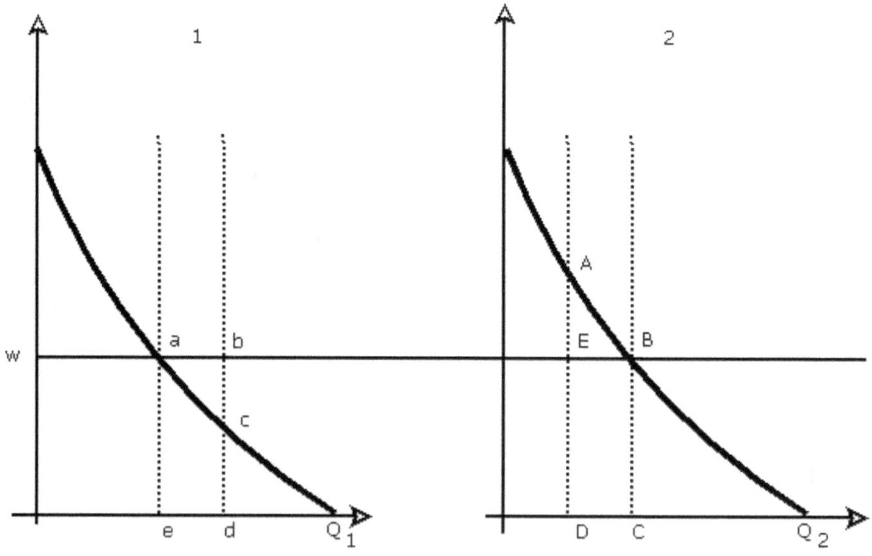

Figure 8.1 Demand for a Food Good in Two Time Periods

Nations (2010) report on regional integration, is taken seriously and implemented by countries and regional groupings within the African continent.

The following discussion is somewhat dry, but it is needed as a reminder of what a market-based policy approach entails. In the market on the left ('1'), we show a price fall to 'c' from 'w' the initial price. Care is taken to ensure that the area abcde in '1' is equal to the area in '2' shown as EBCD at the initial price. The quantity 'ed' is the same as the quantity 'DC'. The price rise is shown in '2', where the price rises to the level associated with point A. Now what are the gains or losses? The gain in total utility from the price fall in the left diagram is the area under the demand curve 'acde', which is less than the area 'abcde', and as area 'abcde' equals area EBCD by construction, it must be that the gain (acde) is less than area EBCD in period '2'. But area EBCD in period '2' is part of the loss in utility from a rise in the price. So at this stage, we know that a lowering of the price gives a lower gain than part of the loss from a higher price in the subsequent period. But there is more. The higher price in the subsequent period ('2') has an additional loss of utility given by the area ABE. The implication of Samuelson's analysis is that it is better to have a common price, and it is not possible to gain by having a low price in one period offset by a higher price in a subsequent period. You cannot avoid the 'best' that the market does, unless you bring resources in from elsewhere.

Against this background, it is now possible to develop a useful framework for thinking about food security. To provide the framework, we reproduce the first period effect in Figure 8.2 below.

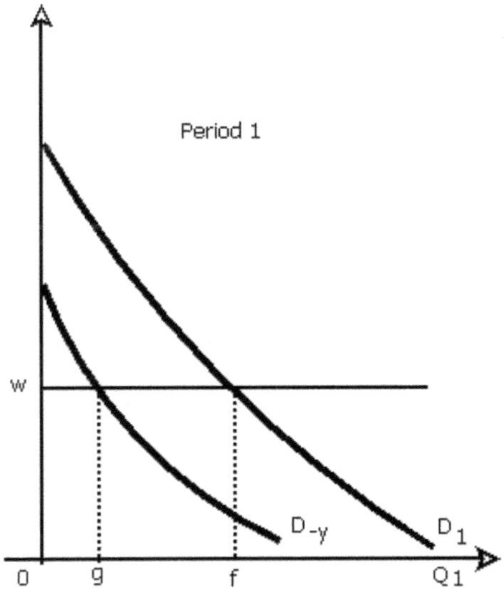

Figure 8.2 Demand for a Food Good in One Time Period

We have already stressed the importance of household income to food security. In Figure 8.2, aggregate income determines the position of the demand schedule. D_1 represents the demand curve, for the good (food in this case) for a modest level of income. The distance 0f is the amount of food bought in the first period. To be 'food secure' requires many time periods of amounts like 0f. For illustrative purposes, we show only one time period. Considering that there is not always a lack of supply, our model focuses on the demand side, namely the inability to buy the good. If individuals lack the purchasing power (despite availability), the situation becomes dire in terms of food security. The possibility of this situation is shown in Figure 8.2 by a leftward shift to D_{-y} resulting in a fall in the purchases of food to 'g'. Thus, the move from 'f' to 'g' reflects the degree of food insecurity due to a lack of income. For a more complete food security model, the notion of choice and nutrition should be acknowledged; namely, that the dietary constituents of Q on the horizontal axis must contribute towards healthy living and allow for some variance in choice.

However, one shortcoming with the analysis of Figure 8.2 is that it has no explicit role for gender. The gender perspective is often overlooked, yet it is extremely important for food security. Women, despite making a critical contribution to household food security as food producers and providers, are most vulnerable and account for over 60 per cent of the world's hungry (World Food Programme 2012). In fact, women are responsible for between 60 and 80 per cent of the food production in the Global South and for half of the world's food production (FAO 1996).

Yet, unfortunately, women are not empowered, despite playing a crucial role towards food security. The recent work by Companion (2010) shows that women in the food supply chain are excluded from lucrative markets. Women also find it difficult to enter more formal labour markets and face challenges in improving their skills or education and training levels. This situation is implicit in the framework of Figure 8.2. Women find themselves crowded at levels such as 'g' where food security is very poor. So given women's limited access to productive resources, in formulating any set of strategies to achieving food security more effectively, policy-makers must emphasize gender equality and women's empowerment. Achieving a more prominent representation of women would contribute significantly to economic growth, poverty reduction and food security.

Another issue that arises is the effect of food aid on domestic price. The impact of aid on domestic prices is of some interest as the issue of effectiveness can be addressed. Getaw and Shively (2009) assess this issue using data for Ethiopia. They find that in crisis periods when food insecurity is high, there are no effects on local prices as long as the aid arrives in a timely manner. We can use the analysis of Figures 8.1 and 8.2 to explain this result. In times of crisis, food aid just meets a critical need and has no impact on the market. But aid should be timely to minimize the adverse effects.

As recent political economy developments in Africa are pushing towards market solutions and this gives rise to challenges (which are covered in more detail below), we need to add the effects of increased trade to this framework. This policy change means greater links to the global economy. But opening up the economy to world markets does mean that local producers of the now imported goods face stiff competition. But household food access can improve as long as incomes do not fall. So it is possible that workers in declining sectors who become unemployed may become food insecure. In addition, small farmers are likely to come under pressure as agricultural production moves to bigger farms. Clearly, these have worrisome implications for food security in ECOWAS. But at least ECOWAS has some structures in place to deal with this concern over the possibility of greater food insecurity. However, in the adjustment period after markets open up, food security is likely to suffer as resources are reallocated to new uses. Thus it is imperative that ECOWAS builds extra capacity to deal with issues of food security if this 'within Africa' market vision takes hold.

Food Security in ECOWAS

We now turn to examine current conditions as regards food security in ECOWAS. Table 8.1 summarizes the food security developments in ECOWAS as of 2012. All countries in ECOWAS have experienced food insecurity in various forms and degrees.

In view of this situation, food aid is vital in smoothing consumption. However, as illustrated in Figure 8.3, on average over an extended time period, excluding the outliers Cape Verde and Liberia, food aid as a proportion of consumption has fallen. However, future aid should not mirror this pattern, especially considering the food crisis in the Sahel region.

The exact cause of food insecurity in the region is difficult to pin down. However, as detailed in Table 8.1, the food insecurity in the region is caused mostly by supply shocks such as conflicts, climate change and exchange rate fluctuations. These problems are compounded by the sharp rise in global food prices, which has severe consequences for the real incomes of the poor.

Figure 8.4 below shows the recent upheavals in global food prices. The large spike in the 2008 food prices has led to significantly higher food prices. A recent report of the World Bank *Food Price Watch* (2012), however, indicates that in the last four months of 2011, global food prices have fallen (8 per cent) due to growth in supplies and uncertainty about the world economy, but remain volatile and high with the 2011 annual index (24 per cent) higher than its 2010 average. Over the same time period, global cereal prices also reached 'historically' high levels. It should be highlighted that cereals are not only a key ingredient in food products but are also a key component of animal feed. Thus, as cereals are an input in the production of other food products, this inevitably feeds into other food product prices (as illustrated in Figure 8.4 where cereal prices are correlated with meat prices) and higher prices for food purchasers mean greater food insecurity.

Table 8.1 Recent Food Security Developments in ECOWAS as of 2012

Country	Situation
Benin	Faces environmental problems; desertification in the northern part and deforestation in the southern part.
Burkina Faso	Reduced output. Affected by conditions in the Sahel region.
Cape Verde	Lower food aid, and higher import prices; more food insecurity in rural areas.
Côte d'Ivoire	Conflict-affected and food security is still a concern. Reliance on humanitarian aid.
Gambia	Reliance on imports and currency depreciation means ongoing food supply problems.
Ghana	Food security is a problem in the rural North.
Guinea	Millions face conditions of food insecurity.
Guinea-Bissau	Rice production higher, other crop revenues higher but prices have not adjusted downwards.
Liberia	Production up but prices constant. Ivorian refugees adding to the food insecurity situation.
Mali	Severely food insecure. Affected by conditions in the Sahel region.
Niger	Cereal production drastically down, thus prices higher. Returning workers from Libya adding to the critical food insecurity situation. Conditions in the Sahel a concern.
Nigeria	Cereal prices are lower, although millet prices are higher. Conditions in the Sahel a concern.
Senegal	Lower production of cereals means higher food prices. Rural areas face food insecurity. Affected by conditions in the Sahel region.
Sierra Leone	Faces higher food prices and dependent on rice imports.
Togo	Rural population suffered the most from floods and sharp increases in food prices.

Source: Food and Agriculture Organization (FAO) of the United Nations, 2012a

The rising global food price is the result of various factors. What is clear is that the basic cause is related to supply and demand. The primary factors : 'Rising energy prices (through mid-2008), subsidized biofuel production, income and population growth, globalization, and urbanization are among the major forces contributing to surging demand' (Robles and Torero 2010). They also point out that demand from China and India pushes up prices.

Beyond these challenges, as illustrated in Figure 8.5, is also the fairly constant agricultural population density, which is relatively low and falling within the ECOWAS region.

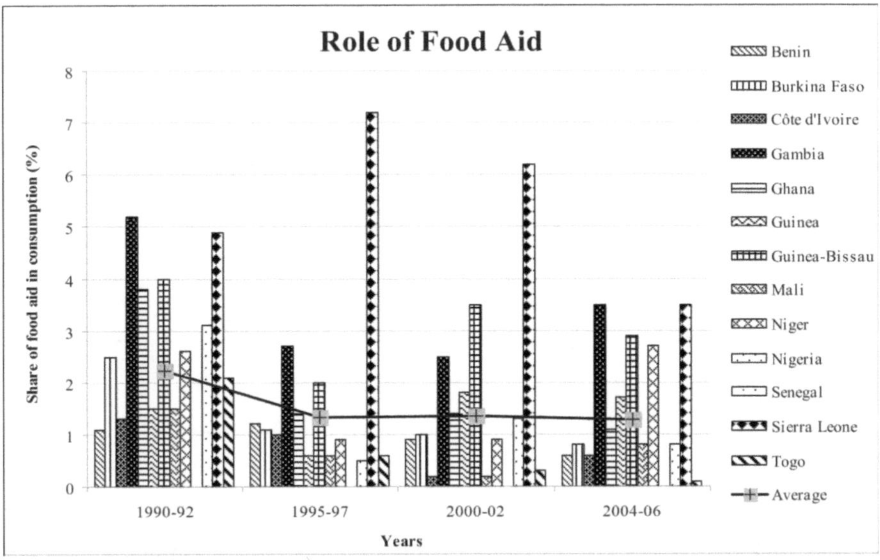

Figure 8.3 **Role of Food Aid: author's compilation based on the Food and Agriculture Organization Statistics Database (2011)**

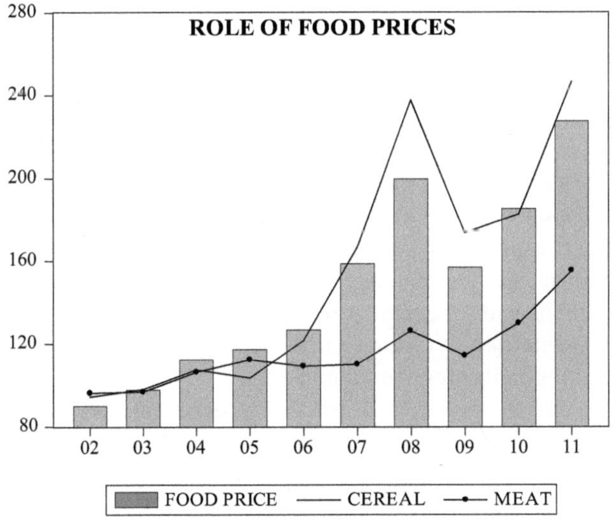

Figure 8.4 **Role of Food Prices: author's compilation based on the Food and Agriculture Organization Statistics Database (2011)**

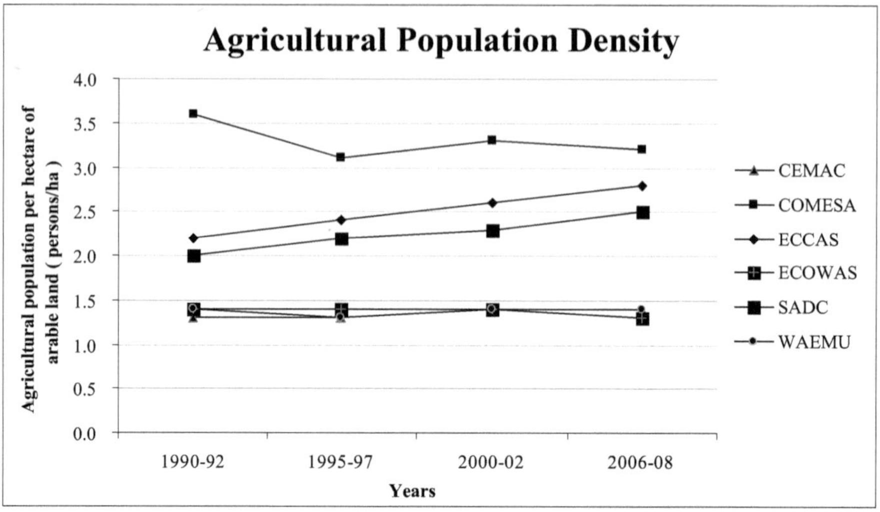

Figure 8.5 Agricultural Population Density: author's compilation based on the Food and Agriculture Organization Statistics Database (2011)

There is hope for a turnaround regarding the future agrarian outlook and food security for ECOWAS with the exciting adoption of the Comprehensive Africa Agriculture Development Programme (CAADP); see, for example, the detailed report of the Republic of Ghana (2009).

CAADP is an ambitious change process of the African Union (AU) and the New Partnership for Africa's Development (NEPAD) that aims to shape African agricultural sector and development, and more specifically, improve food security, nutrition and incomes in Africa's largely agrarian economies. A unique and positive development of CAADP is that it is not imposed by outsiders but is a made-in-Africa response and so should have greater credibility. It is a multi-country initiative and has the support of several partners, including the World Bank, trade unions and producer associations, with provision to finance changes. ECOWAS is committed to ensuring that the made-in-Africa CAADP solution is brought to fruition in its member countries.

ECOWAS has therefore established a programme devoted to agricultural policy called ECOWAP. ECOWAS partners have reacted positively to CAADP, and Ghana for instance has been quick to take advantage of CAADP and has already aligned its national goals to those now contained in ECOWAP by signing an agreement between major role players to coordinate its implementation. The specific goals of the programme over the next three years are to reduce food insecurity by implementing better emergency contingency plans, moving to a more scientific agricultural policy and attempting to reduce income variability through greater crop diversification.

Also, in terms of the nutritional status of ECOWAS, it is pleasing to note, as Table 8.2 shows, some fall in the number of undernourished people. As to the sustainability of their nutritional outlook, this depends upon the ability of institutions in ECOWAS, old or new, to respond effectively to future shocks. However, it is unfortunate that, relatively, SADC countries' nutritional outlook has worsened.

Table 8.2 Undernourished Persons in the World, Including ECOWAS

Undernourishment Number of undernourished persons (millions)				
Country groups	**1990-1992**	**1995-1997**	**2000-2002**	**2006-2008**
World	848.4	791.5	836.2	850.0
Developing countries	831.7	772.1	819.2	838.2
Africa	170.9	193.6	203.3	223.6
Asia developing	607.2	526.2	565.7	567.8
ECOWAS (Economic Community of West African States)	37.8	32.2	34.0	29.0
SADC (Southern African Development Community)	47.9	70.9	80.0	100.4

Source: Food and Agriculture Organization Statistics Database, 2011

The food security developments in ECOWAS should also be considered in the economic context of actual and likely growth rates in the region. According to the World Bank, in a 2012 report titled *Global Economic Prospects: Uncertainties and Vulnerabilities*, countries in the Sub-Saharan region grew at 4.9 per cent in 2011 in line with average growth rates of the previous year. Excluding Liberia, the countries in ECOWAS grew at marginally more (4.94 per cent) than the Sub-Saharan region as a whole.

One can thus say that ECOWAS's performance in 2011 mirrored that of the average performance in the whole of Sub-Saharan Africa (SSA). However, if excluding South Africa from our estimates, the SSA region is now growing at nearly 6 per cent. This is to be expected, considering South Africa's weaker growth performance over this time period.

Challenges for ECOWAS in the Future

The fact that ECOWAS is growing and yet faces problems of food security quickly points to poverty as the underlying problem. The difficulty is then, how does one address the problem of poverty? It is clear that the one approach adopted by many countries and regions is the idea of 'development', where this concept implies that many structural changes need to be made to an economy, or economies linked in some way, and if the changes have the desired effect and growth rates rise, it is possible for the instituted changes to be maintained for as long as they are needed. Recently there have been discussions to move away from the 'development' model towards a freer markets approach for regions in Africa. Whether these changes can be implemented is an issue, but this approach deserves some examination of what is required of regions in Africa. ECOWAS has much of the structure in place, but implementation requires a renewal of democratic approval. Regional solidarity is of paramount importance in times of crisis. Of illustrative value, relating to the food crisis in the Sahel region, ECOWAS and UEMOA have provided monetary aid and some member states have demonstrated their solidarity through food aid and logistical support. However, there is an urgent need for greater solidarity in dealing with food crises and in boosting intra-African trade and African countries' integration in the global economy.

New Regionalism

As ECOWAS is an affiliation of countries in a region, it makes sense to have some idea of the concept of regionalism. We can begin with a somewhat dated view of regionalism, but one that is still important as it is closely allied to debates that took place at the end of the Second World War over the role of markets and planning in the economy. Brannen (1944: 428) states that 'Region (or regionalism) is defined as a geographic area where the people feel that they have more interests and loyalties common to them than they have with other areas, such as are afforded by natural environment, occupation, memory of past triumphs, and alien minority'. The difficulty with this view of regionalism is that it assumes there is a wider entity to which various regions belong and it is that wider entity that is being pulled apart. But more recent developments relating to ECOWAS and the EC seem to indicate a return to this view. Definitions of regionalism have developed and currently there is the idea of a 'new' regionalism. Rugman (2000), in a review of Hettne, Inotai and Sunkel's book *Globalism and the New Regionalism*, published in 1999, states that '"New" regionalism is... "as a multidimensional form of integration which includes economic, political, social and cultural aspects...".' But this definition needs some explanation. Hettne Inotai and Sunkel's definition has roots in the orthodox liberal tradition; however, in a global environment where there is no apex authority to which sovereign states, which may have formed a regional group, belong, or where multilateral authority loses its power, then it is those regions that must take the initiative (or are forced) to interact with other regional blocs. Singly, a region lacks the resources or ability to grow alone and thus looks to economic, social and political measures to form new alliances or sever some older ones, as Hettne and Söderbaum (2006) discuss. The 'new' regionalism is a regionalism that has many dimensions (voting at the AU and new free trade blocks in Africa are two recent examples) and many nations interacting, but where the new multilateral links are set in motion from below at the level of existing regional blocks, rather than from an overarching institution. Paradoxically, it is the logic of market forces across the globe that necessitate this new direction of change from the existing base, rather than an apex authority as was the case in the past. These changes have relevance for food security as this is a problem that needs solutions at many levels given climate change, changes to inter-regional agreements and the slow recovery of the world economy.

Recent Developments in Africa

As already suggested, the focus on economic development implies a reliance on economic growth once institutions change. One form of institutional change is the formation of a group of countries forming a close alliance in a region. These institutional changes can be complex if there are former colonial powers maintaining strong links to the countries concerned. The market-orientated approach is gaining in popularity (although it does have its detractors). It assumes that the best way to produce goods and services that result in a proper allocation (and thus production that is efficient) of resources is a set of institutional arrangements that has a decentralized flow of information via prices for goods. There is a role for the government, as there are externalities that the market cannot deal with, and these (plus disaster relief) are of concern for food security. This hybrid system, where the market plays a central role with intervention and proper policy, must have certain features if it is to sustain growth. To fit in food security as part of the move to market outcomes, poverty must be dealt with by transfers to the poor. Getting to the point that an economy, or region, should be able to generate enough food output might be difficult in the interim. But this move to markets requires certain elements if it is to function fairly.

Agro-Food Standards

Access to export markets requires conformity with a set of standards. Agro-food standards have undergone a series of changes affecting agro-food trade. Agro-food exports are today increasingly regulated with 'double' standards – governmental and private sector requirements.

These 'double' standards have affected African agro-food exports. Standards that are biased against imports favour domestic producers (Fischer and Serra 2000). With public standards growing in numbers, the dominant perspective appears to be that standards are a new form of protectionism (Swinnen and Vandemoortele 2011) and one would expect, therefore, that the least developed countries, such as those in Africa, would be most affected. For instance, a study by Otsuki, Wilson and Sewadeh (2001) argues that the EU standard on aflatoxins will hurt African exports of cereals, dried fruits and nuts to Europe. They claim that the EU standard, which would reduce the health risk by approximately 1.4 deaths per billion a year, will decrease these African exports by 64 per cent.

On the other hand, there is the issue of private sector regulation. Private standards (exacting quality and supply schedules) are today dominated by large multinational food companies, and trade is regulated through standards set by a 'buyer's' market (facilitated by trade liberalization) in global value chains that have little direct contact with producers (Gibbon and Ponte 2005). In the face of this 'new' value chain situation, small-scale farmers who lack the financial, technical and human resources are thus more vulnerable and likely to be excluded or lose export market access. There is evidence of smallholder exclusion in ECOWAS. In Senegal, the 'tightening' of food standards and structural changes in the supply chains has induced a shift from smallholders farming (green beans for export, for example) to large-scale integrated estate production (Maertens and Swinnen 2009). Local policy-makers should therefore aim at strengthening the capacities of smaller operators who lack the productive resources for successful compliance.

A Legal Framework

Part of the role of the legal system is to ensure that property rights are enforced to avoid conflict and resource losses. Obviously, in a regional grouping, careful consideration needs to be given to the role of legal systems. If the local and regional legal structures and the market can help allocate resources, then the resource base can be secure. If the resources in a region are secure, especially the capital stock, then investment can contribute towards the economic growth (and institutional changes) so desperately required in any region and especially those facing problems of food insecurity. An additional problem is that each country's legal system may not be easily accommodated in one regional legal system.

The Link Between Local and Regional Government

At the same time, the legal arrangements are in place or develop, and the state must be strong enough to show leadership in these areas, but also must ensure that the forces of competition are not thwarted by monopoly effects. Regional groupings must be especially careful that former dominant relationships with trading partners to the north do not divide and fracture any regional relationship. Unfortunately, this has begun to occur. But the newer form of government (whatever form it may take without becoming ineffective) for the overall regional grouping must still note that this partly market-based approach requires of it a role in macroeconomic policy that is consistent, and so must not allow different tax structures and must have financial flows that are fair and evenly shared. Fiscal and monetary policies must be aligned (limiting inflation) and, finally, the regional government and each member must be careful to contain expenditure.

Climate Change

Ever since Dalgaard, Hansen and Tarp (2004) noted that the effectiveness of aid depended partly on climate, especially if the country is in the tropics, this has obvious consequences for ECOWAS. Gregory, Ingram and Brklacich (2005) deal with the effects of climate change on food security in addition to supporting the features required of markets. This is important, as global climate change is an issue and greater sensitivity over this issue is needed. Governments, regional groupings (such as ECOWAS) and aid agencies are going to need to adapt policies to deal with climatic effects. This is a challenging task especially in this global economic contraction with donors reducing or postponing their pledges. For ECOWAS, to reduce its food insecurity, it is necessary that the countries of the region cooperate amongst themselves to deal with climate change and to manage their food shortages that threaten them on a regular basis, and in some cases (as in the Sahel region) with increasing frequency and intensity. It is also of utmost importance to strengthen international and regional cooperation and coordination especially regarding humanitarian access in the delivery of food aid and in water resources development. This entails support and changes to the internal structure of ECOWAS or the formation of new regional bodies to deal with climate change.

Food Security and Food Systems

Gregory, Ingram and Brklacich (2005) point out that the concept of food security is supported by the idea of a food system. They define a food system 'as a set of dynamic interactions between and within the biogeophysical and human environments which result in the production, processing, distribution, preparation of food'. A food system comprises the elements related to the supply of food to the consumer; how the consumer expresses which type of food to purchase and how these consumers partly influence prices. A further element covers nutrition, whether the food is safe for consumption and the importance of society's preferences.

With the idea of food systems, Gregory, Ingram and Brklacich (2005) point out that many final sellers of food now obtain much of their product requirements by direct links to producing firms. These firms supplying the retailers can have significant market power. Such international suppliers threaten the ability of domestic governments to legislate their behaviour set against the background of great freedom to trade across internal borders. Regional groupings must form to reduce these effects and much has to change before even ECOWAS moves to the market-based approach already adopted in Asia. In such a developing world, and based on the food system approach, it is likely that the changes to the global climate will have a negative impact on ECOWAS unless it can quickly react and adapt. However, Gregory *et al.* (2005) note that the developing countries have come off worse than developed regions in various models even with changes to the timing and intensity of their production.

Conclusion

Food security is clearly a problem in ECOWAS. Moves in Africa towards a greater reliance on trade and markets, viewed through the lens of new regionalism, means that ECOWAS is facing serious challenges in the future (governance, legal systems, climate and its relationship with the North and the East), all of which have consequences for food security. Whilst these are not really new challenges, the food security problem has been further aggravated by powerful market forces, influential actors and elements of protectionism. First, with these developments in mind, we place the current and future path of economic policy as regards free trade within Africa in a useful theoretical framework that shows that problems of food security may worsen in the immediate future. The second section examines the past and current food security developments in ECOWAS, and although the region faces food security problems, there are regional response mechanisms. Thus, as ECOWAS deepens its market linkages, it is vital that it restructures its response to food security through greater international and regional cooperation and coordination, and considering the food crisis in the Sahel region, humanitarian access in the delivery of food aid should be addressed.

References

Bhagwati, J.N. 1984. Incentives and Disincentives: International Migration. *Weltwirtschaftliches Archiv*, 120(4), 678-701.

Brannen, C.O. 1944. Review of Planning for the South by John V. Van Sickle. *Journal of Farm Economics*, 26(2), 427-429.

Burnside, C. and Dollar, D. 2000. Aid, Policies, and Growth. *The American Economic Review*, 90(4), 847-868.

Companion, M. 2010. Commodities and Competition: The Economic Marginalization of Female Food Vendors in Northern Mozambique. *Women's Studies Quarterly*, 38(3/4), 163-181.

Conway, G. 2008. Presidential Address: The Food Crisis. *The Geographical Journal*, 174(3), 269-273.

Dalgaard, C.J., Hansen, H. and Tarp, F. 2004. On the Empirics of Foreign Aid and Growth. *The Economic Journal*, 114(496), F191-F216.

Easterly, W. 2006. Reliving the 1950s: The Big Push, Poverty Traps, and Takeoffs in Economic Development. *Journal of Economic Growth*, 11(4), 289-31.

Easterly, W., Levine, R. and Roodman, D. 2004. Aid, Policies, and Growth: Comment. *The American Economic Review*, 94(3), 774-780.

Easterly, W. and Pfutze, T. 2008. Where Does the Money Go? Best and Worst Practices in Foreign Aid. *The Journal of Economic Perspectives*, 22(2), 29-52.

Fischer, R. and Serra, P. 2000. Standards and Protection. *Journal of International Economics*, 52, 377-400.

Food and Agriculture Organization (FAO) of the United Nations. 1996. Sustainable Development Department, *Women and Food Security, Release date March 1998.* Available at: http://www.fao.org/sd/wpdirect/wpan0022.htm [Accessed 15 February 2012].

Food and Agriculture Organization (FAO) of the United Nations. 2010. The State of Food Insecurity in the World 2010. Available at: http://www.fao.org/docrep/013/il683e.pdf [Accessed 3 February 2012].

Food and Agriculture Organization (FAO) of the United Nations, FAO Food Price Index. 2011. *The November FAO Food Price Index nearly unchanged from October, Release date 08/12/2011.* Available at: http://www.fao.org/worldfoodsituation/wfs-home/foodpricesindex/en/ [Accessed 4 January 2012].

Food and Agriculture Organization (FAO) of the United Nations, FAO Food Price Index. 2011a. *Crop Prospects and Food Situation*, Number 4 December 2011. Available at: http://www.fao.org/docrep/014/al983e/al983e00.pdf [Accessed 6 February 2012].

Food and Agriculture Organization (FAO) of the United Nations, FAO Food Price Index. 2012. *The State of Food Insecurity in the World, Addressing food security in protracted crises.* Available at: http://www.fao.org/docrep/wfs-home/013/i1683e/i1683e.pdf [Accessed 4 January 2012].

Food and Agriculture Organization (FAO) of the United Nations' Trade and Markets Division under the Global Information and Early Warning System (GIEWS), GIEWS Country Briefs. 2012a. *Western Africa.* Available at: http://www.fao.org/giews/countrybrief/index.jsp [Accessed 6 February 2012].

Food and Agriculture Organization (FAO) of the United Nations. 2012. The State of Food Insecurity in the World 2012. Available at: http://www.fao.org/publications/sofi/food-security-indicators/en. *Release date October 2012.* [Accessed 23 November 2012].

Gibbon, P. and Ponte, S. 2005. *Trading Down: Africa, Value Chains and the Global Economy*, Philadelphia: Temple University Press.

Gibbon, P. and Evelyne, L. 2010. Agro-Food Standards and Africa: An Introduction, in *Global Agro-Food Trade and Standards* edited by P. Gibbon, S. Ponte and E. Lazaro. Basingstoke: Palgrave Macmillan.

Gregory, P.J., Ingram, J.S.I., and Brklacich, M. 2005. Climate Change and Food Security. *Philosophical Transactions: Biological Sciences*, 360(1463), 2139-2148.

Grigg, D. 1997. The World's Hunger: A Review 1930-1990. *Geography*, 82(3), 197-206.

Harms, P. and Lutz, M. 2006. Aid, Governance and Private Foreign Investment: Some Puzzling Findings for the 1990s. *The Economic Journal*, 116(513), 773-790.

Hausmann, R., Pritchett, L. and Rodrik, D. 2005. Growth Accelerations. *Journal of Economic Growth*, 10(4), 303-329.

Hettne, B. and Söderbaum, F. 2006. The UN and Regional Organizations in Global Security: Competing or Complementary Logics? *Global Governance*, 12(3), 227-232.

Maertens, M. and Swinnen, J.F.M. 2009. Trade, Standards and Poverty: Evidence from Senegal. *World Development*, 37(1), 161-178.

Otsuki, T., Wilson, J.S. and Sewadeh, M. 2001. Saving two in a billion: Quantifying the trade effect of European food safety standards on African exports. *Food Policy*, 26, 495-514.

Pilbeam, C.J., Tripathi, B.P., Munankarmy, R.C. and Gregory, P.J. 1999. Productivity and Economic Benefits of Integrated Nutrient Management in Three Major Cropping Systems in the Mid-Hills of Nepal. *Mountain Research and Development*, 19(4), 333-344.

Pross, J., Kotthoff, U., Müller, U.C., Peyron O., Dormoy I., Schmiedl, G. *et al.* 2009. Massive Perturbation in Terrestrial Ecosystems of the Eastern Mediterranean Region Associated with the 8.2 kyr Climatic Event. *Geology*, 37, 887-890.

Republic of Ghana. 2009. ECOWAS Agricultural Policy (ECOWAP)/ Comprehensive African Agriculture Development Programme (CAADP). Available at: http://www.nepad-caadp.net/pdf/Ghana.pdf [Accessed 21 February 2012].

Robles, M. and Torero, M. 2010. Understanding the Impact of High Food Prices in Latin America [with Comment]. *Economía*, 10(2), 117-164.

Rugman, A.M. 2000. Review of Globalism and the New Regionalism by Bjorn Hettne, Andras Inotai and Osvaldo Sunkel. *International Affairs*, 76(1), 146.

Samuelson, P.A. 1972. The Consumer Does Benefit From Feasible Price Stability. *The Quarterly Journal of Economics*, 86(3), 476-493.

Swinnen, J.F.M. and Vandemoortele, T. 2011. Trade and the Political Economy of Food Standards. *Journal of Agricultural Economics*, 62(2), 259-280.

Tadesse, G. and Shively, G. 2009. Food Aid, Food Prices, and Producer Disincentives in Ethiopia. *American Journal of Agricultural Economics*, 91(4), 942-955.

Tavares, R. and Tang, V. 2011. Regional Economic Integration in Africa: Impediments to Progress? *South African Journal of International Affairs*, 18(2), 217-233.

Tol, R.S.J. and Wagner, S. 2010. Climate Change and Violent Conflict in Europe Over the Last Millennium. *Climate Change*, 99, 65-79.

United Nations Economic Commission for Africa. 2010. *Assessing Regional Integration in Africa IV*, prepared jointly with the African Union Commission and the African Development Bank, Addis Ababa: UNECA.

Verdin, J., Funk, C., Senay, G. and Choularton, R. 2005. Climate Science and Famine Early Warning. *Philosophical Transactions: Biological Sciences*, 360(1463), 2155-2168.

Waugh, F.V. 1944. Does the consumer benefit from instability? *Quarterly Journal of Economics*, 58(4), 602-614.

World Bank. 2011. Food Price Watch February 2011. Available at: http://www.worldbank.org/foodcrisis/food_price_watch_report_feb2011.html [Accessed 15 February 2012].
World Bank. 2012. Global Economic Prospects: Uncertainties and vulnerabilities. Regional Summary: Sub-Saharan Africa. Available at: http://siteresources.worldbank.org//INTPROSPECTS/Resources/334934-1322593305595/82871391326374900917/SSARegionalSummary_GEPJan2012_Eng.pdf [Accessed 16 February 2012].
World Food Programme. 2012. Fighting Hunger Worldwide, Hunger Stats 2012. Available at: http://www.wfp.org/hunger/stats [Accessed 15 February 2012].

Chapter 9

Impact of Regional Integration on Human Rights Protection in Africa

Jean-Bosco Ngendahimana

Decades after the United Nations adopted the 1948 Universal Declaration of Human Rights and almost thirty years after the Organization of African Unity (OAU) adopted its own African Charter on Human and Peoples' Rights, hereinafter referred to as 'Banjul Charter', the human rights situation on the African continent is decidedly bleak (Magnarella 2011).

Considering weaknesses associated with the institutions of human rights protection as referred to in the Banjul Charter and other additional protocols, the system that has the protection of individuals at its centre would curb passive complicity among African leaders. Otherwise, achieving genuine respect for human rights constitutes the greatest challenge facing Africans.

Contrary to the lack of commitment experienced at the level of the African Union (AU) in terms of human rights protection, it is encouraging that Regional Economic Communities (RECs) have already granted direct access to individuals in their constitutive treaties.[1] It is with hope that like in any other economic integration, the latter will impact on the cause of human rights in their respective jurisdictions and case courts' decisions are respected by the convicted states, shame or peer pressure mobilized, or other stronger forms of sanctions adopted against recalcitrant states.

Indeed, the history of the world, both ancient and modern, has shown that individual nation-states, left to themselves, cannot be trusted to protect their citizens and other residents against arbitrary, discriminatory and other repressive acts and decisions of state officials acting in the name of the State (Viljoen 2007: 482). It is in this context that this chapter advocates for close trade and other economic links, more likely to be developed at the regional levels, with hope that they may serve as a guarantee of respect for commonly agreed standards, including human rights.

Whereas the researcher wonders whether the African RECs brought any positive influence on the protection of human rights, the general objective of this chapter is to examine both negative and positive impacts of regional integration

1 For ECOWAS, see article 10(c) and (d) of the Protocol and Supplementary Protocol, article 4; COMESA Treaty, article 26; EAC Treaty, article 30; SADC Tribunal Protocol, article 18.

on human rights protection in Africa in order to propose solutions based on the maximization of positive impact. The chapter has the following specific objectives:

1. to explore how human rights issues are addressed in RECs Treaties;
2. to identify the contribution of RECs Courts and Tribunal in the protection of human rights;
3. to inspect how effective the RECs' Courts and Tribunal's decisions are enforced by the member states.

Human Rights and Economic Integration in Africa

It has been argued that the successful enforcement of human rights in Africa will depend, in part, on the development of economic integration among states on the continent. Heyns and Viljoen (1999) argue that as a general principle, the international enforcement of human rights depends for its success on the existence of, among other factors, a web of trade relations between the respective states because only where these exist can their potential severance in cases where human rights violations come to light constitute a real threat to coerce the states to adhere to human rights principles. This justifies the welcoming of the establishment of the AU, which is the highest level of regional integration. Indeed, the AU Act contains provisions that put human rights to the agenda.

Human Rights Provisions in the Constitutive Act of the AU

The provisions of the preamble and those that set out the objectives and principles of the AU Constitutive Act include human rights in very clear terms. The preamble states that African leaders are 'determined to promote and protect human and peoples' rights, consolidate democratic institutions and culture and to ensure good governance and the rule of law'.[2] Furthermore, two of the objectives and at least five of the fundamental principles of the AU incorporate human rights issues in a very explicit manner.

Other guiding principles of the AU that have human rights implications include promotion of gender equality, the promotion of social justice to ensure balanced economic development, and condemnation and rejection of unconstitutional changes of government.[3]

Bearing in mind that AU combines the OAU's political nature and the economic nature of the African Economic Community (AEC), this chapter cannot ignore the human rights aspect of the AEC Treaty.

2 Para 10 Preamble to the Act.

3 Arts 4 (1), 4 (n) and 4 (p) constitutive Act.

Human Rights in the AEC Treaty

The AEC Treaty is more comprehensive than any treaty of other integration schemes in Africa. It adopts an all-inclusive approach to cooperation and integration which takes into account not only the contributions of economic sectors but also non-economic ones.[4]

It is in this context that among its founding principles, the promotion of a peaceful environment, the recognition, promotion and protection of human and peoples' rights, and respect for accountability, economic justice and popular participation in development are believed to be meaningful for the success of the AEC.

It is interesting that the AEC Treaty demonstrates a commitment of the member states to partially surrender their sovereignty for the purpose of integration. Hence, Article 5 records general undertakings of states to create conditions favourable to the attainment of collective goals, and to refrain from unilateral actions that would threaten set objectives.

Considering that the attachment to state sovereignty evident in the Charter of the OAU was a major stumbling block for the attainment of the objectives of the organization and restricted expansion of the powers of the institution even when the situation warranted it, the AEC Treaty could be said to have begun on a better structural foundation by being human rights-friendly.

Further on the structure, Article 6 of the AEC Treaty contains a rather elaborate outline of proposed stages of its implementation, including the establishment or strengthening of RECs in the various regions of the continent.

Relationship with RECs

In specific terms, the AEC Treaty accords multiple functions and responsibilities to the RECs. First, they are the operational arms of the Community in the implementation of programs at the regional level. Second, policies adopted at the regional level are expected to be channelled upwards to the continental level, thereby giving content to the responsibility of the AEC to coordinate and harmonize such policies.[5] This then calls for complementarities and convergence in policies horizontally as between the RECs and vertically as between them and the AEC. It is to ensure that the Assembly of Heads of States and Government, as the supreme body of the AEC, is empowered to take decisions and give directives to the RECs so as to guarantee that AEC objectives are realized.[6]

---

4 These include environment (articles 58 to 60); science and technology (articles 51 to 53); education, training and culture; human resources; social affairs; health; population; and women and development.

5 Article 4 (2) and 6 of the Abuja Treaty.

6 Article 8 (h) of the Abuja Treaty.

Similarly, it may be posited that it is with this need to avoid divergences as contradictions in policy and action at the two levels that the decisions of the Assembly and the regulations of the Council of the Community are made binding on the RECs.[7]

In a concrete way, one may say that the relationship between the AEC and RECs is that the former remains with its own identity and fields of action while also giving the RECs much leeway for operations which are symbiotically integrated, institutionally and functionally into the AEC.

Human Rights in RECs

In this part, the researcher identifies human rights in the objectives and principles of RECs and furthermore shows how the Banjul Charter is the basis of a common regional rights standard.

Human rights as objectives of RECs

Given the people-centred nature of any REC, human rights protection and promotion are both conducive to the achievement of its aims and objectives (Seymour 1997: 23) and its harmony with well-established principles of international law regarding the purpose of trade and development arrangements.

From the point of view of nationals, ceding sovereignty to intergovernmental arrangements has value only if it results in an improvement in their material well-being and if the regional space allows human rights to prosper in ways that were impossible in the nation state.

Human rights as principles of RECs

Although human rights, the rule of law, and good governance do not feature as goals of the RECs, these aspects form part of the way in which the goals have to be attained in a principled way. Developments within the EAC, ECOWAS and SADC are most strikingly illustrative of this change, on the basis of comparing earlier and more recent founding texts.[8] There was no explicit reference to human rights in any of the articles forming the body of the original 1975 ECOWAS Treaty. When the Treaty was amended in 1993, the principle of adherence to human rights was given increased prominence. In 2003, the SADC Summit amended the admission criteria adopted in 1995 by adding the requirement that there should be a commonality of 'observance of the principles of democracy, human rights, good governance and the rule of law in accordance with the African Charter'.

---

7 Articles 10 (2) and 13 (2) of the Abuja Treaty.

8 See Articles 6(d), 7(2) and 3(3) (b) of the EAC Treaty. For more on this, see Sidaway (2003: 64).

Common regional human rights standard

The Banjul Charter is the most representative and legitimate source of reference to ensure regional judicial harmonization. With the exception of Morocco, all African states are party to the Banjul Charter. This explains why most of the regional treaties make reference to the recognition, promotion and protection of human and peoples' rights in accordance with the Banjul Charter as a 'fundamental principle' guiding the accomplishment of their objectives.[9]

Contribution of RECs' Courts and Tribunals in the Protection of Human Rights

Individual access and human rights jurisdiction of RECs' Courts and Tribunals will attract the researcher's attention in his efforts to identify the contribution of RECs' Courts and Tribunals in the protection of human rights in Africa.

Individual Access to RECs' Courts and Tribunals

The importance of individual access is illustrated in the ECOWAS experience. After the adoption of the Protocol on the ECOWAS Court in 1991, and its entry into force in 1996, the Court lay dormant until 2004, when a Nigerian businessman, Mr. Olajide Afolabi, brought a case before the Court. Afolabi alleged that the unilateral closure by Nigeria of the border with neighbouring Benin in August 2003 constituted a violation of his right to free movement as enshrined in the ECOWAS Treaty, the Protocol on Free Movement of Persons and Goods, and the Banjul Charter.[10] Due to the limitation in the ECOWAS Court Protocol that only a state on behalf of its nationals could institute actions before it, the Court decided to forgo the first chance of exercising its mandate. Conscious of the implications of its finding, the Court requested that, in the light of the 'great interest and importance to all member states', these states should all be notified of the judgment date.

An analysis of the arguments presented shows that an activist Court could have viewed the matter differently. Because the protocol does not stipulate in so many words that only states can appear before the Court, the applicant argued that the door was open for an interpretation allowing individuals standing. If only states have standing, a case involving dispute about non-conformity with community law by a member would require that member state to bring a suit as applicant against itself as respondent.

To overcome this absurdity, the argument continued, and to observe 'equity', individuals should be allowed to have standing before the Court. Adopting a different line of argument, the respondent argued that it was a matter of jurisdiction

9 See art. 4 (g) of the 1993 ECOWAS Treaty and art. 6(d) of the 1999 EAC Treaty.

10 *Olajide Afolabi v Nigeria*, Suit no ECW/CCJ/APP/01/03, judgment of 27 April 2004.

rather than standing, and warned that the Court should not usurp the legislative function of redrafting the clear provisions of the Protocol.

Against this background, the Protocol relating to the ECOWAS Court was amended in 2005 to broaden access to the Court to individuals and corporate bodies 'in proceedings for the determination of an act or inaction of a Community official that violates the rights' of the individual or corporate body', and, more broadly, for 'relief for violations of their human rights'.[11]

As the situation stands, individuals may also submit cases directly to the EAC Court of Justice and SADC Tribunal. Individuals may refer the legality of any act, regulation, directive, or decision of the Community or any member state to each of these judicial organs, arguing that it is unlawful or an infringement of the founding treaty.[12]

Under most international law systems, individuals are granted standing only if they have fulfilled some pre-conditions, which usually include the requirement that local remedies must have been exhausted. But what if domestic remedies are not effective or unavailable in practice?[13]

---

11 New article 10 (a) and (b) of the 2005 ECOWAS Protocol (see ECOWAS supplementary Protocol, art. 4)).

12 Article 30 of the EAC Treaty and Article 18 of the SADC Tribunal Protocol.

13 Article 56 (5) of the African Charter on Human and Peoples' Rights requires that communications to the Commission of Human and Peoples 'Rights only after exhausting local remedies, if any, unless it is obvious that this procedure is unduly prolonged'. The African Commission came out with an elaborate jurisprudence in this regard. Thus, in *Communications 25/89, 47/90, 56/91 and 100/93, Free Legal Assistance Group and others v. Zaire* the Commission decided that local remedies are not available or effective in instances of serious or massive violations. The other situation in which complainants may be exempted from exhausting local remedies is where there has been an attempt to oust the jurisdiction of the courts. The Commission has found that 'ouster' clauses render local remedies non-existent, ineffective or illegal, or illusory and create a legal situation in which the judiciary can provide no check on the executive branch of the government. For more details, see *Communications 137/94, 139/94, 154/96 and 161/97, international Pen, Constitutional Rights Project, Interights on behalf of ken Saro-Wiwa Jr and Civil Liberties Organization v. Nigeria*, Twelfth Activity Report 1998-1999, Annex V, para. 76 (Documents of the African Commission, p. 729). The third ground for exemption from exhausting local remedies is illustrated by Communication 60/91, where the Commission found that it would be inappropriate to insist that the complainants seek remedies from sources which do not operate impartially and have no obligation to decide according to legal principles. See *Communication 60/91, Constitutional Rights Project (in respect of Wahab Akamu, G.Adega and others) v. Nigeria*, Eighth Activity Report 1994-1995, Annex VI (Documents of the African Commission, p. 385). The Commission also agreed the Communication as no domestic remedy can give the complainants the satisfaction they seek. See *Communications 137/94, 139/94, 154/96 and 161/97, international Pen, Constitutional Rights Project, Interights on behalf of Ken Saro-Wiwa Jr and Civil Liberties Organization v. Nigeria*, Twelfth Activity Report 1998-1999, Annex V, para. 76 (Documents of the African Commission, p. 729). According to the Commission, it is sensible that a complainant

It is interesting to note that before the ECOWAS Court of Justice, the exhaustion of domestic remedies does not feature as a prerequisite for *locus stand.* It may be argued that this omission derives from the status of the Community law, which is regarded as superior and integral to the law of member states. Thus, in *Ugokwe v Nigeria and others,*[14] the ECOWAS Court stated that 'the distinctive feature' of the ECOWAS legal order is that it 'sets forth a judicial monism of first and last resort in Community law'.

Human Rights Jurisdiction of the RECs' Courts and Tribunals

This point will analyze human rights jurisdiction of three RECs' Courts and Tribunals, namely the East African Community Court of Justice, hereinafter referred to as 'EAC Court of Justice', ECOWAS Court of Justice and SADC Tribunal.

EAC Court of Justice

Under Article 23 of the EAC Treaty, the EAC Court of Justice is the judicial body which shall ensure adherence to law in the interpretation and application of and compliance with the Treaty.[15] One of such provisions that the Court may interpret is Article 6(2) relating to the obligations of the partner States to protect human rights in accordance with the Banjul Charter.

Additionally, the Treaty confers on the Court such other original, appellate, human rights and other jurisdictions as will be determined by the Council at a suitable subsequent date[16] through a Protocol.

So long as the Council of Ministers has not yet decided to equip the Court with human rights jurisdictions, the latter opted for a derivative human rights competence under the EAC Treaty. Indeed, the EACJ used articles 6(d) and 7(2) as the platform to litigate human rights before the Court. The door was opened

---

alleging a violation by way of imprisonment, who escaped the imprisonment and fled to another country, need not exhaust local remedies in the country from which he fled. See *Communication 103/93, Alhassan Abubakar v. Ghana,* Tenth Activity Report 1996-1997, Annex X (Documents of the African Commission, p. 571). Lastly, it is debatable whether a local remedy is available to an individual who does not have the financial means to make use of it and, therefore, whether indigence should absolve a complainant from exhausting local remedies. This question was posed by the Inter-American Commission to its Court, which concluded that 'if legal services are required a person is unable to obtain such services because of his indigence, then that person would be exempted from the requirement to exhaust local remedies'. See *Exceptions to the Exhaustion of Local Remedies, Inter-American Court, OC-11/90,* judgment of 10 August 1990.

14 Case no. ECOWAS/CCJ/APP/02/05, judgment of 7 October 2005.

15 See also Article 27(1).

16 *Idem,* Article 27(2).

in the case of *Katabazi.*[17] While the Court recognized its lack of human rights jurisdiction, it entertained the case in the light of interpreting the Treaty. One commentator compares the EAC Court of Justice and its human rights jurisdiction to a house which has been completed but cannot shelter anyone simply because there should be an opening ceremony before anyone can move in (Mizungo 2011: 74). Compliments to the brave judges, who found a back door to the house such that East Africans can be accommodated in the meantime.

ECOWAS Court of Justice

Within the framework of ECOWAS, there is clearly a link between the construction of an economic community and the issue of human rights. Indeed, this link is perceived by the authors of the revised treaty. Unlike the EAC Court of Justice and the SADC Tribunal, the ECOWAS Court of Justice is vested clearly in human rights jurisdiction.[18]

The Court of Justice is the principal judicial organ of ECOWAS. It generally examines any disputes arising out of the application and the interpretation of the Treaty, but may also be required to examine litigation arising out of human rights violations in the area covered by the Community. It is encouraging that since the establishment of the Court in 1991 and more particularly, since the granting of human rights jurisdiction to the Court in 2005, human rights cases have been the preponderance of the cases before the Court. Thus, as of 25th August 2010, out of twenty nine judgments delivered, fifteen were in respect of human rights.[19]

ECOWAS Court of Justice has gone far in removing barriers for human rights protection. It is in this context that in a number of cases the Community Court of Justice has adopted a simple approach in resolving the paradox of the exhaustion of local remedies, by repeatedly holding that the Supplementary Protocol does not require the exhaustion of local remedies and that the Court cannot read into it, a requirement that is not contained therein.[20] Among the many achievements of the ECOWAS Court of Justice's success in terms of human rights protection, the provisional entry into force of the ECOWAS Court of Justice Supplementary Protocol of 2005 is most inspiring.

Indeed, according to Article 11(1) of the Supplementary Protocol A/SP.1/01/05 Amending the Protocol A/P1/7/91 on the Community Court of Justice, this

---

17 *Katabazi and 21 Others v Secretary General of the East African Community and Another* (Ref. No. 1 of 2007).

18 Article 9 (4) of the Supplementary Protocol A/SP.1/01/05, Amending the Protocol A/P.1/7/91 Relating to the ECOWAS Court of Justice.

19 Interview with Me Tony ANENE MAIDOH, the ECOWAS Court Chief Registrar on 2nd March 2011.

20 Suit No. ECW/CCJ/APP/05/05; Ruling No. ECW/CCJ/RUL/04/07 (20/10/2007). Para. 6; Hadijatou Mani Koraou vs. The Republic of Niger, Judgment No.ECW/CCJ/JUD/06/08, Para. 5; Suit No. ECW/CCJ/APP/11/07; Ruling No. ECW/CCj/RUL/05/09 (30/06/2009) Para 48.

Supplementary Protocol entered into force provisionally upon signature by the Head of State and Government, which allowed the signatory member states and ECOWAS to start implementing its provisions. Paragraph 2 of the same protocol goes far in determining the number of nine ratifications as enough for the definitive entry into force. This activism dissociates from the common practice where ratifications of treaties are delayed by a small number of member states unwilling to be bound by the treaties.

SADC Tribunal

Human rights protection and promotion are not a central goal for SADC, but economy is. However, since human rights have a special role in economic development and this has an impact on investment climate, a need to include human rights was clear in the eyes of this REC. The preamble of the Treaty *inter alia* determines to ensure the progress and well-being of the people through guaranteeing democratic rights, observing human rights and the rule of law. This preambular part is reflected under chapter 3 of the Treaty whereby Article 4(c) requires the member states to act in accordance with principles of human rights, democracy and the rule of law. Apart from the Treaty itself, SADC has adopted different protocols which have, in one way or another, something to do with human rights.

The SADC Treaty under Article 9 establishes a Tribunal before which the rights laid in the Treaty and other instruments of the REC can be enforced. This Tribunal has been given a mandate under 16(1) of the Treaty to ensure adherence to and the proper interpretation of the provisions of this Treaty and subsidiary instruments as well as to adjudicate upon such disputes as may be referred to it. It is by virtue of this broad mandate that the SADC Tribunal rendered the famous *Campbell Case*[21] which was based on the compulsory acquisition of Zimbabwean white farmers' lands, of which the Tribunal found that the Zimbabwean government was in breach of the SADC Treaty obligations.

Compliance with the RECs' Courts Judgments

The success of regional integration is mostly dependent on the willingness of states to embrace, with a real sense of obligation, the core values of the African human rights system and the RECs' mechanisms of human rights protection. This is a two-dimensional obligation. First, it necessitates that states incorporate the provisions of the Banjul Charter into their own municipal law and ensure (through their own municipal courts) compliance with RECs' Courts judgments. Second, it necessitates that states accept and obey the judgments of the RECs' Courts notwithstanding apparent ideological conflict that may exist between their own jurisprudence and that of the RECs' Courts.

21 *Mike Campbell (PVT) Limited and Another V The Republic of Zimbabwe* SADC (T) 2/2007.

Any right or freedom is useful to its addressee or beneficiary, be it a community or an individual, only if it can be enforced. It does not serve any purpose to inform a person that he or she has a given right or freedom, if that person cannot enforce that right or freedom. It is therefore important that a clear articulation of various rights and freedoms be closely linked with and followed by a well-established mode of implementation or enforcement. Absence of such an enforcement mechanism reduces the right or freedom to pure nothingness (Peter 1995: 81).

In a number of cases existing in the African human rights jurisprudence, one finds that reparations ordered are not solely focused on the victims; they may be community-centred or benefit the society as a whole. Among many reparations that may be guaranteed to the victim such as those of a financial character, constitutional reform of provisions that do not comply with the State's freely assumed international human rights obligations, the clearance of the name of victims who have often been maligned by the State is of paramount importance. Thus symbolic acts, such as organizing a public ceremony in memory of victims or naming streets or schools after victims or creating memorials, are of commendable importance.

Talking of judgments' compliance in RECs, judicial activism found in both the EAC Court of Justice and SADC Tribunal is of paramount importance.[22] Indeed, judges in recognizing their lack of jurisdiction in adjudicating human rights refrained from abdicating the exercise of the jurisdiction interpretation. Accordingly, they based their findings on the violation of the principle of the rule of law instead of embarking on a direct determination whether the human rights of the applicants have been violated.

The political will found in ECOWAS when it comes to the execution of judgments is of a commendable character. In fact, despite the provision in the ECOWAS Treaty calling for the appointment of the national authority in each member state to deal with execution of the ECOWAS Court's decisions, the practice shows that such an authority is no longer needed.

More importantly, the attitude of the complainants *in Louis Karel Fick & Others v Republic of Zimbabwe* and the South African High Court in enforcing the SADC Tribunal's decisions is of an inspiring character.[23] Indeed, neighbouring countries are well placed to help in executing the RECs Courts' decisions since pariah States' properties of commercial nature can be attached upon the request of the complainants.

It goes without saying that enforcement of RECs' Court judgments encounters many difficulties, among which is the nature itself of international law and luck of political will, exacerbated by the political interference in the proper work of

22 See above, *Katabazi Case* and *Campbell Case.*

23 After the Zimbabwean Government ignored and refused to be bound by the SADC Tribunal's ruling, the applicants proceeded to make an application to the High Court of South Africa in order to register and enforce the Tribunal's main rulings in Campbell in terms of Article 32 (1) of the Protocol.

RECs' Courts and Tribunals. On this point, the speeding-up of the review of the SADC Tribunal's functions is much needed, as is the adoption of enforcement measures to address issues of non-compliance and the observance of international obligations in good faith.

The independence of judges of RECs' Courts being a cornerstone of the activities of the latter, the appointment process of ECOWAS judges[24] is recommendable for the other two RECs under study. In fact, considering the judges' mode of appointment in the EAC Court of Justice and SADC Tribunal, the risk of political interference remains strong. Appointing judges to such a supranational position should not ignore the intervention of the civil society in vetting candidates of potential judges.

Concluding Remarks

The successful enforcement of human rights in Africa will depend on the development of economic integration among states on the continent. Indeed, the international enforcement of human rights depends for its success on the existence of, among other factors, a web of trade relations between states which results in a threat whenever a pariah state contravenes with the community values, among which is the protection of human rights.

To have Courts' orders complied with depends on a number of issues which are to be introduced into the African RECs' mechanisms of human rights protection. Thus, follow-up measures on behalf of the REC Court or Tribunal to ensure each State's compliance with the Court's findings, either by reminding letters, promotional visits or visits for protective reasons, follow-up by the complainant to avoid *alibi* from pariah governments that they could not locate the victims to be compensated, system of governance allowing an independent judiciary, the rule of law, an active civil society and the involvement of the press. All these

24 According to Article 3 of the Supplementary Protocol A/SP.2/06/06, the ECOWAS Court of Justice is composed of seven independent judges selected from nationals of the Member States who are persons of high moral character and possess the qualification required in their respective countries for appointment to the highest judicial offices, or are jurisconsults of recognized competence in international law, particularly in areas of Community Law or Regional Integration Law. Furthermore, article 3, new Paragraph 2 requires candidates to the posts of Judge of the Community Court of Justice to have a total of no less than 20 years' professional experience, and no two members of the Court shall be nationals of the same member state. Article 3, new Paragraph 4 provides for a Judicial Council of the Community composed of the Chief Justices of Member States to which the posts have not been allocated, or their representatives; among other missions assigned to the Judicial Council is the selection of three candidates per country from among nationals of the countries to which the posts have been allocated, to interview the candidates and propose their appointments by the Authority of Heads of State and Government through the Council of Ministers, and last but not the least, to decide on the judges' disciplinary matters.

factors encourage States to comply with the Courts' orders with good faith to avoid international shaming process that would lead to negative publicity.

References

Magnarella, P.J. 2011. *Achieving Human Rights: The Challenges for the New Millenium*, [Online]. African Studies Quarterly, 4(2), Summer 2000. Available at http://www.africa.ufl.edu/asq/v4/v4i2a2.htm [Accessed on 4/10/2011].

Mkizungo, J. 2011. *The Role and Significance of the East African Court of Justice in the Promotion and Protection of Human Rights,* LL.M Dissertation Paper, Dar es Salaam: UDSM.

Peter, C.M. 1995. Enforcement of Fundamental Rights and Freedoms: The Case of Tanzania, *African Yearbook of International Law, Vol. 3*, The Hague/London/Boston: Martinus Nijhoff Publishers.

Seymour, V. 1997. Regional Economic Integration and Human Rights: SADC and South Africa, in *Democracy, human rights and economic development in South Africa*, edited by N. Steytler, Cape Town: Community Law Centre.

Sidaway, J.D. 2003. *Imagined Regional Communities: Integration and Sovereignty in the Global South*, 2nd edition, New York: Taylor & Francis.

Viljoen, F. 2007. *International Human Rights Law in Africa*, Oxford: Oxford University Press.

Viljoen, F. and Louw, L. 2007. African Commission on Human and Peoples' Rights, 1994-2004. *American Journal of International Law*, 101(1), January, 12-30. Heyns, C. and Viljoen, F. 1999. An overview of international protection of human rights in Africa. *South African Journal of Human Rights*, 15(3), 425-433.

Chapter 10

The Role of Regional Parliaments in Enhancing Democracy in the South

Andrea Cofelice and Stephen Kingah

Democracy is a fraught concept. It is understood differently in various parts of the world. Even when colloquially considered as people power as it is in the West, it tends, in certain cases, to produce results that may be regarded to be less appealing. And there is indeed a strong view that electoral democracy, especially in resource-rich developing countries, may actually be a recipe for instability particularly in countries where tribal lines are cast in stone and patronage is past time. But what we understand in this chapter as the minimum conditions for democracy (human rights, strong civil society and free elections) encapsulate what the solid majority of people in societies that aspire to democratic rule hope for.

The kind of democracy that has been embraced in many countries around the world is one that is contingent on the precept that decisions are taken in any polity based on the will of the majority of the people involved either as those who will shape or be affected by the decisions. The nature of our current societies today entails that to uphold such a democratic ideal, a system needs to be undergirded by a number of crucial elements including respect for human rights, especially those of the vulnerable, accommodation of an active civil society and the organization of free and fair elections.

The respect for human rights is a vital aspect of democracy. Previously, attention was often placed on civil and political rights or the first generation form of rights. Increasingly there are greater demands from the left that emphasis should also be on securing and protecting the second generation of rights or the economic, social and cultural rights. So governments are not only judged by the provision and respect for civil liberties, they are also expected to the best of their ability to provide for the welfare of the public with the available resources. Respect for human rights also entails that there should not be discrimination based on sexuality, gender, ethnic belonging or religion. In the current tough current economic situation, the danger that some of these precepts will be violated becomes very real. It is often said that the quality of a society can be determined by how it treats its weakest members. Such vulnerable sections of the public are often most exposed to the fallout of economic hardship and so vigilance in protecting them becomes very salient.

The existence of a vibrant civil society is also salient in fostering democracy. What matters here is that civil society and citizens are aware of the critical issues that affect their lives in the polis. A vibrant civil society is one that uses the tools of communication technology to engage leaders and other vital stakeholders in society. When regarded from a broad perspective, civil society involves non-state actors including faith-based organizations, cultural fraternities, professional groups, and grassroots organizations, amongst others. Increasingly in African circles, the Diaspora is regarded as an important part of civil society. But civil society as a term of art also poses some challenges. First, civil society entities tend to back specific interests which may not always be in sync with the broader goals of the majority. In many instances, civil society organizations can actually be used to serve parochial and insular goals. Second, it is not always clear that such entities have the wherewithal to appositely serve the broader interests of society.

The most patent indicator of the openness of a democratic system are free and fair elections that are used to make important choices such as legislative and executive leaders. Ensuring that the elections are free and fair has become an important preserve or attribute of many regional parliaments. Some of them are now adept at constituting small teams of elections, observers or monitoring groups. However important the electoral process, it must not hedge the point that the most important phase is actually after the electoral process is expunged.

A closer examination of all these precepts mirrors a biased element in favour of neo-liberal economic determinism behind popular choice. Neo-liberal traits such as economic liberalization; the preponderance of free markets; privatization and acute competition assumes that a society is driven by market pressures contingent on individual drive and choices. Yet this perspective cannot be challenge-proof. The current economic crisis affecting most parts of the world today indicates the limits of the current models of representative democracy that is undergirded by market economy. But what exactly are some of the flaws of representative democracy? The first is that representative democracy may not always be a true mode of reflecting the will of the common good or the majority. Current affairs are marked by examples of influence that is brought to bear on law makers and politicians through lobby groups that represent special interests rather than the wider good or welfare of society. Second, representative democracy is a mode of decision making that tends to focus more on electoral cycles rather than the crucial non-electoral phases of life that dominate the existence of people.

Third, it tends to be slow in responding to the challenges of our day. For instance, the US's democratic system is often hailed as admirable but the nature of the political machine in that country is such that gridlock in crucial decisions can either be facilitated by factors such as filibusters and political brinkmanship. This has meant that in vital areas, such as decisions to adopt revision of the debt ceiling; reform of healthcare; and the cutting of the budget deficit amongst others, what has marked the conversation has been complete stasis from the Congressional arm of government. In such scenarios, the system can be held hostage by a fringe of society (for instance, Tea Partiers) with very specific interests and power to shape electoral politics on which politicians tend to focus. So faced with monumental challenges, representative democracy can be a slow machine in contrast to benevolent autocracies where decisions tend to be prompt and implemented expeditiously as in China. This is not to extol autocratic systems and dictatorships. What counts is that leaders should have a benign common vision and a way to reach the same.

Fourth, representative democracy can also be expensive. Activities such as elections tend to serve as badges for true democracy. So actors, both internal and external, dedicate stupendous resources to ensure (or give the impression) that the elections were free and fair. Democracy soon becomes an exercise in the next electoral phase. This distorts the real concerns of the majority of the people. Finally, while important democratic elements such as respect for human rights are vital, one cannot discount the possibility that the respect of the rights of minorities in a democracy tend to be problematic.

That being said, and as Churchill once averred, democracy can be the worst system of government, with the caveat that it remains the best of the available alternatives. The problem is that modern-day democracy that is inter-linked with neo-liberal market principles and practices is often regarded in the South as prescriptions from the North. They are regarded to be artificial and not home-grown. They are perceived as too Western and detached from the concerns of the people. So the perception of democracy matters, and even more so when it is regarded as the product of the predilections of external players. Such a perception can be mitigated when demands for greater democratic reforms emanate not so much from external actors as from regional institutions including regional organs like the parliaments.

Section two presents regional parliaments in the current context of a strong global demand for people power marked of late by the occupying Wall Street Movement. It will also provide insights on the current literature on the role of regional parliaments in enhancing elements of democracy. A typology of the regional parliaments is also presented. Section three will consider each of the parliaments treated in terms of what they do in forging democracy in their member states.

Regional Parliaments: Theoretical Considerations, Context and Typology

The growing theoretical interest towards international parliamentary institutions (IPIs) and their potential contribution to the promotion of democratic processes, both at the national and international level, is strictly interconnected to the field of studies on globalization, global governance and what has been termed 'international democracy deficit'.

Since the 1990s, indeed, the question of the democratic legitimacy of the international system has been increasingly tackled by scholars and researchers of International Relations, who have started to question the value of even the most democratic institutions at the nation state level when so many important decisions respecting citizens' life are more and more taken beyond states' borders, mainly by international (either governmental or non-governmental) institutions that are not strictly subject to any democratic control or accountability (Beetham 2006). This issue is elucidated in the following paragraph from the United Nations Report 'We the Peoples: Civil Society, the United Nations and Global Governance – Report of the Panel of Eminent Persons on United Nations–Civil Society Relations' (Cardoso Panel 2004):

> Concerning democracy, a clear paradox is emerging: while the substance of politics is fast globalising (in the areas of trade, economics, environment, pandemics, terrorism, etc.), the process of politics is not; its principal institutions (elections, political parties and parliaments) remain firmly rooted at the national or local level. The weak influence of traditional democracy in matters of global governance is one reason why citizens in much of the world are urging greater democratic accountability of international organizations.

The awareness of an international democratic deficit was raised as a consequence of the progressive affirmation at the international level (especially by the United Nations and some prominent regional organizations) of the human rights law, involving a set of 'democratic rights', so that some scholars started to refer to democracy 'as a human right' (Franck 1992, Henkin and Hargrove 1994). The Universal Declaration of Human Rights, indeed, proclaims the right of all individuals to take part in government, to have equal access to public service, to vote and be elected, as well as the right to equality before the law, to freedom of opinion and expression, and to freedom of peaceful assembly and association. It further states that

> The will of the people shall be the basis of the authority of government; this shall be expressed in periodic and genuine elections which shall be by universal and equal suffrage and shall be held by secret vote or by equivalent free voting procedures (art. 21.3).

Moreover, Art. 28 of the Declaration projects the validity of these rights at the international level, too.[1] At the regional level, different organizations have attempted a variety of ways to obviate criticisms for allegedly democratic deficit. The most visible of this has been the creation and empowerment of regional parliamentary institutions. These attempts have been perceived by scholars as a response of national parliaments to the globalization process and the erosion of their power: in other words, 'they attempt to shift parliamentary control of governments of the international level' (Finizio, Levi and Vallinoto 2011: 3). As Rittberger puts it, de-parliamentarization at the domestic level and re-parliamentarization at the international or supranational level are insolubly linked:

1 Art. 28 states: 'Everyone is entitled to a social and *international order* in which the rights and freedoms set forth in this Declaration can be fully realized' (emphasis added).

> Where the procedural legitimacy of a democratic polity is challenged, political elites will feel compelled to press for compensatory mechanisms, either at the domestic or supranational level. In this sense, both processes mark the two sides of the same coin (Rittberger 2005: 199).

What does the regional parliaments' contribution to the strengthening of democracy consist of? The Universal Declaration on Democracy adopted by the Inter-Parliamentary Council in September 1997 recognizes that:

> Democracy is founded on the right of everyone to take part in the management of public affairs; it therefore requires the existence of representative institutions at all levels and, in particular, a Parliament in which all components of society are represented and which has the requisite powers and means to express the will of the people by legislating and overseeing government action.

David Held is probably amongst the first scholars who considered international parliaments as having the potential to establish themselves as a contributor to a more democratic and transparent global governance. In his model of cosmopolitan democracy, he envisages, among other tools,

> [T]he creation where feasible of regional parliaments and governance structures (for example, in Latin America and Africa) and the enhancement of the role of such bodies where they already exist (the European Union) in order that their decisions become recognized and accepted as legitimate independent sources of regional and international regulation (Held 1995: 272-273).

Several authors also emphasize their legitimating role of international organizations:

> Parliamentarians, as the directly elected representatives of their constituents, are for international organizations an essential link to international public opinion. Without such a link it has become extremely difficult to build recognition, understanding and support for international efforts […]. At the same time, by carrying the views and concerns of their constituents to the international arena, parliamentarians offer a direct channel for increasing the legitimacy, responsiveness and effectiveness of international organizations. Situated between citizens of States and the community of States, and by definition committed to dialogue, discussion and agreement, parliamentarians are a direct and motive force for democratization at the international level (Boutros-Ghali 1996: 36-37).

Similarly, Kissling affirms that international parliaments

> Provide moral legitimation for international decision-making by making it more transparent, accountable and participatory. They put public pressure on mighty governments, which is sometimes remarkable and has real political effects, regardless of any entitling legal rights. Moreover, as bodies composed of elected representatives that are accountable to their constituents, IPIs in principle make sure that the people are not ignored and that public participation is secured. At last, they bring the world closer to national decision-making, whereas they are, at the same time, better attuned to take decisions in favour of the common good, rather than being based solely on national interests (Kissling 2005: 52).

According to Stavridis and Ajenjo, one of the main roles of a regional assembly is to monitor the various agreements that are made within its corresponding international organization. In addition, they identify less traditional functions, as follows: a) parliamentary bodies as 'moral tribunes';[2] b) parliamentary input in election monitoring; c) the role of parliamentarians in the so-called 'socialization effect';[3] d) conflict resolution (Stavridis and Ajenjo 2010: 15).

However, international parliamentary institutions are not a panacea. Slaughter, for instance, argues that they are rather weak (2004: 128-129): they may have some success in certain areas (e.g. in addressing the 'democratic deficit' in trade organizations, or as catalysts for regional cooperation), but generally they 'exercise little official power and rarely find themselves in situations where they can use the mechanisms of soft power – information exchange, deliberation, persuasion – with much impact' (Slaughter 2004: 122). Kissling, moreover, admits that even if they may be endowed with extensive oversight and legislative powers, 'they generally lack continuity through their periodical elections and are sometimes hampered in their effectiveness through structures that favour tedious participatory procedures and debate'. He adds that general 'ignorance of their actions and importance is widespread and makes IPIs less relevant than they could be. And the overabundance of information and issues to be addressed overstretches the capacities of IPIs, just as is frequently the case with regard to other governmental, public or private institutions' (Kissling 2005: 52).

More generally, Finizio, Levi and Vallinoto recognize that 'a parliament represents only one side of democracy and, although it is a necessary one, it is not enough'. They further surmise that 'a working international democracy needs a government, a court, a constitutional charter, and all the elements that

2 International parliaments 'tend to bring a moral dimension to international politics that transcends narrow definitions of the national interest, particularly in their principled support for democracy and human rights' (Beetham 2006: 11).

3 'In the existing literature, the "socialization effect" is usually referred to a process that has taken place in situations where parliamentarians from democratic countries mix with their counterparts from undemocratic or partly democratic ones. Such institutional frameworks are supposed to socialize the non-democratic members over time in democratic practices' (Stavridis and Ajenjo 2010: 15).

constitute a democratic system: a gender democracy, a participatory democracy, a social democracy, an electoral democracy, cultural democracy, an information democracy and a cosmopolitan democracy' (2011: 4).

In summary, it is possible to identify the following domains where international and regional parliaments may give a substantial contribution to the promotion of democracy:[4] control of governments at the international level; legislation; representation of citizens and legitimization of international organizations and deliberation, including a declaratory and consultative role. The domains also include advocacy, in particular by lobbying governments and national legislatures to accede to international legal instruments; election monitoring; confidence building and socialization; conflict resolution; and finally training.

Before dealing with the specific topic of promotion of democracy, it is necessary to point out that the parliamentary institutions treated belong to three different categories (rather than levels) of IPIs. First, the group of assemblies composed of the PAP, EALA, ECOWAS Parliament, CEMAC Community Parliament and ACCP are *international parliamentary organs*, i.e. they are institutional branches of regional/sub-regional organizations, established through an intergovernmental agreement (either the same treaty as the international organizations they belong to, or a separate treaty), whose members may be appointed by national assemblies or directly elected to that office. The second category covers assemblies with loose institutional links to the main organization. For instance, the SADC Parliamentary Forum is an *international parliamentary organization affiliated to an intergovernmental organization*. This category is composed of independent parliamentary organizations, ruled by a formal founding act generally agreed upon by national parliaments (more rarely governments), whose members are national parliamentarians who act in their official capacity and have been designated as delegates by national legislatures. They meet on a regular basis, and the statute may provide for a formal structure (including permanent headquarters), giving members the right to periodically elect a governing body and a secretariat in order to ensure the continuity of the work. However, although formally independent, they have established working relationships with an intergovernmental organization. This affiliation must be approved by the intergovernmental organization's decision-making bodies through a formal act (decision, resolution, declaration etc.). Finally, the ACP-EU Joint Parliamentary Assembly is an *institutionalized inter-regional parliamentary assembly*, composed of parliamentarians from different regional parliaments and/or national legislative assemblies that meets on a regular basis

4 We share Malamud and Stavridis' opinion that 'a parliament is a multi-member institution that performs four main functions within a political system: representation, legislation, control of the executive, and leadership recruitment and socialization' (2011: 106). Accordingly, functions 'are neither exclusive to, nor characteristic of, parliamentary institutions. If regional parliaments are to be enhanced, the distinction between their constitutive and supplementary functions is worth acknowledging' (Malamud and Stavridis 2011: 106).

and has a formal structure (Co-Presidents and Vice Presidents, a Bureau, Standing Committees).

This typology matters because different categories of IPIs tend to display different functions and powers. For the purpose of this chapter, it is interesting to note that only international parliamentary organs, given their inclusion within intergovernmental systems and their continuous interaction with their governmental counterpart, will have more incentives and chances to acquire and expand a significant deal of legislative powers in addition to their declaratory role. In practice, however, only EALA and the CEMAC Community Parliament have some legislative functions. EALA is the legislative organ of the Community and, as such, is responsible for, among other things, approving budgets of the EAC, debating audit reports, performing an oversight function and initiating bills in the Assembly. Once a bill has been enacted by the Assembly and assented to by the Heads of State or Government, it becomes an act of the Community. On its part, the CEMAC Community Parliament may not only invite the Commission to develop or modify existing Community policies, or to initiate new ones, but must also be consulted in a list of issues, including the accession of new member states, negotiations of association agreements with third countries, the Community's budget, Community sector policies, the right to settle and the right of free movement of people, goods and services, the election modalities of the Parliament's members, and all the issues related to Community taxes and levies. Regarding new memberships, free movement rights and agreements with third countries, the Parliament's assent is even mandatory. PAP, ECOWAS Parliament and ACCP have only consultative and declaratory functions.

The Parliaments and Efforts to Forge Democracy

ACP-EU Joint Parliamentary Assembly (JPA)

The JPA has played an important declaratory function in the human rights field: through the work of *ad hoc co-rapporteurs* and Vice Presidents for human rights, it managed to adopt many reports and resolutions on several human rights-related aspects (such as on children's rights, 2003; the role of regional integration in the promotion of peace and security, 2005; small arms and light weapons and sustainable development, 2005; migration issues, 2006; freedom of association, 2007; right to food, 2009), which in some ways has had a considerable impact, contributing to the adoption by the Council of strategic guidelines that States are supposed to follow (as happened in 2003 with the guidelines on children in armed conflicts). It has regularly conducted fact-finding missions to assess human rights and humanitarian situations on the ground. These missions generally lead to the adoption of a report and a resolution urging States to adopt the necessary measures to address the most serious concerns. However, the Assembly, in some cases, has failed to adopt a unified stance due to sharp divisions between the

European Parliament (EP) and ACP delegations. This happened, for instance, in Nigeria, Togo and the Democratic Republic of Congo in 1997, Sudan in 1999, and in Zimbabwe in 2002. On certain occasions, the Assembly also acted as mediator in resolving conflicts peacefully and offered its full support to international and regional negotiators, as happened in Ethiopia and Eritrea between 1998 and 1999.

As for civil society, the Rules of Procedure clearly state that the Assembly's role shall consist of facilitating regular contacts and consultations between EU and ACP representatives and civil society actors.[5] Accordingly, on the one side it has repeatedly called for an increasing involvement of civil society in the taking of decisions and the management of EU-ACP cooperation as a key factor in guaranteeing a successful and sustainable development process, promoting regional and sub-regional meetings to consult with different non-state actors and fully involving them in regular monitoring work carried out by the Assembly's Committee on Economic Development, Finance and Trade with regard to the ACP-EU Economic Partnership Agreements. Also, the Assembly passed many resolutions calling for the protection and promotion of those rights that are particularly sensitive for civil society's activities, such as freedom of speech, information, and assembly, amongst others. In the area of elections, field missions have been conducted to enhance electoral transparency through election observation that has regularly been conducted in several ACP countries since the 1990s.

Pan-African Parliament

The African Union was created in 2002 following the adoption of its founding treaty or the Constitutive Act (CA) in 2000. It replaced the Organization of African Unity (OAU) that was regarded as an institution which had outlived its usefulness. One of the strictures that the OAU received was that it was a talking shop for the elites (Murithi 2008). So the creation of the AU and the incorporation of a Pan-African Parliament (PAP) was regarded as a welcome relief for those who were keen to see greater representation of the African people in the institutional architecture of any continental organization (Cilliers and Mashele 2004). The PAP is the foremost AU organ that seeks to reflect the demographic composition of African people as a whole (AU CA, Art 17). From its creation, the PAP has been endearing as an organ to many. During its inception, some states contested in a tough competition to host the PAP. These included Egypt, Libya and South

5 Art. 28 states: 'The Assembly shall take steps to ensure that the ACP States and the European Union have regular contacts and consultations with representatives of the ACP-EU economic and social partners and the other actors of civil society, in order to obtain their views on the attainment of the objectives of the Partnership Agreement. These representatives of civil society shall have the opportunity to attend regional and sub-regional meetings and standing committee meetings and take part in workshops. The Bureau will examine, in each case, the conditions under which invitations should be addressed to them'.

Africa. Thanks to the determined efforts and commitment of former South African President Thabo Mbeki and Frene Ginwala, South Africa was retained as the host nation. It remains a staunch backer of the organ (Mashele 2005). The institution itself started operations in 2004.

The modalities on its operations are included in the PAP Protocol to the Treaty of African Economic Community. The Protocol stipulates that the Parliament shall represent the people of Africa. It makes clear that its members will not be elected through universal suffrage but will serve as delegates from the national assemblies. This implies that the individual terms of members stop running once they are elected out of national office. While the cost-related reasons for this modality can be understood, such delegated representation is not a decent basis on which to solidify the institutional memory of the young organ. All the 230 representatives of PAP have a consultative role but the Protocol envisages an evolution of this role into a more legislative attribute.

In the area of human rights, the PAP has been very vocal in declaratory statements about the need for countries to adhere to their international obligations. In the violent events that unfolded in Kenya and Côte d'Ivoire following the declaration of elections in those countries, the PAP underscored the importance of the main protagonists to respect the rights of citizens, especially those of the most vulnerable including minorities, women and children.

The PAP has exposed a strong will and actually made outreach efforts to civil society organizations (CSOs). In a meeting held in Midrand in 2007, civil society organizations urged it to be more active in enhancing a strong continental governance agenda.[6] CSOs that are working closely with the PAP include IDASA and the Open Society Institute. Amongst the areas on which it has joined efforts with CSOs has been on the adoption and ratification of the AU Charter on Democracy. It teamed with CSOs and visited countries like Uganda, Chad and Zimbabwe to push for the AU Charter ratification. Both sides have also been active in the creation of an African Youth Parliament. This being said, the PAP's engagement with CSOs and outreach to African people is hamstrung by a lack of adequate resources to support inclusive initiatives.

With respect to free and fair elections, the PAP has been active in electoral monitoring. It has monitored elections in Kenya, Zimbabwe, Angola, Swaziland, Ghana and Namibia and its impact on these have been well reported and are duly respected. That said, it has also been tainted in its efforts with mediocre results recorded in its efforts in missions like those in Sudan, Mauritius, Burundi, Guinea and Ethiopia which have been marked by problems of cooperation with the AU Commission. For instance, in the case of Ethiopia its members reported that they

6 Submission from Civil Society Organisations to the Pan-African Parliament on the Proposal for Continental Government, 14 May 2007, Gallagher Estate, Midrand, South Africa.

were treated with contempt by AU Commission staff.[7] During the Ethiopian mission, the PAP members were sent to the most remote areas with little logistical, transport and translating support. These experiences have pushed some PAP members to propose separate future electoral missions that will be completely independent of those of the AU Commission.[8] Craving greater independence in this regard is further fuelled by the fact that post-electoral reports of the PAP have to be endorsed by the AU Commission before they are sent to the Assembly of heads of state and government.

Many problems still affect the general performance of the PAP. First and foremost is the fact that its members are still highly dependent on the whims and caprices of the political masters in their various capitals and few leaders in these countries take the parliaments seriously. In many countries, parliaments simply rubber stamp government initiatives given that the parties of the presidents are often dominant in the national parliaments. This weakness inevitably has fallout at the PAP level. Second, PAP is afflicted by the problems of inadequate financial and human resources (Interview: Dahab 21 February 2011). Such problems are not helped by the fact that many African countries also belong to many regional entities which also have their own parliaments. All these mean a drag on scarce resources in a time of great economic stress. What is more, PAP has been very invisible to many African citizens and the organ has not been amply aggressive in exposing the merits of its actions to a wider audience beyond the tribe of African elites.

Assembly of Caribbean Community Parliamentarians (ACCP)

The ACCP had a very short life to produce something relevant on human rights, free elections and civil society. Inaugurated in 1996, it held only two sessions in 1999 and 2000, and since 2002 it has virtually ceased to function. During its inaugural meeting, a motion was discussed to consider a proposal for Caribbean Non-Governmental Organizations to be granted observer status in the ACCP. An attempt to reinvigorate the Assembly has been carried out by a Technical Sub-Group on the ACCP, established in 2003 to follow up on the decisions adopted by

---

7 See interventions of Hob Mbutoh Njingum, Second Legislature, Third Session, Debates of the Pan-African Parliament, 11 October 2010, at p. 4.

8 The opinions of members like Hon Rachid have been strong: 'Members of Parliament are the cream of society; they represent the people of Africa, they are the pulse of our democracy, they are people whom we have to uphold, to show respect and reverence for, in terms of building a democratic transition in Africa. So, if they go out there, using economy tickets and flying in the economy, going without the needed facilities and materials to work with, it is an indictment on the very foundation and principle of PAP and our strive to democratize Africa. I want to say that we need, without any option to relook at this and to rethink and ask ourselves whether we need it or not. If we do not need it, we do not go for it, if we go for it because we need it, we have to ensure that we fully sponsor it, and that Members are comfortable when they go out there to observe'.

the CARICOM Heads of Government at their 24th meeting held in Montego Bay. It is interesting to note that, in recognition of some weaknesses in the functioning of the Assembly, it was proposed that support should be sought for the establishment of an ACCP Research Centre in order to develop an appropriate research capability in respect of issues such as governance, human rights, parliamentary practice, and regional integration as well as overall development. However, no political and institutional steps followed after this report was adopted in October 2003.

ECOWAS Parliament

In the area of human rights, the ECOWAS Parliament has to be consulted prior to the adoption of important decisions on the matter.[9] The organization, like the PAP, has created a human rights committee within the parliament of the region. ECOWAS Parliament adopted policy strategies on child trafficking and child soldiers (2001), gender equality (2010), parliamentary oversight of the security sector (2011), and in the near future it will work on a 'Policy plan of action and draft Humanitarian Response mechanism' and ECOWAS Emergency fund for the region responding to crisis situations, as well as on drug abuse.

ECOWAS has developed an institutional *modus operandi* for dealing with CSOs. It has an elaborate framework in dealing with non-state actors. In Articles 81 and 82 of the revised treaty, the Community not only commits to cooperating with non-governmental and socio-economic organizations, but in both instances, also commits to setting up mechanisms for consultation[10] with organizations such as the West African Civil Society Forum (WACSOF). Details about such consultations are articulated in a separate ECOWAS decision which introduces regulations for granting observer status to non-governmental organizations to participate in the Community's institutions. Under the decision, organizations are divided into two categories (A or B) depending on their level of interest in ECOWAS activities. An organization qualifies for an 'A' designation if it (1) has a basic interest in the activities of the Community; (2) is closely linked with the social and economic life of the area which it represents; and (3) has made sustained contributions towards the attainment of Community aims and objectives. In comparison, 'B' certifications are given to organizations which only have a general interest in the activities of the Community.

The difference between the two designations is essentially that 'A' observers have privileged access to the ECOWAS Council of Ministers whereas 'B' observers are only accredited for institutions other than the Authority and the Council. Having the privileged 'A' observer status entitles an organization to: i) send observers to all public meetings of the Council; ii) be invited by the Council

9 ECOWAS Protocol relating to the Parliament, art. 6.2.

10 ECOWAS Decision A/DEC.9/8/94 Establishing Regulations for the Granting to Non-Governmental Organizations (NGOs) the Status of Observer within the Institutions of the Economic Community of West African States (1994).

to make oral presentations; iii) dispatch documents to Members of the Council; iv) be invited to collaborate with any Committee as may be established by the Council; v) submit questions or views for insertion in provisional Council agendas for all meetings except those of the Authority; and vi) consult with the Executive Secretariat on matters of mutual concern.[11]

Election observation (and election assistance) also represents an important aspect of its activity for the ECOWAS Parliament. Examples of the missions hitherto conducted include those in Togo (2005), Sierra Leone (2007), and Liberia (2011). However, these missions have been sometimes criticized, especially for their gaps in the observation methodology, conflicts of interest, inexperience and the absence of coordination with other electoral players (Bittiger 2005).

The East African Legislative Assembly

The EALA is the parliamentary arm of the East African Community (EAC). The EAC itself has strong historical roots as it was the erstwhile British East African Federation. It was active in the 1960s as the East African Federation and then the Community. But in the late 1970s, it closed shop largely due to the shenanigans of Idi Amin. Unlike any of the other IPIs, EALA has the power and mandate to adopt legislative bills that are then applicable in the member states.

Since its launching in 2001, the EALA has not adopted many bills on human rights but this has been changing. The first mark of change was the adoption of the *East African Parliamentary Institute Bill (EAPI) 2011*. The object is to establish an institute to provide training on parliamentary procedures and practices, and to promote recognition and respect for democracy in the EAC region and beyond. The second has been the elaboration of the *East African Community Human and Peoples' Right Bill 2011*.[12] It seeks to establish a regime to give effect to clauses of EAC human and peoples' rights in accordance with the provisions of the African Charter on Human and Peoples Rights. Advocates of the text hope the bill will foster the process of deepening and widening of integration by guaranteeing human and peoples' rights in the social, economic and political spheres. What is more, the EALA has shown resolve in dealing with these topics under its declaratory and consultative role. Since 2001 it has adopted, *inter alia*, the following resolutions for implementation by the Council of Ministers: a resolution seeking the appointment of an East African Peace Committee for Uganda with the mandate to bring to an end the violence in Northern Uganda in May 2003; a resolution urging EAC Partner States to ratify the United Nations Convention on the Rights of Persons

11 Courtesy, comments from GIZ's ECOWAS Technical Advisor, Monika Pottgiesser (August 2009).

12 The Bill covers six categories: Dignity rights (torture and privacy etc); Freedom (conscience, assembly and association etc); Equality; Social rights; Citizen rights (freedom of movement etc); Justice/guarantee rights (refer to power of the states not to harm the individual).

with Disabilities; a resolution urging the partner States to develop a joint policy to protect the environment; a motion urging the EAC Heads of State Summit, through the Council of Ministers, to review Economic Partnership Agreement Negotiation (EPAs); a resolution urging EAC Partner States to take action against the practice of Female Genital Mutilation/Cutting (FGM/C) for non-medical reasons; and a resolution urging peaceful solution of the Conflict in Migingo Island.

In terms of its ties with CSOs, efforts have also been made of late to enhance cooperation. The EALA organizes Public Hearing workshops to consult civil society organizations on issues related to the implementation of the policies and activities outlined in the Protocol/Treaty for the Establishment of the EAC. Since 2006, this process has been enhanced by the establishment of the *East African Civil Society Organizations Forum* that brings together many organizations of the region: EALA's representatives regularly participate in the annual civil society's forum in order to exchange views on the process of East African integration. Many thematic roundtables have also been organized over the years. EALA and NGOs agreed to collaborate for the betterment of human rights standards in the region, including information dissemination, scale-up of promotion and protection of human rights, enhanced monitoring and linking up with citizens to share best practices. However, the goal of a formal seat at the EAC's table remains a priority for the Forum.

Finally, the Treaty for the Establishment of the East African Community (1999) provides, amongst others, that the EAC Partner States shall cooperate in a broad range of identified areas, including cooperation in political matters (which encompasses election observation). In pursuit of this objective, EALA representatives led EAC observer missions to several member and non-member countries including Zanzibar (2005), Tanzania (2005), Kenya (Referendum, 2005), Uganda (2006), Kenya (2007), Zimbabwe (2008), Rwanda (2008), Kenya (Referendum, 2010), Burundi (2010) and Sudan (Referendum, 2011).

CEMAC Parliament

CEMAC rules also demand that the regional parliament be consulted before decisions and measures are adopted that have fallout on human rights.[13] The document that gives birth to the assembly stipulates clearly that it will be a promoter of human rights. The main text that gives birth to the CEMAC Parliament makes clear that the organ has a representative role and the organ is peculiar in this regard because the members represent CEMAC population as a whole. In addition, the parliament also has the attribute of oversight and control. In terms of this latter duty, the parliament can call on the Commission to respond to specific questions and it can also mandate commissions of inquiry on specific issues. Finally, the organ has the attributes of an advisory body but with very limited law-making powers even if it has powers to issue directives on certain areas of concern.

13 CEMAC Parliament's Convention, art. 25.

SADC Parliamentary Forum (SADC PF)

The SADC PF has also developed a strong critical mass in recent years in the field of democracy promotion. Its involvement in human rights issues has been unique. In the area of human rights, the PF has been active in fostering the efforts of a right to health and has engaged the public on dealing with the problem of AIDS. It has also been very active in advocating better protections of the rights of women. In its activities, it has developed strong bonds with CSOs working in various areas including health and education. Moreover, through its election observation programme it has monitored, and often criticized, several elections since 1999. Its 2001 *Norms and Standards for Elections* is widely considered a very important and comprehensive policy instrument for promoting good governance in the region.

Conclusions

Democracy cannot be by fiat. It is never a done deal but a constant process of negotiation to arrive at a decision that will reflect the interest of the commonweal. Arriving at a consensus may entail a chaotic ride. But the most important point is that the project and process should be owned by the people who will be most affected by the outcome of the process. In this sense, therefore, one has to be realistic in terms of the expectations from regional parliaments to enhance democracy. Care is warranted in any effort to extrapolate EU Parliamentary experiences to other regions dominated by young nations which cherish their sovereignty. That said, the role that regional parliaments play in the area of democracy promotion is interesting to study because in as much as the regional parliaments may be regarded as external actors to the state, they are composed by the same states. Put simply, they have an important role to play in enhancing democracy from inside and from outside. Yet their mandate is often constricted, narrow and limited. In the area of human rights, all the assemblies are making efforts to make their positions clear through declarations. The PAP, ECOWAS and the ACP-EU JPA have committees that deal mainly with human rights matters and this is to be encouraged. But in this area, regional parliaments are often bereft of any clout to reverse perverse flows of events, be these in the realm of human rights violations in Zimbabwe or flawed elections in Burkina Faso and Togo, amongst others. In the area of engagement with CSOs, they are now making strides to forge outreach to such groups with PAP and ECOWAS parliaments embedding regional institutions with links to CSOs. This is an encouraging development to the extent that the CSOs are not co-opted by the public institutions for more parochial ends. But one should also be guarded against the possibility of CSOs that in turn can use narrow agendas and insular motives to divert the hijack public office. Finally, in terms of elections, this is also an area where critical mass is being developed in many regional parliaments with the PAP taking the lead, constraints notwithstanding.

References

African Union. 1991. Treaty Establishing the African Economic Community, (AEC Treaty 1991), 3 June 1991.

African Union. 2001. Protocol to the Treaty Establishing the African Economic Community Relating to the Pan African Parliament, (PAP Protocol 2001), 2 March 2001.

Beetham, D. 2006. *Parliament and Democracy in the Twenty-first Century.* Geneva: Inter-Parliamentary Union.

Bittiger, T. 2005. *Election Observation in West Africa: The ECOWAS Experience.* Available at http://aceproject.org/today/feature-articles/election-observation-in-west-africa-the-ecowas-experience [Accessed 2 October 2012].

Boutros-Ghali, B. 1996. *An Agenda for Democratization.* New York: United Nations Dept. of Public Information.

Cilliers, J. and Mashele, P. 2004. The Pan African Parliament: A Plenary of Parliamentarians. *African Security Review* [Online], 13(4). Available at: www.iss.co.za/pubs/asr/13no4/ECilliers.htm [Accessed 2 October 2012].

Civil Society Organisations to the Pan African Parliament on the Proposal for Continental Government, 14 May 2007, Gallagher Estate, Midrand, South Africa.

Dahab, K. 2011. Interview: Director of Communications, Pan African Parliament, (15.00-15.30, 21 February 2011), Midrand, South Africa.

The Economist. 2011. The African Union: Short of cash and teeth. *The Economist*, 29 January.

Finizio, G., Levi L. and Vallinoto N. (eds.) 2011. *First International Democracy Report 2011.* Torino: Centre for Studies on Federalism.

Franck, T.M. 1992. The Emerging Right to Democratic Governance. *The American Journal of International Law*, 86(1), 46-91.

Held, D. 1995. *Democracy and the Global Order: From the Modern State to Cosmopolitan Governance*, Cambridge: Polity Press.

Henkin, L. and Hargrove J.L. (eds.) 1994. *Human Rights: an Agenda for the Next Century*, Washington DC: American Society of International Law.

Kissling, C. 2011. *The Legal and Political Status of International Parliamentary Institutions*, Berlin: Committee for a Democratic U.N.

Mashele, P. 2005. The 3rd Pan-African Parliament Session: Utility or Futility? *African Security Review* [Online], 14(2), Available at: www.iss.co.za/pubs/asr/14no2/CMashele.htm [Accessed 2 October 2012].

Murithi, T. 2008. The African Union's Evolving Role in Peace Operations: The African Union Mission in Burundi, the African Union Mission in Sudan and the African Union Mission in Somalia. *African Security Review* [Online], 17(1), Available at: www.iss.co.za/uploads/17NO1MURITHI.PDF [Accessed 2 October 2012].

Rittberger, B. 2005. *Building Europe's Parliament: Democratic Representation Beyond the Nation State.* Oxford: Oxford University Press.

Slaughter, A.M. 2004. *A New World Order.* Princeton: Princeton University Press.
Stavridis, S. and Ajenjo, N. 2010. EU-Latin American Parliamentary Relations: some Preliminary Comments on the EUROLAT, *Jean Monnet/Robert Schuman Paper Series*, 10(3).

Chapter 11

Regional Economic Integration in Africa: Impediments to Progress?[1]

Rodrigo Tavares and Vanessa T. Tang

Pan-Africanism, or the idea of a united Africa, was a direct response to European slavery and colonialism (Londsdale 1968, M'bayo 2004, Muchie 2003, Landsberg 2004, and Murithi 2005). At the beginning of the twentieth century, the voices of Peter Esedeke, W.E.B. Du Bois, George Padmore and Léopold Senghor spearheaded political campaigns against the destructive legacies of the Berlin Conference (1884-1885) and triggered the belief that Africans, whether born on the continent or abroad, should be unified as part of a global African community.

Since the early years of independence, the goal of creating a single African economic community has been one of the most enduring priorities of many African leaders and also a rallying call for Africans. Economic regionalism or regional economic integration was seen as a means to overcome the structural disadvantages of many African countries in terms of small economic size, fragmentation of national markets and in view of the disillusionment with the international economy and political system, both perceived as unfavourable to developing nations (Oyejide *et al.* 1997).

The creation of the Organization of African Unity (OAU) in 1963 warranted initial hopes that the continent was set for integration. However, pushed by countries such as Ethiopia, Nigeria and Liberia (the so-called 'Monrovia group'), the OAU from the beginning advocated an idea of unity that was intent on retaining the colonial demarcations of the new independent states and envisaged the formation of an 'alliance' of African states rather than a 'United States of Africa' (Makinda and Okumu 2008: 28 and Tavares 2010: 21). To reinforce the prevailing vision, the charter of the OAU specifically called for the respect of national borders and non-interference in the domestic affairs of its members.

Although political expectations ran low, the economic potential of integration was perceived as great. Hence, since the early 1960s, the United Nations Economic Commission for Africa (UNECA) has encouraged African states to combine their economies into sub-regional markets, or Regional Economic Communities (RECs), which would ultimately form one Africa-wide economic union (FAO 2003). These aspirations were followed by the OAU, which sponsored various

1 This chapter is a revised and updated version of a paper published in the South African Journal of International Affairs, 18(2): 217-233, October 2011.

resolutions and declarations – namely in Algiers in September 1968, in Addis Ababa in August 1970 and May 1973, and in Kinshasa in December 1976 – that identified the need for the economic integration of the continent as a pre-requisite for the realization of the objectives of the Organization.[2] As we shall see in this chapter, in the decades that followed the drive and efforts of the OAU and the African Union (AU) led to the adoption of several treaties and programmes that aimed at fostering regional integration. However, achieving that goal has proved difficult and slow, mostly due to Africa's many daunting challenges, including the lack of economic diversification, inadequate financial resources, macroeconomic instability, poor governance, conflicts and war, the high incidence of HIV/AIDS, and the existence of numerous and overlapping sub-regional organizations (UNECA 2010: 7).

There are numerous organizations in Africa, and a significant number of African states have opted to simultaneously belong to two or three integration arrangements. As acknowledged by the UNECA and the AU, 'overlapping mandates, objectives, protocols, and functions create unhealthy multiplication and duplication of efforts and misuse the continent's scarce resources – making regional economic communities very inefficient' (UNECA 2006: 110).

This chapter assesses this conundrum and is structured as follows. Discussion first views Africa within the world economy and considers some constraints to economic development and trade before tracing the historical formation of the African RECs. The chapter then evaluates major impediments to an effective continent-wide economic integration before considering a retrospective look and possible scenarios for the future.

Africa in the Global Economy

Africa has the lowest share of world trade of any region, at only 3.2% in 2011. Africa's share of developing regions trade in merchandise, for instance, has fallen from 6% in 1980 (its highest level in five decades) to 3% in 2011 (see Figure 11.1). By these measures, Africa is underperforming in terms of exports.

Much of African trade, through 2011, has been driven by exports from the Southern African countries and more specifically the Southern African Development Community (SADC) group of countries (as illustrated in Figure 11.2). Whether this will change as China and other emerging economies explore trading relationships with African nations across the continent remains to be seen.

African RECs' share of world exports is also very low and fluctuates around less than 1.1%. The low trends in Africa's exports performance are partly attributed to the degree of 'protectionism that is by no means confined to the

2 In addition, at its 27th Ordinary Session in 1976, the OAU Council of Ministers by paragraph 2(a) of its Resolution CM/Res. 464(XXVI) also decided that 'there shall be five regions of the OAU, namely, Northern, Western, Central, Eastern and Southern.'

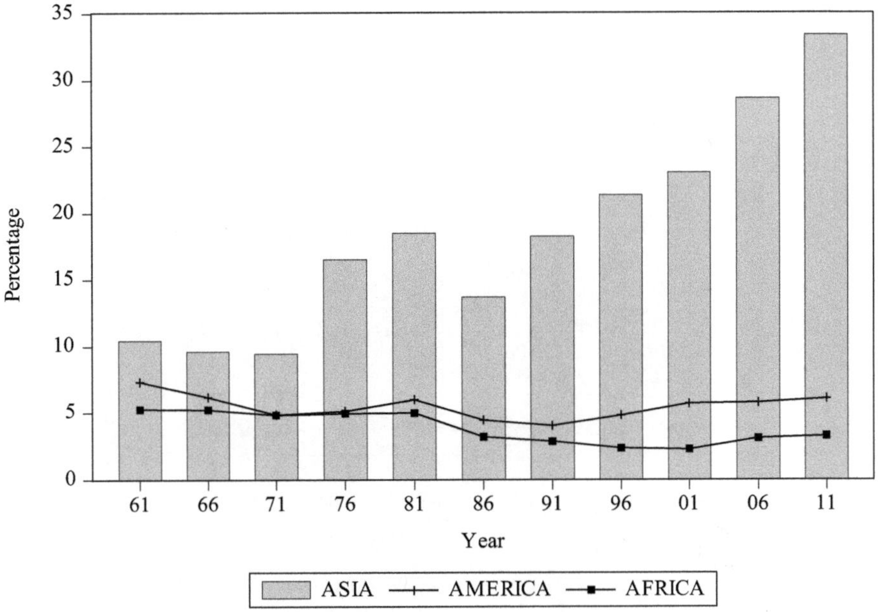

Figure 11.1 Shares of Developing Regions in World Merchandise Exports, 1961-2011

Source: Authors' compilation based on UNCTAD (United Nations Conference on Trade and Development), United Nations Conference on Trade and Development handbook of statistics Database, database, 2012

developed world, and encompasses, among other things, "buy local", government stimulus packages, tariff increases and increased resort to trade remedies' (Draper 2010: 5). As a result, African countries are 'compelled to pursue bilateral and regional trade agreements even though their economic benefits remain a matter of contention' (Holden and Tang 2010:12). Bilateral and regional trade arrangements have therefore, not surprisingly, been concluded with diverse and geographically distant partners.

Southern African Custom Union (SACU) members, for instance, are party to a free trade agreement (FTA) with the European Free Trade Association (EFTA) as well as a preferential trade agreement (PTA) with the Southern Cone of the Americas (the Common Market of the South – MERCOSUR). The December 2010 entry of South Africa to the Brazil, Russia, India and China (BRIC) group, which is reportedly including in its discussion the goal of 'strengthening economic and trade cooperation among members' (Badasi 2011), illustrates this competitive trend within African regionalism.

Intra-continental trade in Africa as a share of total foreign trade has consequently been low compared to other regions (UNCTAD 2009). The exception is SADC,

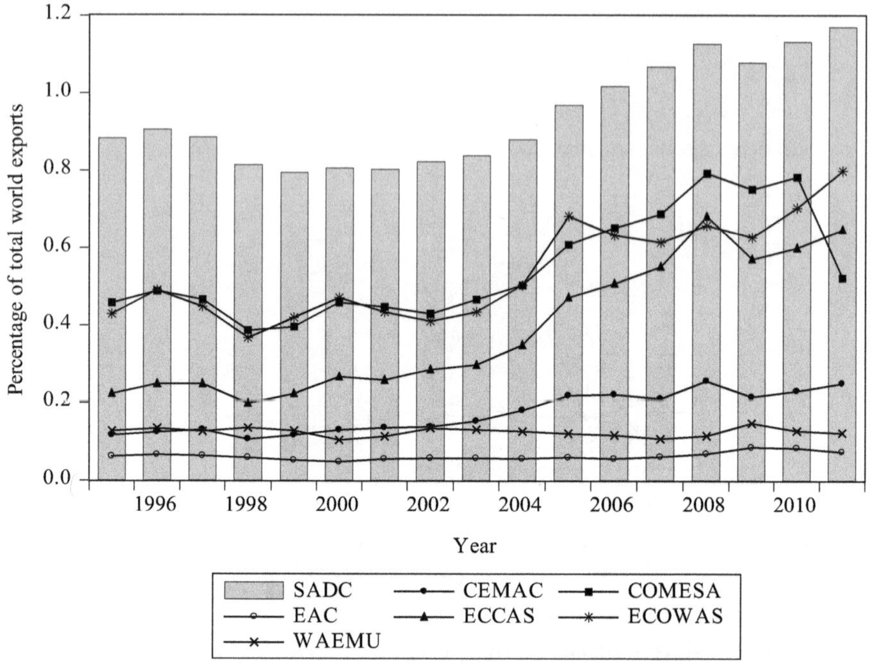

Figure 11.2 Share of African RECs' Merchandise World Exports, 1995-2011
Source: Authors' compilation based on UNCTAD (United Nations Conference on Trade and Development), United Nations Conference on Trade and Development handbook of statistics Database, database, 2012

the lead regional player in trade, whose exports by value are mostly destined for countries in its own geographical group (see Figure 11.3).

According to the UN Conference on Trade and Development (UNCTAD), intra-African trade is low mostly due to 'the lack of product complementarities among members' (UNCTAD 2010:11). Africa's relatively low level of trading can also be attributed to its low productivity (Sachs *et al.* 2004) and its inability to diversify its exports. It is argued here that for RECs in Africa to be truly effective in increasing trade, they should increase their efforts to diversify their exports. Taking a look at the African RECs Herfindahl-Hirschman index[3] by 2011, the Economic Community of Central African States (ECCAS) group is the least diversified followed by the Central African Economic and Monetary Community (CEMAC),

3 The Herfindahl-Hirschman index (H2) is a measure of the degree of market concentration and can be expressed as where S_i represents the share of the market of the ith firm, and N denotes the number of commodities exported. A H2-index value closer to 1 indicates a concentrated market (less diversified). On the contrary, a H2-index value closer to 0 shows a lesser concentrated market (more diversified).

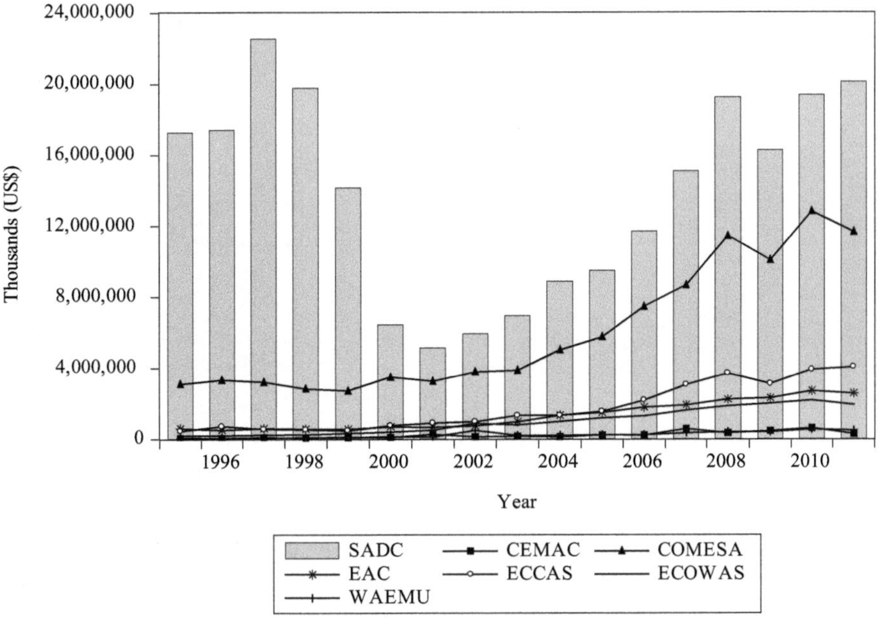

Figure 11.3 Shares of SADC Merchandise Value of Exports, 1995-2011 (US$)

Source: Authors' compilation based on UNCTAD (United Nations Conference on Trade and Development), United Nations Conference on Trade and Development handbook of statistics Database, database, 2012

Economic Community of West African States (ECOWAS), Southern African Development Community (SADC), Common Market for Eastern and Southern Africa (COMESA), West African Economic and Monetary Union (WAEMU) and the East African Community (EAC) (see Figure 11.4). Diversification efforts have been relatively weakest among the Central African States.

Additionally, the high cost of trading in the region has been highlighted (UNCTAD 2003: 8) as one of the major deterrents of trade with African countries. In addition, Africa's high prevalence of a wide range of contagious diseases including HIV and AIDS, malaria and tuberculosis has been a constant strain in Africa's economic development, affecting directly both productivity and mobility of people (Krueger 1997). The Sub-Saharan African region is known for the highest incidence of HIV/AIDS in the world, accounting for over two thirds of the global total. Figure 11.5 shows the prevalence of HIV/AIDS infection in Sub-Saharan Africa within the most active working age population group (15 to 49 years).

Since 1990, the annual percentage from among the total population of Sub-Saharan Africa who are living with HIV/AIDS has more than doubled, from around

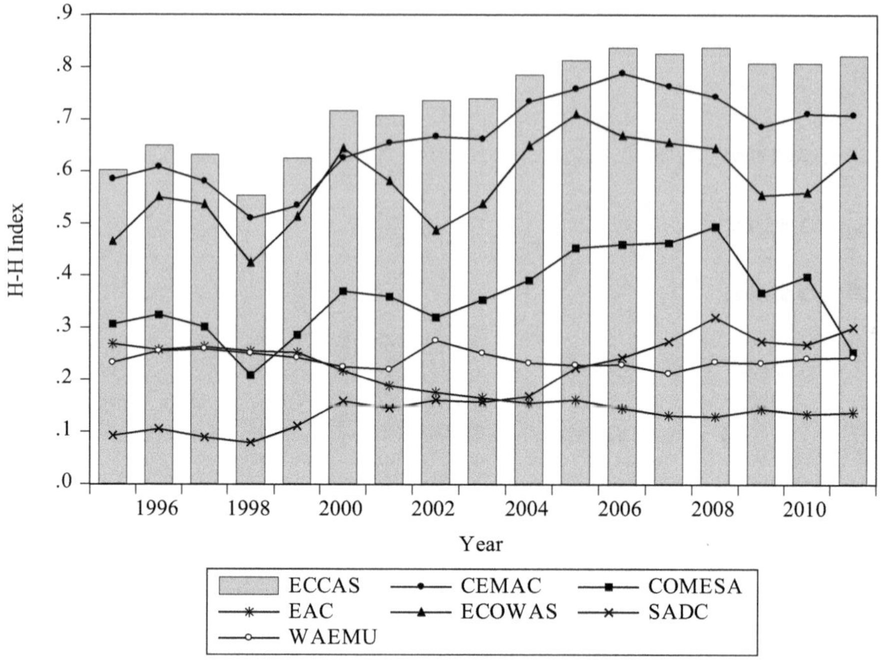

Figure 11.4 Concentration Index of Exports, 1995-2011

Source: Authors' compilation based on UNCTAD (United Nations Conference on Trade and Development), United Nations Conference on Trade and Development handbook of statistics Database, database, 2012

2% in 1990 to 5% in 2007. Since the beginning of this century, the prevalence of HIV/AIDS has been slowly declining, most likely due to the beneficial effects of antiretroviral therapy. Demographers are predicting a hike in life expectancy in Africa, subject to continued efforts in combating not just HIV/AIDS but also other diseases, including early childhood infectious diseases.[4] The commensurate savings in human lives, as well as a turn around on health care costs and the detriment to the labour force, are almost incalculable in terms of their impact on economic growth.[5]

4 See the Atlas on Regional Integration trends and recommendations on communicable diseases (OECD 2007).

5 See Oldstone, Michael B A, *Viruses, Plagues & History* for further discussion of the effects of illness, including HIV/AIDS, on global migration, economic development, and social cohesion.

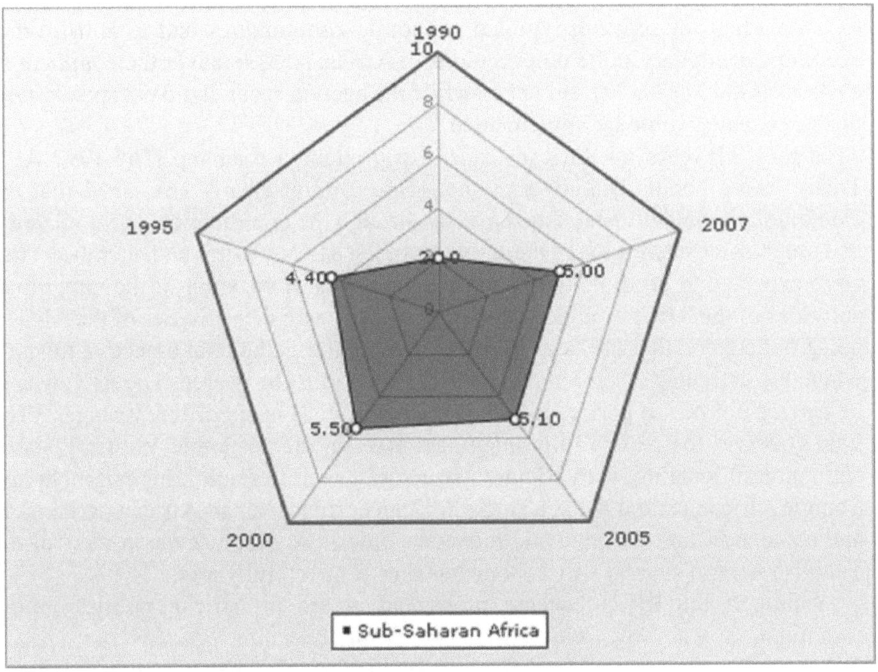

Figure 11.5 Prevalence of HIV/AIDS in Sub-Saharan Africa, 1990-2007 (Percentage of population aged 15-49)

Source: Authors' compilation based on UNCTAD (United Nations Conference on Trade and Development), United Nations Conference on Trade and Development handbook of statistics Database, database, 2010

A Brief History of RECs in Africa

The RECs are intergovernmental organizations set up by groups of countries to foster stronger economic ties and cooperation. The stated goal of UNECA was that, in Africa, these would eventually lead to the creation of one African Economic Community (AEC). Although regional economic pacts started to emerge in the 1960s (the OAU in 1963 and the Economic and Customs Union of Central Africa in 1964), the conscious decision to strengthen the RECs was only set in motion with the adoption in 1980 of the *Lagos Plan of Action* (LPA) and the *Final Act of Lagos* (FAL), two continental initiatives that made provisions for the future establishment of the AEC by the year 2000, 'so as to ensure the economic, social and cultural integration of [the] continent'.[6] The Plan committed member states

6 After the LPA and FAL, several other resolution have also instructed African leaders to strengthen the REC, namely: (i) Resolution CM/Res.1043 (XLIV) of the 44th Ordinary Session of the Council of Ministers (1986), requested in paragraph 7 'the OAU

to 'strengthen the existing regional economic communities and establish other economic groupings in the other regions of Africa, so as to cover the continent as a whole' (OAU 1980: 99). However, while the agenda is out, it did not specify how the agreements would be implemented.

It took 11 years for African leaders to produce a roadmap. The 1991 AEC Treaty (more popularly known as the *Abuja Treaty*) clearly envisaged that the Community would be established mainly through the coordination, harmonization and progressive integration of the activities of the RECs.[7] To this end, member states were expected to promote the coordination and harmonization of the integration activities of the RECs of which they are members with the activities of the AEC, it being understood that the establishment of the latter is the final objective towards which the activities of existing and future RECs must be geared. The AEC was to be carried out over a period of 34 years (1994-2028) in six different stages.[8] The final goal was to create a fully integrated area (in the economic, political, social and cultural domains) with common structures, facilities and function, including a single African central bank, a single African currency, a pan-African parliament, and a pan-African economic and monetary union.[9] Arguably, even in view of the establishment of several RECs, none has thus far been fully met.

Although the RECs became prominent actors in African politics in the meantime, it was only with the *Protocol on Relations between the African Economic Community and the RECs*, signed in 1998, that they were clearly named and identified. The signatories of the document were ECOWAS, COMESA, SADC, and the Intergovernmental Authority on Development (IGAD). The ECCAS, the East African Community (EAC), and the Community of Sahel-Saharan States (CEN-SAD) signed the protocol later, in contrast to the Arab Maghreb Union (AMU) which opted out due to the objections by one of its members (Morocco).

Secretary General, to examine the practical and operational modalities for coordinating and harmonizing the activities and programs of existing sub-regional economic groupings'; and (ii) The Heads of State and Government, in paragraph 7 of Resolution AHG/Res.161 (XXIII) adopted at the 23rd Ordinary Session in 1987, requested the 'Secretary General of the OAU, the Executive Secretary of the ECA, and the authorities of sub-regional and regional economic groupings, particularly ECOWAS, PTA, SADCC and ECCAS to take the necessary steps to ensure coordination, harmonization and rationalization of activities, projects and programs of all the African inter-governmental cooperation and integration organizations in their respective regions in order to avert overlaps, power conflicts and wastage of efforts and resources'.

7 See Chapter IV, article 28 on 'Strengthening of Regional Economic Communities'.

8 The six stages envisage: (i) Full continental coverage of the existing active pillars; (ii) strengthening of intra-REC integration and inter-REC harmonization; (iii) establishing free trade areas and customs unions in each existing REC; (iv) establishing a continent-wide customs union; (v) establishing a continent-wide common market and (vi) establishing a full economic and monetary union and parliament.

9 See Chapter II, article 6 on 'Modalities for the Establishment of the Community'.

Nevertheless, the AU ended up recognizing the existence of the eight RECs (including the AMU).[10]

The 1998 Protocol turned out to be a cosmetic document, however, and did not lead to the implementation of any new state of affairs. But soon African leaders re-engaged with their ambition to integrate the continent and adopted several instruments for that purpose. In 1999, OAU leaders signed the Sirte Declaration, which announced the establishment of the African Union and carried the promise to strengthen the RECs 'as the pillars for achieving the objectives of the African Economic Community'. This ambition was reiterated in 2000, in Togo, when the General Assembly of the OAU showed its resolve to rationalize the different RECs as a means to engage Africa with the world economy. Two years later, the New Partnership for Africa's Development (NEPAD) was adopted by the AU and was aimed at providing an overarching vision and policy framework for accelerating economic development, cooperation and integration among African countries – economic integration was arguably one of its overarching objectives.

Additionally, in 2003, the AU Maputo Summit requested the AU Commission to accelerate the preparation of a new draft protocol to replace the 1998 version. The much-needed new version was signed in January 2008 – after much technical and political negotiation – by the seven RECs that had recognized the legal value of the first protocol. Once again, the Arab Maghreb Union decided against the signing of the protocol and remained an outsider.[11] The protocol was preceded by the symbolic adoption of the Accra Declaration of 2007, where AU leaders agreed on a 'Union Government for Africa' which would presuppose the rationalization and strengthening of the RECs. Despite the fanfare, commitment was ephemeral and consensus regarding the establishment of a 'United States of Africa' remains elusive. Still, work continues within the AU to pave the way.

Currently, the AU efforts on rationalization of REC activities are anchored in the work of the annual Conference of African Ministers in Charge of Integration (COMAI), which was institutionalized in 2006. Thus far, the COMAI has met in Ouagadougou (2006), Kigali (2007), Abidjan (2008), Yaoundé (2009), and Tripoli (2010). Each conference, progressively, (i) recognized the important role played by RECs as central pillars for achieving continental integration; (ii) underscored the need to rationalize and harmonize the activities and programmes of RECs, with a view to accelerating the African integration process; and (iii) underlined the need to ensure that Africa's partnership engagements work in favour and not against its integration objectives.

10 In 2006, the AU Assembly in Banjul, The Gambia recommended recognizing the eight RECs, putting a moratorium on the new RECs and focusing on rationalizing and harmonizing REC policies and programmes. Also, it should be noted that the AU fails to recognize SACU as an official REC.

11 It should be noted that although recognized as RECs, EAC, IGAD and CEN-SAD do not satisfy the criteria of 'region' as per the OAU Resolution 464.

The several drawbacks of overlapping membership in African regional integration arise from the contradictory or conflicting obligations that numerous memberships entail for countries and regions (Guinea and Galvez 2011: 14). With multiple regional integration arrangements (RIAs), the task of applying different rules of origin for each regional agreement becomes cumbersome, draining the gains from trade liberalization and postponing the deepening of regional trade agreements (Krueger 1997). For instance, in West Africa, for the three economic communities – ECOWAS, Union Economique et Monétaire Ouest Africaine/West African Monetary and Economic Union (UEMOA) and the Mano River Union (MRU) – not only do their regional groupings overlap and compete with each other, but each economic community also operates a different scheme in the removal of tariff and non-tariff barriers. These schemes were conceived to operate with different rules of origin and compensation plans, so with the operation of different liberalization schemes in the same region, this has inhibited their effective integration and potential development of trade. This type of rationalization issue was also recognized at the highest level by the First COMAI in Ouagadougou in 2006.

Additionally, as at 2010, out of the 53 African countries, 27 are members of two regional organizations, 18 are members of three and one (Democratic Republic of Congo) is a member of four (Bundu 1997). On average, 95% of the members of a regional economic community belong to another community. An obvious question is whether national policymakers are aware of the consequences of multiple and overlapping memberships. Survey evidence clearly shows that more than a quarter of the countries that are members of more than one regional economic community say that multiple memberships make it difficult to meet their contributions and obligations to the various regional economic communities (UNECA 2006: xvii). Another 23% say that multiple memberships are the reason behind low implementation of their programs. Two other major problems from multiple memberships are low attendance of meetings and duplicated or conflicting programme implementation (UNECA 2006). And why do countries still join more than one regional economic community given these problems? Half cite political and strategic reasons as the main determinant. Economic interests rank a distant second, with only 35% of countries citing it. Geography, which is a key consideration in the Abuja Treaty, is cited by only 21% (UNECA 2006: xvii). The extent of multiple overlapping memberships is illustrated in Figure 11.6.

Different Speeds and Capabilities, or Slow Progress Towards Supranational Institutions and the Sharing of Sovereignty

All RECs have lent legal validity to the objective of establishing the African Economic Community. In their constitutional treaties, the AEC is universally recognized as one of the objectives of the organizations. For instance, the Revised Treaty of ECOWAS states clearly that: 'The integration of the region shall constitute an essential component of the integration of the African continent.

Member States undertake to facilitate the coordination and harmonization of the policies and programmes of the Community with those of the African Economic Community' (Chapter 17, Article 78). In a similar vein, the Agreement Establishing IGAD declares that one of the aims of the organization is to 'Promote and realize the objectives ... of the African Economic Community'. And in the EAC Treaty is expressed that 'The Partner States reiterate their desire for a wider unity of Africa and regard the Community as a step towards the achievement of the objectives of the Treaty Establishing the African Economic Community'.

Despite this harmony at the legal level, the application has been less than constant. The Abuja Treaty anticipated that the AEC was to be achieved through six consecutive stages. But the pace of implementing these stages varies. For instance, stage three, to be completed by 2017, requires establishing an FTA and customs union in each regional bloc. Although all the RECs, with the exception of IGAD, AMU and CEN-SAD, have launched FTAs, some member states have not yet joined the FTA, 'which has serious implications for intra-REC trade flows' (UNECA 2010:11). As an AU audit underlines, 'the approach to integration seems to be based more on deadlines than concrete achievements' (AU 2007a:127).

Indeed, the RECs are not progressing towards the AEC at the same pace, nor are they following similar procedures and processes to reach that aim. There appears to be no clear evidence that existing RECs have the long-term continental integration in view, or that there is the political will within all the RECs to submit their regional concerns to the overriding imperatives of the AU. This is largely due to members' low level of development and priorities. For instance, in East and Southern Africa, 'SADC has focused on infrastructural constraints, whereas COMESA has tackled harmonization of standards and customs procedures as well as trade facilitation' (UNCTAD 2010: 11).

Despite the rhetoric regarding a continental government conveyed by the former President of the Assembly of the AU, Colonel Muammar Gaddafi, African leaders still regard sovereignty as the best defence against uninvited foreign interventions (Herbst 1996). Indeed, given the prevalence in Africa of weak states and political opposition to sharing sovereignty, it is not surprising that integration arrangements are characterized by loose supranational bodies and that virtually all institutions are intergovernmental. Regionalism has been mainly led by public sector organizations and, in most cases, has lacked the support and involvement of the private sector. Cooperation is perceived to entail bloated and expensive bureaucracies, rather than opportunities for growth and development. It seems that, lacking a sense of regional identity, trust and common interests, regional institutions are only what individual member states wish them to be.

Most African states have suffered from severe macroeconomic disequilibrium, foreign debt service burdens, over-valued currencies, lack of trade finance, and a narrow tax base, with customs duties forming a substantial source of revenue. The protective import substitution strategies adopted by most countries since independence has resulted in a host of regulations restricting trade such as licensing, administrative foreign exchange allocation, special taxes for acquiring

RECS	UMA	CEMAC	COMESA	EAC	ECCAS	ECOWAS	IGAD	SACU	SADC
UMA									
Algeria	√		..						
Libya	√		√						
Mauritania	√								
Morocco	√								
Tunisia	√								
CEMAC									
Cameroon		√							
Central African Rep		√			√				
Chad		√			√				
Congo		√			√				
Equatorial Guinea		√			√				
Gabon		√			√				
COMESA									
Burundi			√	√	√				
Comoros			√						
Dem Rep Congo			√		√				√
Djibouti			√				√		
Egypt			√						
Eritrea			√				√		
Ethiopia			√				√		
Kenya			√	√			√		
Libya			√						
Madagascar			√						
Malawi			√						
Mauritius			√						√

RECS	UMA	CEMAC	COMESA	EAC	ECCAS	ECOWAS	IGAD	SACU	SADC
Rwanda			√	√					
Seychelles			√						√
Sudan			√				√		
Swaziland			√					√	√
Uganda			√	√			√		
Zambia			√						√
Zimbabwe			√						√
EAC									
Burundi				√	√				
Kenya				√					
Rwanda				√					
Uganda				√					
Tanzania				√					√
ECCAS									
Angola					√				√
Burundi					√				
Cameroon					√				
Central African Rep					√				
Chad					√				
Congo					√				
Dem Rep Congo					√				√
Equatorial Guinea					√				
Gabon					√				
Rwanda					√				
Sao Tome & Principe					√				

RECS	UMA	CEMAC	COMESA	EAC	ECCAS	ECOWAS	IGAD	SACU	SADC
ECOWAS									
Benin						√			
Burkina Faso						√			
Cape Verde						√			
Ivory Coast						√			
Gambia						√			
Ghana						√			
Guinea						√			
Guinea Bissau						√			
Liberia						√			
Mali						√			
Niger						√			
Nigeria						√			
Senegal						√			
Sierra-Leone						√			
IGAD									
Djibouti							√		
Eritrea			√				√		
Ethiopia			√				√		
Kenya			√				√		
Somalia							√		
Sudan			√				√		
Uganda			√				√		
SACU									
Botswana								√	√
Lesotho								√	√

RECS	UMA	CEMAC	COMESA	EAC	ECCAS	ECOWAS	IGAD	SACU	SADC
Namibia								√	√
South Africa								√	√
Swaziland								√	√
SADC									
Angola									√
Botswana								√	√
Dem Rep of Congo			√						√
Lesotho								√	√
Malawi			√						√
Mauritius			√						√
Mozambique									√
Namibia								√	√
Seychelles			√						√
South Africa								√	√
Swaziland			√					√	√
Tanzania				√					√
Zambia			√						√
Zimbabwe			√						√

Figure 11.6 African Regional Economic Communities Multiple Overlapping Memberships
Source: Authors compilation based on United Nations Conference on Trade and Development (UNCTAD 2009: 12)

foreign exchange, and advance import deposits. Such an economic context has been unfavourable to the development of regional commitments.

To some extent, poor regionalism can also be due to the region's low developmental capacity. As noted by Franke, 'given the desolate state of Africa's public finances and governmental structures, its organizational deficits and inexperienced leaders as well as wide-spread corruption and clientelism, it is hardly surprising that its institutions did not develop as clearly, strongly or professionally as they did elsewhere' (2007:11). In the same vein, the COMAI has identified that insufficient financial resources are a major obstacle slowing down the process of integration. Although much of the financing is provided by African member states and supported by development partners, these resources remain inadequate. It was against this background that in 2009 the African Ministers in Charge of Integration mandated the AU Commission, in collaboration with the African Development Bank (AfDB) to prepare a study exploring the possibility of establishing a special continental fund for the implementation of the Minimum Integration Program.

Fragmentation

The Economic Partnership Agreement (EPA) negotiations with the European Union have also highlighted particular challenges associated with regional integration. Though EPAs are meant to strengthen regional integration and development, among other aims, their immediate impact has been the further fragmentation of existing regional economic communities across Africa – Southern Africa in particular. For instance, one now sees a case scenario of original SADC members such as Zimbabwe negotiating not within the SADC framework, but under the Eastern and Southern African (ESA) regional banner. Others such as Tanzania have joined the EAC. SADC now negotiates the EPA with only half of its members: Mozambique, Angola and the SACU countries – South Africa and the BLNS countries (Botswana, Lesotho, Namibia and Swaziland). It is also problematic that half of SADC members are members of COMESA. The signing of the SADC Interim Economic Partnership Agreement (IEPA) in June 2009 by Mozambique and the BLS countries (Botswana, Lesotho and Swaziland) has caused tensions within SACU and frictions among the SADC EPA group (Kumalo and Mulleta 2010). These scenarios are indicative of the different economic interests and unclear regional agendas within the Southern African region. There is also a serious conflict of interest if one considers the fact that South Africa's scope of liberalization and its trade and industrial policies are neither in line with the EU nor the BLNS agenda (Draper and Khumalo 2009). The EPA negotiations configurations are not conterminous with existing RECs. This places further stress on an already delicate situation in which institutional capacities are already overstretched and consequently threatens to divide the region even further (Draper *et al.* 2007, Ndomo 2009).

Many have questioned the rationale for being a party to the EPAs. On the one hand, despite the slow pace of progress in the World Trade Organization (WTO)

Doha round of negotiations, the EU is a major trading partner for most African countries and the EPA could be quite beneficial. Both trading partners expect to improve significantly their market access and investment opportunities and both aim to enhance the economic growth and development in their member states. On the other hand, despite the EU's commitment to strengthening regional integration and economic development among ACP countries,[17] one should not overlook the EU's articulated need and aim to ensure a sustainable and unrestricted supply of raw materials and energy for the competitiveness of the EU economy.[18] Opportunities are obvious in view of Africa's considerable natural resource endowment and its population of nearly one billion (15% of the world's population), constituting a sizable market.

For Africa, in line with the Abuja Treaty, trade and integration are essential components for an Africa-wide development. In the case of EPAs, however, most African countries seem primarily motivated by preserving their preferential market access (Khumalo and Mulleta 2010). Unlike the earlier Europe-ACP arrangements, the EPA represents a fundamental shift from the traditional EU-African trading relationship: EPAs involve reciprocal trade, and aid takes a subordinate role. This reciprocal trade regime (between the EU and seven ACP regional groupings) aims to conform to the trade rules of the WTO. Conformity with Article XXIV of GATT/WTO means that the EPA should cover 'substantially all trade' within a 'reasonable period of time'. However, the differing views on the interpretation of the terms 'substantially all' and 'reasonable period' make the legal context of the EPA negotiations all the more complicated. This has slowed the pace of EPA implementation and the deepening of African economic integration. However, as the EPA implementation process picks up pace, African countries will have to pay careful attention to their external liberalization policies.

Another feature of the EPA negotiations that has hindered progress and attracted much attention is the principle of most favoured nation (MFN). The MFN clause has sparked much criticism since the inclusion of this clause requires parties to the EPA to extend to the EU any trade concessions that they may accord to third parties. This added provision effectively gives the EU the power to slow down the deepening of African integration.

Meanwhile, EPA negotiations continue between the EU and sub-regional blocs in Africa, and these are some of the most contentious issues that have not been finalized.[19] Further, an Africa-wide benefit will depend upon the capacity for RECs to address their supply constraints and trade-related reforms. That said, the multiplicity of overlapping regional initiatives coupled with divergent economic

---

17 See communication from the European Commission (2008).

18 See the recent interview with the EU Trade Commissioner Karel De Gucht (Trade Negotiation Insights 2010).

19 So far, with the exception of the Caribbean, none of the regions have managed to conclude a full EPA.

interests places an undue burden on African countries' capacity to effectively exploit and manage these initiatives.

Besides EPAs' implementation problems, institutional disarticulation is also visible in the fact that five countries – Eritrea, Somalia, Madagascar, Gabon and Djibouti – have not signed or ratified the Abuja Treaty, although they are full members of the AU, which in its Constitutive Act, incorporating the Abuja Treaty, provides for the RECs to serve as the vehicles for accelerated integration. However, they are members of several RECs, adding further obscurity to the integration process. Moreover, Morocco is a full member of AMU and CEN-SAD, the two leading regional communities in Northern Africa, but due to the Western Saharan situation, it has opted for not joining the AU. This disarticulation raises important legal issues. The institutional disarticulation is often accentuated by the fact that more RECs tend to perceive the AU as being both slow and a rival. As a 2007 Capacity Needs Assessment report to the AU noted, RECs tend to be hypnotically focused on their own regions 'with continental aspirations receiving little attention' (African Union 2007c: 13).

A Retrospective, and Future Scenarios

A number of studies have underscored the sensitive nature of the rationalization debate and have demonstrated how the multiplicity of overlapping regional arrangements has slowed down Africa's integration process (Draper *et al.* 2007, Ndomo 2009). The AU Commission itself has undertaken several studies on this matter, such as the 'Rationalization of the Regional Economic Communities (RECs): Review of the Abuja Treaty and Adoption of the Minimum Integration Programme', which was completed in April 2007. The study, which was presented to the Second COMAI in Rwanda, in July 2007, tends however to underestimate the need for firm criteria in order to implement policy decisions and is focused on economic and technical matters. A more recent study, also by the AU, on the quantification of scenarios for the rationalization of RECs in terms of advantages and costs was presented during the Fifth COMAI held in Tripoli, Libya, in October 2010.

In retrospect, it seems doubtful that there exists the institutional will and capacity in Africa to push the integration process for an ultimate single African economic community. Regional economic integration in Africa is a shallow integration. This is most likely to continue as long as: (1) the multiple memberships and the multiplicity of regulations co-exist; (2 the complementary trade structure and diversification efforts remain low; (3) member states' capacity and level of preparedness are not at the same level and remain weak; (4) local trade policies and protocols are unattractive; (5) there is an absence of collective agreement on rationalizing and harmonizing regional initiatives; (6) the institutional framework remains inadequate, and (7) the region lacks effective political will and leadership.

Even so, analysts consider there to be three scenarios currently on the table: (i) the status quo, (ii) the Abuja Treaty approach, and (iii) an anchor community approach.

The first scenario presupposes that all economic communities and groupings of regional vocation should be considered as RECs. This has the 'advantage' of not upsetting the established order, but on the other hand it encourages duplication of programmes and policies. The second scenario limits the economic integration entities to the five regions mentioned in the Abuja Treaty (North, West, Central, East and Southern) and entails the exclusive selection of five regional organizations. This policy would reverse the proliferation of RECs and strictly align the integration process with the stages defined in the Abuja Treaty, but it would likely be marred by political controversies and tensions during the rationalization process.

The third scenario presupposes the singling out of a regional lead organization that will effectively spearhead matters of socio-economic development through what has been referred to as an anchor community. Regional decisions would hence be formulated and taken within the framework of the anchor community and only such decisions would be recognized by the AU. But this would not necessarily imply the dismantling of other regional organizations. According to a study conducted by the African Union, 45% of the RECs consulted favoured this anchor community scenario, whereas 22% preferred either the Abuja Treaty or the status quo.

The idea of an 'anchor community' has an operational or strategic value considering especially that this chapter has shown that African RECs lack a certain 'regional order'. An 'anchor community scenario' can possibly ease trade and promote economic development, and offer the best opportunities for African RECs to grow. With this framework in mind, the UN could potentially be (in the short run) an anchor community. This view is based on the UN's operational capacity and its support of Africa in various fields including social and economic development, as well as regional integration.

Conclusion

Africa's efforts towards a continent-wide economic integration have been constrained and undermined by overlapping regional arrangements and the absence of collective agreements on rationalizing and harmonizing regional initiatives. This has been further undermined by the non-complementary trade structure and low degree of diversification and member states varying economic interests clearly indicated by the ongoing EPA negotiations. Although it is commonly accepted that trade and regional integration are key components of African development strategies, it may be more appropriate to be somewhat cautious about Africa's push for a rapid pursuit of integration. Several constraints exist, including issues of sovereignty, MFN, and fragmentation of economic markets on the continent.

Moving forward, African integration has to be addressed in a credible manner, with attention paid to the speed and sequencing of its implementation efforts and reforms, which ultimately are highly dependent on effective leadership and the capacity of both regional organizations and member states.

References

African Union. 2007a. *Audit of the African Union*. Addis Ababa: AU.

African Union. 2007b. *Rationalization of the Regional Economic Communities (RECS): Review of the Abuja Treaty and Adoption of Minimum Integration Programme*. AU: Addis Ababa.

African Union, 2007c. *Long-Term Capacity Needs Assessment of the AU and RECs in Their Promotion and Maintenance of Peace and Security*, Report produced to the AU and the EU by a team of consultants, Addis Ababa: African Union.

Badasi, P. 2011. *Third BRICS Leaders' Summit, 17 April 2011*. [Online]. Available at: http://devterms.co.za/news/third-brics-brazil-russia-india-china-south-africa-leaders%E2%80%99-summit/ [accessed: 8 May 2011].

Bundu, A. 1997. ECOWAS and the future of regional integration in West Africa, in *Regional Integration and Cooperation in West Africa: A Multi-dimensional Perspective*, edited by R. Lavergne. Trenton, New Jersey and Ottawa: Africa World Press and International Development Research Centre.

Draper, P. 2010. *Whither the Multilateral Trading System? Implications for (South) Africa. Occasional Paper Nr 64*. Johannesburg: South African Institute of International Affairs (SAIIA).

Draper, P. and Khumalo, N. 2009. The future of the Southern African Customs Union. *Trade Negotiations Insights*, 8(6). [Online]. Available at: http://acp-eu-trade.org/library/files/TNI_EN__8-6.pdf [accessed: 7 February 2011].

Draper, P., Halleson, D. and Alves, P. 2007. *SACU, Regional Integration and the Overlap Issue in Southern Africa: From Spaghetti to Cannelloni? Trade Policy Report Nr. 15*. Johannesburg: South African Institute of International Affairs (SAIIA).

European Commission. 2008. *Regional Integration for Development in ACP countries*, October 2008, [online]. Available at: http://europa.eu/legislation_summaries/development/general_development_framework/dv0002_en.htm [accessed 18 April 2011].

Food and Agriculture Organization of the United Nations (FAO). 2003. *Regional Integration and Food Security in Developing Countries*. Rome: FAO.

Franke, B.F. 2007. Competing regionalisms in Africa and the continent's emerging security architecture. *African Studies Quarterly*, 9 (3).

Guinea, O. and Galvez, R. 2011. *Understanding African Regionalism: The Case of Overlapping Membership*. Paper to the Conference: Whatever Happened to North-South?, the IPSA-ECPR joint conference, Sao Paulo, February 2011.

Herbst, J. 1996. Responding to state failure in Africa. *International Security*, 21(3), 120-144.

Hichert, T., Draper, P. and Bertelsmann-Scott, T. 2010. *What Does the Future Hold for SACU? From Own Goal to Laduma! Scenarios for the Future of the Southern African Customs Union, Occasional paper Nr. 63*. Johannesburg: South African Institute of International Affairs (SAIIA).

Holden, M. and Tang, V. 2010. *Competitive Bilateralism or Regionalism: A South African Perspective.* Paper to the ACP-NETRIS Conference, Durban, September 2010.

Khumalo, N. and Mulleta, F. 2010. Economic partnership agreements: African-EU negotiations continue. *South African Journal of International Studies*, 17(2) 209-220.

Krueger, A.O. 1997.Problems with overlapping free trade areas, in *Regionalism Versus Multilateral Trade Arrangements*, edited by T. Ito and A.O. Krueger. Chicago: University of Chicago Press.

Landsberg, C. 2004. The fifth wave of Pan-Africanism, in *West Africa's Security Challenges: Building Peace in a Troubled Region*, edited by A. Adebajo and I. Rashid. Boulder, Colo.: Lynne Rienner, 117-143.

Londsdale, J. 1968. The Emergence of African nations: A historiographical analysis, *African Affairs*, 67(266), 11-28.

M'bayo, T. 2004. W.E.B. Dubois, Marcus Garvey, and Pan-Africanism in Liberia 1919-1924. *The Historian*, 66(1), 19-44.

Makinda, S.M. and Okumu, F.W. 2008. *The African Union: Challenges of Globalization, Security, and Governance*. London and New York: Routledge.

Muchie, M. (ed.) 2003. *The Making of the African-Nation: Pan-Africanism and the African Renaissance*. London: Adonis and Abbey Publishers.

Murithi, T. 2005. *The African Union: Pan-Africanism, Peacebuilding and Development.* Aldershot, UK: Ashgate.

Ndomo, A. 2009. *Regional Economic Communities in Africa: A Progress Overview*. Study Commissioned by GTZ.

OECD. 2007. *Atlas on Regional Integration trends and recommendations on communicable diseases, 2007* [online]. Available at: http://www.oecd.org/data oecd/56/39/40997324.pdf [Accessed 18 April 2011].

Organization of African Unity (OAU). 1980. *Lagos Plan of Action for the Economic Development of Africa*. Addis Ababa: OAU.

Oxfam International. 2006. *Unequal Partners: How EU–ACP Economic Partnership Agreements (EPAs) Could Harm the Development Prospects of Many of the World's Poorest Countries*, September 2006. [Online]. Available at: http://www.oxfam.org.nz/imgs/whatwedo/mtf/unequal%20partners.pdf [accessed: 7 February 2011].

Oyejide, A., Elbadawi, I. and Collier, P. 1997. Introduction and overview, in *Regional Integration and Trade Liberalization in SubSaharan Africa, Vol. 1, Framework, Issues and Methodological Perspectives*, edited by A. Oyejide, I. Elbadawi and P. Collier. London: MacMillan Press.

Sachs, J.D., McArthur, J., Schmidt-Traub, G., Kruk, M., Bahadur, C., Faye, M. and McCord, G. 2004. Ending Africa's poverty traps. *Brooking Papers in Economics*. 1, 117-216.

Tavares, R. 2010. *Regional Security: The Capacity of International Organizations*. London and New York: Routledge.

Trade Negotiations Insights. 2010. Interview with EU Trade Commissioner Karel De Gucht. *Trade Negotiations Insights* 10(9), December 2010-January 2011, [online]. Available at: http://acp-eu-trade.org/library/files/tni_en_9-10.pdf [Accessed 7 February 2011].

UNCTAD. 2003. *Economic Development in Africa: Trade Performance and Commodity Dependence*. Geneva: UNCTAD.

UNCTAD. 2009. *Economic Development in Africa: Strengthening Regional Economic Integration for Africa's Development*. Geneva: UNCTAD.

UNCTAD. 2010. *Addressing the Commodity Problematique through Trade-Related Policies*. Geneva: UNCTAD.

United Nations Conference on Trade and Development (UNCTAD). 2010. *Addressing the Commodity Problematique through Trade-Related Policies*. Geneva: UNCTAD.

United Nations Conference on Trade and Development (UNCTAD). 2012. Available at: http://unctadstat.unctad.org/TableViewer/ [accessed: 02 January 2013].

United Nations Economic Commission for Africa (UNECA) and African Union (AU). 2006. *Assessing Regional Integration in Africa II – Rationalizing Regional Economic Communities*. Addis Ababa: UNECA.

United Nations Economic Commission for Africa (UNECA), African Union (AU) and African Development Bank (AfDB). 2010. *Assessing Regional Integration in Africa IV – Enhancing Intra-African Trade*. Addis Ababa: UNECA.

Chapter 12
Regional Formations and Global Governance[1]

Luk Van Langenhove and Maria Cristina Macovei

This chapter aims to provide a framework for understanding the growth and changing character of regional governance. Section one explores how governance has evolved from an essentially state-led pre-occupation into a complex phenomenon that involves many other actors and that is characterized by inter-linkages between different (geographical) levels of policy-making. It will be argued that we are witnessing the transition from a single world of states towards a multiple world of states and regions. Important actors in this new world order are the world regional organizations and regional arrangements between states that have resulted from regional integration processes. Section two discusses three main varieties of regional integration that currently exist. First, there is the regional integration by removing economic obstacles, a process that has resulted in a multitude of regional trade arrangements all over the world. Second, there is the regional integration by building institutions and regulations that often go beyond economic and trade policies and that can be described as a 'pooling' of sovereignty at a transnational level. Third, there is regional integration by building a geopolitical identity and actorness. Here the 'world region'[2] behaves as an actor on the global scene, both through its own 'foreign' policy and through its presence in global institutions. The final section will then begin the exploration of the consequences of these varieties of regionalism for social policy. It will be argued that regionalism aimed at only creating free trade areas can put severe pressures on existing national social policies of the countries involved. On the other hand, the development of a broader and deeper form of regionalism (often referred to as 'new regionalism') can act as a driver towards regional social policies. Moreover, in those – rare – cases where regionalism involves global actorness, the regional external policy can contribute to the development of global social policies as well. By way of conclusion, it will be argued that in theory, regional integration can act

1 A version of this chapter was previously published in B. Deacon, M-C. Macovei, L. Van Langenhove and N. Yeates, World-Regional Social Policy and Global Governance. New Research and Policy Agendas in Africa, Asia, Europe and Latin America. Abingdon and New York: Routledge. 2010.

2 In the text, the 'world region' concept refers to supranational entities.

both as a building block and as a stumbling stone towards a global social policy that makes globalization more 'fair'.

The Changing Face of Governance

In our globalized world, societies are affected more and more extensively and deeply by events of other societies. Debates on globalization raise questions regarding the appropriate political response for dealing with both its negative and positive effects. One of the fundamental questions is at what level action should be situated. Actions can be taken by the national and local authorities, but as is often the case, these authorities are limited in their ability to tackle global and thus transnational problems. On the other hand, there are the global worldwide institutions such as the UN and the Bretton Woods institutions. And in between both, there are the regional institutions (such as the EU, MERCOSUR, Association of South East Asian Nations (ASEAN), Asia Pacific Economic Cooperation (APEC), Southern African Development Community (SADC), African Union (AU), North American Free Trade Agreement (NAFTA), etc.), and perhaps it is exactly at that level that there is increasing interest in and focus on dealing with the effects of globalization.

This may seem surprising as at first sight it could only be the UN who as a global institution offers a political answer to globalization. After all, the UN was founded in 1945 in an attempt to create a multilateral world forum where sovereign states can resolve differing opinions and where common actions about peace and development can be stimulated. Today, however, the world is dramatically different from that of the post World War II period in which the UN was founded. First of all, the geopolitical stability of that system disappeared with the end of the Cold War. Second, a lot more countries are now members of the UN than used to be the case (from the original 51, the number has raised to 192 Member States), which means that the functioning of the General Assembly is not getting easier. Third, states now have to share their hegemony on governance and their capacity to regulate economic transformation more and more with local governments, supranational groupings and nongovernmental actors.

One can observe that nowadays there are emerging problems that are beyond the national or regional borders. Therefore, the problématique is how to deal with the rapid emergence of collective problems with cross-border dimensions, in particular those ones that are global in scope or potentially so. Global governance can be an answer to this problématique, as it refers to 'cooperative problem solving arrangements on a global plane' (Thakur and Van Langenhove 2006: 233). Global governance is characterized by a complex matrix of institutions, both formal and informal, of mechanisms, and of processes between and among states, markets, citizens, and of organizations, both intergovernmental and nongovernmental ones. In the global governance system, the collective interests are wrought, the rights and obligations are set up, and the differences are mediated (Thakur and Van Langenhove 2006). The need for global governance is very present in today's world; however, the idea of a centralized world government is not embraced by many people. In this respect, as underlined by Thakur and Van Langenhove (2008: 22), the goal of global governance 'is not the creation of world government, but an additional layer of consultation and decision-making' of governments and intergovernmental organizations. The organizing principle of global governance is multilateralism, and the UN represents the hub of the multilateral system of global governance. The world needs global governance in order to deal with non-passport issues, like human rights, chronic poverty, migration, and other social problems. Global governance can be seen as a 'chameleonic-like' concept that can be adapted to different meanings. The goal of global economic governance, for instance, is to manage the economic activity of the world without undermining state sovereignty, preserve international financial stability, and promote cooperative solutions to global problems, among others. Global security governance aims to minimize conflicts and violence across the planet, again respecting the sovereignty of the nation state (Thakur and Van Langenhove 2006). By the same token, global social governance, without harming the sovereignty of the nations, seeks to protect the well-being of all people, including issues like social protection, education, health, and try to solve the inequality and poverty dilemmas via intergovernmental modalities. Indeed, the world is 'stumbling towards the articulation of global social policy of global redistribution, global social regulation, and global social rights' (Deacon 2007). Global redistribution can be achieved via tax and income transfers, regional funds, and overseas development assistance (ODA). Global social regulation is encompassing the core labour standards advanced by the ILO in 1998 and the UN Conventions. Global social rights are about citizenship empowerment, which refers to UN Conventions of the Rights of the Child, UN International Covenant on Economic, Social and Cultural Rights (Deacon 2007 and 2008).

The current debate (WCSDG 2004, Farrell *et al.* 2005, Thakur and Van Langenhove 2006 and 2008, UNU-CRIS 2008) is advocating for a global governance build on regional integration. This approach is of particular interest for the debate on advancing (regional) social policy (Deacon 2007, Yeates 2005, 2008, Yeates and Deacon 2006, Deacon, Ortiz and Zelenev 2007). The regional level is becoming a level of governance actively involved in policy implementation and then policy elaboration. Multi-level governance or 'the dispersion of authoritative decision-making across multiple territorial levels' (Hooghe and Marks 2001: xi) is the new paradigm to explain this phenomenon. From this perspective, European integration, for example, is a 'polity-creating process in which authority and policy-making influence are shared across multiple levels of government – sub-national, national, and supranational' (Hooghe and Marks 2001: 2). The weakening of the state and the shift of competences to the new sub-national and supranational levels of government is the result of a dual process:

> European integration has shifted authority in several key areas of policy-making from national states up to European-level institutions. Regionalization in several countries, including the most populous ones, has shifted political authority from the national level down to sub-national level of government. (Hooghe and Marks 2001: XI)

One of the main characteristics of the sovereign state is that it has had for a long time a quasi-monopoly on the provision of public goods within its territory. The beneficiaries of public goods are not limited to a single consumer or a specific group or consumers, but are available to all. The benefits of different public goods, like legal systems and institutions, defence systems, and nationwide highways, are extended to the entire population of a specific state (R.A. Musgrave and P.B. Musgrave 2003: xi). Part of these public goods deal also with social policy. For instance, national poverty eradication programmes, national education programmes, national social security systems, etc are examples in this sense.

A main debate has always been on how far a state should go in developing instruments of social policy. The two extreme positions in that debate have been (i) states need to be strong to tame the negative consequences of market-forces, and (ii) states need to refrain from interfering where markets can do a better job. States versus markets has been a dominating political theme and has long been the main point of difference between left and right. But recently, two major (inter-related) events have shaken that old paradigm of state/market balance. On the one hand, markets have increasingly become globalized. As a result, many aspects of industrial production and of trade escaped the control of national states. On the other hand, states have increasingly become stripped of some of their powers and competences as a result of a double movement. In many cases, there has been devolution of power from the (central) state level to federalized entities. In a country such as Belgium, the majority of governmental policy domains are now situated at the level of the regions. Next to that, there have been strong tendencies to somehow 'pool' sovereignty across states into larger regional entities. The EU is the most developed example of this trend, though other examples of how this pooling/cooperation is taking place across world regions exist as well. As a result, a complex web of inter-related levels and spheres of governance has emerged with many actors. For a person living in Belgium, for example, this means that policies are situated at the local level of the commune, the level of the provinces, the regional level, and the level of the language community, the national (federal) level, the level of the Benelux group of countries, the European and global level.[3]

Notwithstanding the above, in the foreseeable future, states will remain important centres of governance. Nevertheless, in an attempt to face the challenges

3 While this concept of levels captures an element of the emerging process of multi-levelled governance, it is also important to recognize that higher level actors can and do take part in lower level decisions and vice versa. Some kinds of actors are more likely to jump scale such as representatives of global financial institutions or policy consultants.

of globalization, states can turn to sub-national and world regions to complement and even strengthen their power. As such, the world of states will gradually become a world of states and regions. A world of states and regions could be an innovative approach that holds the promise of a renewed and better system of global and local governance. Within this development, regional integration has taken an important place since the mid-1980s. There has been not only a proliferation of various forms of regional integration processes on a global scale but also an unprecedented deepening of the process of European integration. The EU is the world's most advanced form of supranational regionalism. It has managed to develop a model that incorporates political elements in a deep economic integration, and as such challenges existing assumptions about governance.

This has important consequences for social policy. On the one hand, there is the issue of migration of some elements of social policy from the state level to either the supranational or sub-national level. On the other hand, there is the problématique of the interaction between these different governance levels. Progressively, the idea that the EU should strengthen its competences in the social area over the national member states has indeed gained ground. In this sense, the first steps made have been the introduction of the legally enforceable 'acquis communautaire' and the softer 'acquis', the Open Method of Coordination (OMC)[4] to promote coordinated social policy-making. But all in all, the European integration process as far as social policy is concerned is not as advanced as for other policy domains.

Although not the model for the rest of the world, the EU can be seen as an example of regional integration with cooperation spanning culture, politics, security, economics, social policies and diplomacy, and is often taken as a model for political and economic efforts in other regions to achieve stability and prosperity. Not surprisingly then, an interest in the social dimension of regional integration turns to the EU to see how social policy has been handled in the European integration process.

But regional integration is a worldwide phenomenon, and the regions should not be seen just as formal institutions, but rather as (re)constructed organizations in the process of global transformation. The regions, therefore, should be seen as 'dynamic in their development and open to change and adaptation' (Farrell 2005: 8).

In Latin America, for instance, the idea of a Latin American unity by regional economic integration has been on the agenda since the end of World War II. Prominent organizations in the region are MERCOSUR and the Andean Community, next to other forms of regional integration. MERCOSUR can be considered as a 'network regionalization' scheme, where the regional identity is a response to globalization, and relies primarily on non-institutionalized or intergovernmental working methods (Warleigh-Lack 2008). The Asunción Treaty establishing MERCOSUR in 1991 does not provide a special cluster of integration-

4 See also Deacon, B. (2007: 165).

related social issues. In 2004, however, the issue of the institutionalization of the social dimension began to form part of the agenda, with proposals and actions in this connection. This resulted in the creation in 2000 of the *Social MERCOSUR*, which consists of Ministers and Authorities in charge of Social Development of MERCOSUR. The social dimension of MERCOSUR underlines the importance of an integration process that has real implications for human and social development (SELA 2008). In contrast with MERCOSUR, the social dimension of integration was part of the Andean Community (CAN) since its conception in 1969. The whole Andean integration process was accompanied by social and labour issues, followed by health-related ones. CAN also started to deal with border problems and education-related issues, and it was in 2003 and 2004 that the Andean Community approved its first decisions regarding its social development plan (SELA 2008).

In Asia and the Pacific, the most notable examples of regional integration are ASEAN and APEC. According to Warleigh-Lack (2008), ASEAN, as well as MERCOSUR, is a network regionalization process. With its *ASEAN Vision 2020*, ASEAN leaders vow to establish a community of caring societies with a common regional identity. In October 2003, they returned to Bali to update the original Bali Concord that laid the foundation for ASEAN cooperation. The declaration of *ASEAN Concord II* (*Bali Concord II*) provided for the establishment of an ASEAN community with three pillars, the ASEAN Security Community (ASC), the ASEAN Economic Community (AEC) and the ASEAN Socio-Cultural Community (ASCC). APEC is basically a forum to facilitate trade and investment. Labour issues in APEC have been mostly limited to human resources, productivity, worker training, and education issues. A Human Resources Development Working Group (HRD), established in 1990, aims at facilitating recognition of qualifications between the participating members. It also fosters links and strengthens collaborative initiatives between the members by organizing regular meetings of education ministers. One major outcome in the field of professional recognition so far has been the APEC Engineers Register.[5]

In the African continent, regional integration schemes have taken place both at continental and sub-continental levels. The main drivers of continental integration are the UN Economic Commission for Africa (ECA) and the Organization for African Unity (OAU), now known as the African Union (AU). The second wave of African regionalization started in the 1980s and led to the creation of a patchwork of overlapping sub-continental organizations, such as Southern African Development Community (SADC) and The Economic Community of West African States (ECOWAS). The original ECOWAS Treaty included, as it does today, a Social and Cultural Affairs Commission designed to 'provide a forum for consultation generally on social and cultural matters affecting the member states' (Art. 49). The AU is the umbrella organization for all African regional

5 See APEC website http://www.apec.org.

arrangements.[6] The AU is designed as an intergovernmental organization and was established in 2002 to promote unity and solidarity of African states, to spur economic development, and to promote international cooperation.

On a world scale, the picture of regionalization is thus complex. There exist many regional organizations, and quite a lot of them overlap with other regional integration schemes (i.e. the overlapping membership in the case of Regional Economic Communities (RECs) in Africa). Most of the existing schemes, however, are little more than 'paper tigers': they have weak structures and powers and all too often there is a gap between the integration discourses and the actual practices. Nevertheless, it is possible to identify differences in the nature of the ongoing integration processes.

Varieties of Regional Integration

Regional integration is a complex process of interactions between a group of (mostly) neighbouring countries that can be driven by state interventions or by interactions between citizens. As a merely European endeavour after the World War II, it has its origins in a political pre-occupation to bring peace and security in Europe, based upon a common economic policy. Since then it has not only spread around the globe, it has also developed into instruments of economic cooperation. As a result, regional integration schemes come in many different forms. Based upon the three generations of regional integration as identified by Van Langenhove and Costea (2007), one can classify the many varieties of regionalism into three broad categories: (i) regional integration by removing economic obstacles, (ii) regional integration by building institutions and regulations, and finally, (iii) regional integration by building a geopolitical identity and actorness.

Regional Integration by Removing Economic Obstacles

If one considers the building of a supranational region, then several obstacles exist. Perhaps the most important one is the concept of sovereignty as it limits – de jure – the possibility of 'interference' in internal affairs of each of the concerned states. Identity can also be a major obstacle, as it – de facto – will limit the urge towards integration. And then there are the borders: fixed boundaries that limit jurisdictions of each state that can be used to control and limit the flow of goods, people, and money across borders.

One of the main drivers towards regional integration has always been trade, for obvious reasons: if one has goods to sell, why limit oneself to a market that coincides with a certain national territory? In principle, market expansion does

6 Eight RECs are accredited to the AU: ECOWAS, COMESA, ECCAS, SADC, AMU, IGAD, CEN-SAD, EAC (First Conference of African Ministers of Economic Integration in March 2006, Ouagadougou, Burkina Faso, CAMEI/Consol. Report (I)).

not want to be limited by borders. States have had a general tendency to limit free trade across borders for a long time, partly out of protectionism (limiting the inflow of goods should increase the internal sales) and partly because trade across borders can generate income for the state through tariffs and custom duties. However, during the 1980s and 1990s, most policy makers agreed that allowing a maximum of free trade across borders would generate more benefits for all parties involved. More recently, this approach has come to be questioned and some now put forward a case for a degree of regional protectionism for the purposes of social development.

Not surprisingly then, an important manifestation of regional integration has been and still is the economic integration of neighbouring states which consists of the incremental lowering of all internal boundaries for trade and the establishment of common external boundaries. Such a form of regional integration is based upon the idea of a linear process of economic integration involving the merging of separate (national) economics into larger world economic regions. This process begins with a Free Trade Area in which states agree to remove all custom duties and quotas on trade passing between them, while keeping the right to determine unilaterally the level of custom duties on imports coming from outside the region. The next stage is the Customs Union where a common level of duty on external trade arrangements is applied. The following stage is the common market where the free movement of goods and factors of production are added to the agreement on free trade. And finally there is the Economic Union where a common market is installed that also has a complete unification of monitory and fiscal policy. Mattli (1999: 41) has defined such an economic regional integration as 'the voluntary linking in the economic domain of two or more formerly independent states to the extent that authority over key areas of domestic regulation and policy is shifted to the supranational level'.

The classical example of this linear evolution of economic integration is offered by the evolution of Western Europe after the Second World War: the creation of the European Economic Community (EEC) with the Treaty of Rome in 1957 removing the tariffs and quotas on intra-EEC trade, the achievement of a Customs Union in 1968 with the establishment of a common external tariff (CET), the creation of a Single European Market in the mid-1980s eliminating the barriers still existing to trade, and the establishment of the 'four freedoms' of circulation (persons, goods, services and capital). The economic union is in the process of being completed following the creation of the single currency, although, even in the EU, unification is still needed in important fields such as fiscal policy.

There are nevertheless numerous other examples worldwide of agreements which can be placed at different levels on the above-mentioned spectrum of economic integration. The European market integration became a trigger for the creation of similar common markets and free trade areas in the Middle East, Africa, the Pacific, and the Americas during the 1960s and early 1970s. The surge in these agreements has continued since the early 1990s. With the current suspension of the Doha global trade negotiations in 2008, the road towards more economic regionalism lies open as it seems that such regionalism is a 'natural response to the diversity in the world of economy' (Ahearne *et al.* 2006).

Regional Integration by Building Institutions and Regulations

Economic integration as described above is not the only possible driver for building a world region. There are also domains in which states want to cooperate in order to facilitate their dealing with common problems or in order to create win-win situations. In addition, feelings of belonging to joint cultural or language groups can foster regional integration. In principle, there is not a single aspect of the social realm that cannot be the subject of integration processes. This implies not only state-driven integrations but also integration from below; that is, when the initiative comes from citizens. Of course, much citizen-driven integration can only occur to the extent that states allow such integration to occur.

While economic integration in the strict sense is mostly a story of removing obstacles, non-economic integration more easily involves specific institution building or regulations that promote or facilitate integration in fields such as justice, security, culture, education, social protection etc. For instance, if two or more countries want to build a common security policy, this involves not necessarily merging the separate armies but it will necessitate building a common security infrastructure such as a centralized command.

In some – still limited – cases, economic regionalization has been broadened towards other areas of society because it is believed that a truly economic integration cannot be achieved if trade and economy are isolated from the rest of society. If for instance one wants to create a competitive economic union, this implies achieving a good innovation system, which in turn is linked to research and development. So one might consider a move from national socio-economic policy research towards a regional research area. Consequently, as research is linked to the higher education system, so again there can be a tendency towards unifying the educational system, without having a centralized educational body. Some scholars have called this 'new regionalism': a form of supranational regional integration that involves a deep economic integration as well as integration in many other domains.

Once again, the European Union is the first and most developed case of such an integration that is not only multidimensional but also based upon building a strong institutional and legal framework. It is a political model that challenges conventional assumptions about governance all over the world and is related to a transformation of the nation state and 'the dispersion of authoritative decision-making across multiple territorial levels' (Hooghe and Marks 2001: xi).

Regional Integration by Building a Geopolitical Identity of Actorness

The two ways of achieving integration described above have in common that they focus upon internal procedures. Nevertheless, a transnational region can also act in the international arena in a more or less unified way. This implies working towards a recognized regional identity at the geopolitical level as well as achieving a regional coherence in how to address global issues. Such a form of regional integration is difficult to achieve as it goes against one of the main principles of state sovereignty, its foreign policy.

However, one can observe that there is a trend towards such a form of regional integration that could have at least three main characteristics, which would distinguish it from the previous generations. First, the institutional environment for dealing with 'out of area' consequences of regional policies would become fully consolidated, by for instance developing a regional organized 'diplomatic force'. Second, regions would become more proactive, engaging in interregional arrangements and agreements going beyond purely trade issues with a multidimensional character, and having the potential to affect more relations at the global level. Finally, regions would become more actively engaged as a single entity of the UN and other world bodies.

In other words, while the first generation of regional integration was of an 'introverted' and protectionist nature, exclusively focusing on the creation of economic benefits for its members, the second generation brought in a more extroverted form of regionalism, opening integration to new domains although the focus is still mainly on the consolidation of internal political integration. Finally, the third generation would produce the extroverted level of regionalism, with a clear focus on external projection of the region and inter-regionalism. Even though second generation integration is still a limited phenomenon, the EU shows that the contours of a third generation of regionalism are becoming apparent. It recognizes that next to economic and internal political integration, there is also integration in external policy with the ambition to participate in the global institutions as a single entity with a single voice and the promotion of inter-regionalism.

While first generation regional integration was generally a top-down process led by national governments and economic élites, with a strong emphasis on the process of government, the 'new regionalism' is characterized by the multiplication of actors involved in the regional integration building, including national and regional civil society actors in a bottom-up process focusing on regional governance. Third generation regional integration would go further in this respect, by adding as a new category the transnational actors involved in the processes of interregional cooperation. The emphasis is rather on the promotion of the region's identity in global governance and in countries and geographical regions outside its own continent.

The EU Moving Towards Third Generation Regionalism?

Despite the difficulties in ratifying the most recent Lisbon Treaty, the EU is consolidating its position as most advanced integration scheme in the world and moving further towards third generation regionalism. This is visible in the two domains discussed below, as well in the EU growing role in interregional relations.

The Development of an Adequate Foreign Policy Institutional Design

In 'third generation' regionalism, the institutional environment for dealing with 'out of area' consequences of regional policies would become fully consolidated. Despite the problems of ratification, the European Constitutional Treaty, signed in Rome on 29 October 2004, was the first step in bringing the EU closer than ever to unifying its foreign policy representation through the intermediary of several institutional innovations. The proposed Treaty of Lisbon to replace the Constitutional Treaty would represent a major further step in developing a unified foreign policy.

The Treaty creates a new High Representative for the Union in Foreign Affairs and Security Policy, who will conduct the Union's common foreign and security policy presiding over the Foreign Affairs Council while acting also as a full member and Vice-President of the European Commission. This should ensure better coordination between the Council's foreign policy and security competences, ruled at present by a purely intergovernmental method and the Commission's work in external relations, development, and foreign trade dominated already by the supranational method. In fulfilling the mandate, the High Representative shall be assisted by a European External Action Service, made up of officials from relevant departments of the General Secretariat of the Council and of the Commission as well as staff seconded from national diplomatic services of the Member States. Furthermore, the European Council will become a fully fledged institution with a President appointed for two and a half years. The possibility of closer structured cooperation in the field of defence policy is newly introduced. At the same time, the Treaty of Lisbon, if ratified, will offer the EU a legal personality and create therefore the first ever regional organization that has the jurisdiction to act as a supranational organization within the framework of the UN.

If ratified and implemented by all member states, these institutional innovations have the potential to unify the European foreign policies currently undermined by the existing fragmentation between the Council, the Presidency, and the Commission's work. This could also help address the current 'frustrating ambiguity' (Telò 2005) about EU's foreign policy identity choice between 'civilian power' and military power. By achieving a complete 'package of capabilities'[7] combining both 'soft power' and 'hard power' elements, the EU could promote

7 In 2002, Javier Solana, the EU High-Representative for CFSP, stated in the Spanish journal Politica Exterior: 'La mejor manera de afrontar muchos de los retos que en materia de seguridad se presentan en el siglo XXI será la aplicacíon coordinada y coherente de un "paquete de capacidades" que incluya recursos económicos, diplomáticos, civiles y militares. La UE avanza de manera adecuada para reunir los componentes de tal paquete' (Solana 2002).

a quite unique vision of international affairs, in which multilateralism should prevail over unilateralism, and a specific strategy of conflict prevention combining civilian and military aspects.

The Role of Regional Actors Within Global Institutions such as the UN

Finally, in the third generation form, regions would become more actively engaged with the UN. The European Union's commitment to multilateralism has been gradually consolidated as a defining principle of its foreign policy identity. The European Commission Communication from 9 September 2003, *The European Union and the United Nations: The choice of multilateralism*, underlines Europe's attachment to multilateralism – and to the United Nations, as the pivot of the multilateral system. The communication also highlighted two aspects, in particular, of the EU's contribution to the effectiveness of multilateral legal instruments and commitments established under UN auspices that could be further developed. The first is the EU's ability to act as a 'front-runner' in developing and implementing multilateral instruments and commitments. Second is support, where necessary, for the capacity of other countries to implement their multilateral commitments effectively (European Commission 2003: 5). The communication also stated the need to lay the foundations for a wider EU-UN partnership going beyond development and to build cooperation in peace and security: conflict prevention, crisis management, peacekeeping, and peace building. However, the presence of the EU in the UN will always be limited to the extent that the UN is an organization that brings together states and the EU is not a state.

Nevertheless, in the context of the UN reform debates, a number of developments are going on that could pave the way for this aspect of third generation regionalism (Thakur and Van Langenhove 2006: 233-40). The High-Level Panel on Threats, Challenges and Change (2004) recognized that regional organizations can be a vital part of the multilateral system, and this was confirmed by the former UN Secretary General Kofi Annan in his 2005 report *In Larger Freedom: Towards Security, Development and Human Rights for All*. In addition, the UN member states called for a stronger relationship between the UN and regional organizations at the Millennium Review Summit in 2005. It was even suggested that regional organizations should be involved in the proceedings of the Security Council. Meanwhile, the existing high-level meetings between the UN and regional organizations have become annual since 2006 and coordinated with meetings of the Security Council (SC). This decision was undertaken in October 2005, when the Council adopted resolution 1631, in which the Council expressed its intention to have regular meetings with regional and sub-regional organizations. This is the first resolution on the UN and regional organizations.[8] The main areas for

8 See http://www.securitycouncilreport.org/site/c.glKWLeMTIsG/b.2616247/k.893B/Update_Report_No_3BR_The_UN_and_Regional_OrganisationsBR_23_March_2007.htm.

discussion stated in the resolution are standby arrangements, rapid deployment, small arms and light weapons, counter-terrorism and capacity-building assistance. Though 'some action has been taken and a number of countries have committed funds to African organizations, in particular ECOWAS, the progress at the general level is minimal' (Thakur and Van Langenhove 2006: 233-40). Moreover, the Secretary General requested to submit a report on the issue to the Security Council. As a result, in July 2006 it was issued as the report *A Regional-Global Security Partnership: Challenges and Opportunities* (United Nations 2006).

All of these recent developments go back to the UN Charter where the so-called 'Chapter VIII' already foresaw a specific role for regional organizations. Scholars such as Graham and Felício (2006) and Tavares (2006) have argued that the time is ripe to take Chapter VIII as the basis for a new global-regional security system. Of course, this cannot be seen independently of the hot issue of the reform of the Security Council (SC). A regional framework for SC membership could facilitate UN-regional organization cooperation and allow regional actors such as the EU to play a greater role in international politics.

In other words, a number of developments within the UN are gradually allowing regional organizations to act much more as an international actor just as states do.[9] One would expect the EU, as currently the most advanced form of second generation in the world, to fully take advantage of this and support the UN reform processes that create a space where it can manifest itself as a third generation integration scheme. This seems, however, not to be the case. The main reason for this seems to be that the EU does not want to be identified as a 'Chapter VIII' agency. Given its current special status within the UN, accepting 'Chapter VIII' status would somehow be perceived as degradation, putting the EU at the same level of, say, the African Union or the League of Arab States (Graham and Felicio 2006).

Regional Social Policies

Regional integration thus comes in many varieties. On the one hand, there are the pure Regional Trade Agreements (RTAs). More than 400 RTAs are currently notified to the WTO. On the other hand, there are supranational regional arrangements that go beyond pure economic integration. Such integration schemes exist and the EU is currently the most developed example. And finally there seems to be an emerging regionalism that finds its place as an actor in the multilateral system, next to nation states; again, the EU is in the forefront of this development, its objection to 'Chapter VIII'[10] status and its failure to ratify the Lisbon Treaty notwithstanding.

---

9 See also Van Langenhove, L (2003).

10 The Charter of the UN refers to regional arrangements in its 'Chapter VIII'. Article 52.1 of 'Chapter VIII' states that 'Nothing in the present Charter precludes the existence of

All of these developments are challenging social policies. First, there is the impact of the proliferation of first generation integration scheme on national social policies. Second, there is the development of regional social policies in the framework of second generation integration scheme. And third, there is the emergence of regional integration as a catalyst of global social policies.

Regional Integration as a Factor Affecting National Social Policies

Whether regional integration has positive or negative impacts upon national social policy is much contested with claims and counterclaims. Some draw attention to the downward pressure on social and labour standards resulting from economic competition. Others draw attention to the levelling up of national policies through legally binding regional directives.

Downward pressures

Regional trade agreements have brought with them an increasing openness to global competition. It has been argued that this has imposed costs on unskilled labour in industrial countries through downward pressure on wages, erosion of social security systems, weakening of trade unions and labour standards. The creation of 'internal' regional markets has given birth to a fundamental economic dilemma:

- it is in the interest of companies to move business from high wage to low wage countries;
- it is in the interest of workers to move from low wage to high wage countries.

Furthermore, companies move from countries with high labour standards to countries with low labour standards. In developing countries, this increased openness has exacerbated child labour and other violations of core labour standards as established by the ILO (Granger and Siroën 2006).

Incorporating labour rights provisions in regional trade agreements

Attempts by the ILO to establish at a global scale legally binding regimes of social standards have not until now been successful. Opposition to a multilateral regime for social standards has come from developing countries that feared that it would undermine their comparative advantages in low wage, labour-intensive industries

---

regional arrangements or agencies for dealing with such matters relating to the maintenance of international peace and security as are appropriate for regional action, provided that such arrangements or agencies and their activities are consistent with the Purposes and Principles of the United Nations'. For more information, see http://www.unhchr.ch/html/menu3/b/ch-chp8.htm.

(Dasgupta 2000). The possibility of such standards being developed at a regional level is opened up.

At the regional level, however, even in the EU, the most advanced model of regional integration with a social dimension, member states have still maintained a large sovereignty over labour legislation. Nevertheless, the EU has developed a series of directives governing social issues that deal with free movement of labour, social security, equal treatment of men and women, protection of safety and health at the workplace and the introduction of a 'social dialogue' between industrial management and labour representatives at the European level. The European charter of Fundamental Social Rights, incorporated in the 1993 Maastricht Treaty, has given enlarged competence to the EU to legislate in a number of areas.

Regional Integration as a Driver Towards Regional Social Policies

The main characteristic of the 'second generation' of regionalism or 'new regionalism' is the development of the political dimension. The political dimension has to be understood in the way in which Hettne (1999) uses to define 'new regionalism', as a: 'multidimensional form of integration which includes economic, political, social, and cultural aspects and thus goes far beyond the goal of creating region-based free trade regimes or security alliances. Rather, the political ambition of establishing regional coherence and identity seems to be of primary importance.' As underlined by Van Langenhove and Costea (2007), the idea behind 'new regionalism' relies on the fact that trade and economy cannot be isolated from the rest of the society. Integration is also about non-economic matters, like social, cultural, and environmental issues. The more the economies become integrated, the more there will be a need for common policies in the social field.

Regional integration through institutional building has been most prominent in Europe. Nevertheless, the EU institutions have played a relatively minor role in social policy compared to their powers in purely economic matters such as trade, competition and monetary policy. Since the 1980s, under pressure from social groups, the EU social policy has been gradually built up. However, the key moment of developing a coherent set of regional social policies was the Lisbon Summit in 2000. The heads of the member states adopted the Lisbon Strategy aimed at turning the EU into 'the most competitive and knowledge-based economy in the world capable of sustainable economic growth with more and better jobs and greater social cohesion' (Zeitlin, Pochet and Magnusson 2005). Therefore, the EU model has been redefined to include high economic growth, and a high level of social and economic cohesion. This is Europe's response to globalization in order to make business and labour more competitive and better able to take advantage of the opportunities arising from globalization.

The Lisbon Strategy, however, represents the materialization of progressively EU initiatives regarding labour and employment issues. The 1992 Maastricht Treaty is the moment when it was decided to form the Monetary Union. Moreover, the multilateral surveillance procedure was introduced for aligning national decisions. Based on the new provisions of the Amsterdam Treaty in 1997, which includes for the first time a chapter on employment policy, the Luxembourg European Council in 1997 paved the way for the European Employment Strategy (EES). The EES is designed to function as the main tool to give direction and ensure coordination of the employment policy priorities to which member states should subscribe at EU level.

The EES represents the foundation of a new soft working method at EU level – the Open Method of Coordination (OMC), launched at the Lisbon Summit in 2000. The OMC is a new and broadly applicable instrument of EU governance that addresses common European concerns while taking into consideration national diversity. Moreover, it is a tool to translate the European guidelines into national and regional policies. The main areas covered are employment, social inclusion, pensions, health, research and innovation, and education and training.

Regional Integration as Catalyst of Global Social Policies

In terms of a region as an actor seeking to influence global policy, the EU is our most developed example. Since the beginning of the millennium, the EU 'has indeed taken a more systematic and assertive approach to advancing the social dimension of globalization' (Orbie and Tortell 2008: 21). The EU as global player together with ILO has been instrumental in injecting Decent Work (including social protection) into the Millennium Development Goals (MDGs) targets, and since 2005 has included social cohesion in its external development assistance (Delarue 2006). Moreover, the EU plays an important role in promoting social clauses throughout its trade and development policies. A significant objective of the EU's global social agenda is deepening the cooperation with the ILO. Thus the EU as a global actor is promoting the effective application of core labour standards at a global level. Moreover, the strategy aims at helping developing countries to apply core labour standards for achieving social development (European Commission 2001). An example in this sense is the Cotonou Agreement, signed in 2000 with the ACP countries, which makes specific reference to the ILO core labour standards (CLS).

The EU's international position on health, gender, children's rights, and corporate social responsibility has many progressive features. The European Commission is given as an important example within the World Commission on the Social Dimension of Globalization (WCSDG), which issued in 2004 the report: *A fair globalization. Creating opportunities for all*. The 'European social model', the Lisbon Strategy, and the Open Method of Coordination are given as models for international social governance.

In the field of development, the EU is supporting the UN sustainable development policies and is committed to achieve the UN MDGs. By adopting *The European Community's Development Policy*, the European Commission strengthened the role of the EU in promoting regional integration, alongside five other activities (European Commission 2000). In this respect, 'the EU has clearly acknowledged [the] link between regional integration and development in its policies towards African countries [...] by including regional integration among the focal priorities for poverty reduction mentioned in the Cotonou Agreement' (Van Langenhove and Costea 2007: 71).

However, Orbie and Tortell (2008: 21) note that:

> in relation to initiatives such as the inclusion of labour standards in bilateral agreements, the social dimension of the Union's enlargement and neighbourhood policies, the implementation of gender mainstreaming in development aid and the achievements of the MDG , the EU's actions are still at a preliminary stage.

Moreover the EU has been argued to be an *obstacle* to a fair globalization in its trade policies even as it argues for a fairer globalization. Thus it has been argued that the EU's attempts at creating Economic Priority Areas between itself and former ACP states is not conducive to enabling African and other poorer countries to develop the social and labour dimension of their own regional integration (Keet 2007).

A third position argues that the EU as a global social policy player is neither an effective actor for progressive global social policies based upon the EU model, nor an obstacle because of its trade policies, but is indeed irrelevant because European social welfare ideas and ideals are not transferable to other world regions. Thus

> In the light of the peculiar religious-historical roots of social policy in the West, we must reassess the transferability of Western institutions to countries with a different cultural foundation as well as standards of measurement of progress in the development of a welfare state. (Rieger and Liebfried 2003: 326)

In fairness, the EU insists it does not seek to export its own social model or to promote harmonization with its own social standards. In addition, together with the World Commission on the Social Dimension of Globalization, it strictly refuses any sanctions-based approach to labour standards in international trade agreements (European Commission 2004).

Conclusions

Regional integration can act both as a building block and as a stumbling stone towards a global social policy that makes globalization more 'fair'. The report of the WCSDG, *A fair globalization: Creating opportunities for all*, strengthens the idea that regional integration can contribute to a more equitable pattern of globalization, but only if regional integration has a strong social dimension (WCSDG 2004). The WCSDG referred quite extensively to the need to strengthen regional governance, based on principles of participation and democratic accountability:

> Representative bodies, such as regional parliaments, have an important role to play. We believe that regional integration should be advanced through social dialogue between representative organizations of workers and employers, and wider dialogue with other important social actors, on the basis of strong institutions for democratic and judicial accountability. The creation of tripartite or wider councils and forums at the regional level [...] provides an important institutional framework for such dialogue. (WCSDG 2004: 73)

At least in theory, regional integration offers a number of possibilities for the development of

> regional social, *regulation, rights and redistribution schemes* (Yeates and Deacon 2006) in the form of regional *social, health and labour regulations*, regional mechanisms that give citizens a voice to challenge their governments in terms of *social rights*; regional intergovernmental forms of *co-operation in social policy*; regional cross-border *investments* in the area of social policy; regional *coordination of economic and developmental policies*; regional initiatives in *capacity building and innovation* to strengthen the capabilities of people; or *inter-regional* agreements and arrangements related to social issues. (UNU-CRIS 2008:1)

A general tendency that can be observed is the need for more new initiatives in the area of social policy at the regional level. More shallow forms of regional integration and interregional relations introduce social issues as part of the broader attempts to manage and regulate intra- or interregional flows of goods and services (trade), capitals (investment), and people (migration). In deeper, broader and more institutionalized forms of regionalism, more or less embryonic forms of what could be called regional social policies can and do emerge, through policy approximation, coordination and/or convergence. However, policy spill-over mechanisms and policy sequencing within regional integration processes are still not very well understood, mainly because they remain under-studied – even if some new trends in regionalism studies are emerging to address these important questions.

References

Ahearne, A., Pisany-Ferry, J., Sapir, A. and Véron, N. 2006. Global Governance: an Agenda for Europe, *Breughel Policy Brief* 2006/07, Brussels: Breughel.

Dasgupta, A. 2000. Labour Standards and WTO: A New form of Protectionism, *South Asia Economic Journal*, 1(2), 113-129.

Deacon, B. 2007. *Global Social Policy and Governance*, London: Sage.

Deacon, B. 2008. Global and Regional Social Governance, in *Understanding Global Social Policy*, edited by N. Yeates. Bristol: The Policy Press, 25-48.

Deacon, B., Ortiz, I. and Zelenev, Z. 2007. Regional Social Policy, *DESA Working Paper*, No. 37, ST/ESA/2007/DWP/37, New York: UNDESA.

Delarue, R. 2006. ILO-EU Cooperation on Employment and Social Affairs, in *The United Nations and the European Union: An Ever Stronger Partnership*, edited by J. Wouters, F. Hoffmeister and T. Ruys. The Hague: T.M C Asser Press.

European Commission. (2003) *Communication from the Commission to the Council and to the European Parliament. The European Union and the United Nations: The choice of multilateralism*, COM 526 final: 5, Brussels: European Commission.

Farrell, M. 2005. The Global Politics of Regionalism: An Introduction, in *Global Politics of Regionalism. Theory and Practice*, edited by M. Farrell, B. Hettne, and L. Van Langnehove. London: Pluto Press.

Graham, K. and Felício, T. 2006. *Regional Security and Global Governance*, Brussels: VUB Press.

Granger, C. and Siroën, J.-M. 2006. Core Labour Standards in Trade Agreements: From Multilateralism to Bilateralism, *Journal of World Trade*, 40(5): 813-836.

Hettne, B. 1999. The New Regionalism: A Prologue, in *Globalism and the New Regionalism,* edited by B. Hettne, A. Inotain and O. Sunkel. London: Macmillan.

Hooghe, L. and Marks, G. 2001. *Multi-level Governance and European Integration.* Lanham: Rowman and Littlefield.

Keet, D. 2007. Alternative Regional Strategies in Africa, *Global Social Policy*, 7(3): 262–5.

Keet, D. 2007. *Economic Partnership Agreements: Responses to the EU offensive against ACP Developmental Regions.* The Hague: Trans National Institute.

Mattli, W. 1999. *The Logic of European Integration: Europe and Beyond.* Cambridge: Cambridge University Press.

Orbie, J. and Tortell, L. (eds.) 2008. *The European Union and the Social Dimension of Globalization, How the EU influences the World.* London and New York: Routledge.

Rieger, E. and Leibfried, S. 2003. *Limits to Globalization, Welfare States and the World Economy*. Cambridge: Polity.

SELA. 2008. *Social Dimension of Integration: Guidelines for an Action Plan in the Areas of Health, Education, Housing, and Employment, UNU-CRIS Working Papers W-2008/4*, [Online]. Available at: http://www.cris.unu.edu/fileadmin/workingpapers/W-2008-4.pdf [accessed 10 January 2009].

Solana, J. *Politica Exterior*, Marzo/Abril 2002, XVI (86), 10.

Tavares, R. 2006. *Understanding Regional Peace and Security: A Framework for Analysis*. Gothenburg University: unpublished Ph.D dissertation.

Telò, M. 2005. *Europe: A Civilian Power? European Union, Global Governance, World Order*. Houndmills: Palgrave Macmillan.

Thakur, R. and Van Langenhove, L. 2006. Enhancing Global Governance through Regional Integration. *Global Governance*, 12(3): 233-40.

Thakur, R. and Van Langenhove, L. 2008. Enhancing Global Governance through Regional Integration, in *Regionalization and Global Governance. The taming of Globalisation?*, edited by A. Cooper, C.W. Hughes and P. De Lombaerde. London and New York: Routledge.

United Nations. 2006. *Report of the Secretary-General A regional-global security partnership: challenges and opportunities*, document S/2006/590, New York, 28 July 2006. New York: United Nations.

UNU-CRIS. 2008. *Deepening the Social Dimension of Regional Integration: An Overview of Recent Trends and Future Challenges in the Light of the World Commission on the Social Dimension of Globalization, ILLS Discussion Paper, No. 188*, [Online]. Geneva: ILO. Available at: http://www.ilo.org/public/english/bureau/inst/download/dp18808.pdf [Accessed 28 August 2008].

Van Langenhove, L 2003. Regional Integration and Global Governance. *UNUnexions*, August 2003: 1-4.

Van Langenhove, L. and Costea, A.C. 2007. The EU as a Global Actor and the Emergence of "Third-Generation" Regionalism, in *Managing a Multilevel Foreign Policy*, edited by P. Foradori, P. Rosa and R. Scartezzini. Lanham: Lexington Books.

Warleigh-Lack, A. 2008. Studying Regionalization Comparatively: A Conceptual Framework, in *Regionalisation and Global Governance. The taming of globalization?*, edited by A.F. Cooper, C.W. Hughes, and P. De Lombaerde. London and New York: Routledge.

WCSDG 2004. *A Fair Globalisation: Creating Opportunities for All*. Geneva: International Labour Office – World Commission on the Social Dimension of Globalisation.

Yeates, N. 2005. *Globalisation and Social Policy in a Development Context: Regional Responses, Social Policy and Development Programme Paper, No. 18*, Geneva: United Nations Research Institute for Social Development.

Yeates, N. 2008. *Understanding Global Social Policy*, Bristol. Policy Press.

Yeates, N. and Deacon, B. 2006. *Globalism, Regionalism and Social Policy: Framing the Debate, UNU-CRIS Occasional Papers (O-2006/6)* [Online]. Available at: http://www.cris.unu.edu/fileadmin/workingpapers/20060418154630.O-2006-6.pdf [Accessed 20 September 2008].

Zeitlin, P., Pochet, P. and Magnusson, L. (eds.) 2005. *The Open Method of Coordination in Action: The European Employment and Social Inclusion Strategies*, Bern, Berlin, Bruxelles, Frankfurt am Main, New York, Oxford, Wien: P.I.E.-Peter Lang.

Conclusion
New Regionalisms: Beyond NETRIS[1]

Timothy M. Shaw and Vanessa T. Tang

> For a long period the study of regions and regional orders occupied a small if not insignificant place in international relations theory and scholarship. Now we have [...] books which argue that regions are central to our understanding of world politics. (Acharya 2007: 629)

> The regionalist strategies of states, businesses, non-governmental organizations (NGOs) and social movements are key to understanding the complex relationship between contemporary globalization and social policy processes [...] to advance a wider appreciation of the significance of regionalist and regionalization processes in the making of global social governance and policy. (Yeates 2007: 251)

The three-year opportunity to interact through the EU-ACP Network of Regional Integration Studies (NETRIS) constituted an unrepeatable, fleeting challenge to engage with analysts from the trio of continents in the Global South. It was also unexpectedly timely as the EU crisis of the eurozone coincided with the continued rise of the BRICS, and the continuing fall-out from the 'global' crisis of the end of the first decade of the new century: i.e. regional divergence was undeniable. The juxtaposition of original analyses from the South with the palpable difficulties of the North makes for a unique legacy with relevance for comparative studies of regional development in the 21st century. This concluding reflection seeks to go beyond the overview in our introduction to suggest a range of regional scenarios for the Global South beyond the second decade of the 21st century; these will increasingly impact the North as well as *vice versa.*

The potential of NETRIS was not so apparent when we first met in Dar es Salaam in mid-2009; but it had become palpable by our finale in Addis Ababa in late-2011 (see Appendix). Symbolic of regional divergence in the new decade as we met in Africa Hall of the UNECA was Africa's assertive declaration to advance towards 'developmental states' (Kyung-Sup, Fine and Weiss 2012 and UNECA and AU 2011a) combined with its reluctance to sign EPAs with the EU. These came together in the *dirigiste* African Mining Vision (UNECA and AU 2011b) (www.africaminingvision.org). Simultaneously, the prestigious journal *Global*

1 This is a revised, updated and extended version of a brief Foreword by Tim Shaw to Lorenzo Fioramonti (ed) 2012. *Regions and Crises: new challenges for contemporary regionalisms.* London: Palgrave Macmillan. viii-x.

Environmental Policy in mid-2012 published a special issue on the prospects for 'regional environmental governance' (Balsiger and Vandeveer 2012); this balanced the innovative regional focus on social policy advanced by Yeates (2007), Deacon (2009) and Deacon (2012). Seemingly, 'new' regionalisms were unstoppable, including Africa's articulation and advocacy of a Tripartite FTA, possibly constituting a new 'African regional paradigm' (Hartzenberg 2012). This ambitious dream to combine a trio of RECs – COMESA, EAC and SADC – would create the largest-ever region on the continent of 26 states with implications for the established groupings; there are also questions about whether its three pillars – market integration, infrastructural development and industrialization – will boost intra-African trade.

The increasingly multidisciplinary 'political economy' of 'new regionalisms' is emerging as one way to approach and understand the contemporary 'global' crisis and its related restructuring/rebalancing (Lorenzo 2012 and Van Langenhove 2011). Unlike the so-called 'Asian crisis' at the end of the last century confined to one 'distant' region (Robertson 2008), the current one underlines contrasts between old North and new South, serving to unsettle established inter-regional hierarchies.

The unfolding crisis has had divergent inter-regional incidences and impacts: the 'old' North has suffered contraction whereas the 'new' South has experienced further expansion. The trans-Atlantic advocates of 'extreme' liberalization first endured the most 'shocks' or contractions, since the EU of 27 including the PIIGS has also been in decline. By contrast, the original four BRICs, if not all five BRICS, especially the pair in Asia – i.e. China and India – have continued to grow impressively and relentlessly. Moreover, Africa has benefitted from the interest and demand from China and India, even if their rising labour costs and growing competition may yet lead to trade wars, now ranking as another growth region – of 'lion kings' (www.mckinsey.com)! – leading *The Economist* (2011) to revise its 'hopeless' label or lament of the turn of the century and recognize that Africa at the start of the second decade of the new millennium was now part of the burgeoning Global South – the 'East-South turn' of Pieterse's opening citation – in something of a renaissance (Shaw 2012).

So lessons can begin to be derived about contemporary development from Asia and Africa as indicated in this reflection from NETRIS as suggested in two recent collections on IR (Waever and Tickner 2009) and IPE (Philips and Weaver 2010). Similarly, one of us has just co-edited with others two relevant original collections on African IR (Cornelissen, Cheru and Shaw 2012) and on varieties of regionalisms (Shaw, Grant and Cornelissen 2011). These, along with a series of titles, both articles and books, by Amitav Acharya *et al.* on Asian IR and regionalisms (Acharya 2001, Acharya and Johnston 2007), resonate with the present collection.

And analysts/advocates of social policy increasingly focus on the intermediate regional level (Deacon *et al.* 2012, Yeates 2007); likewise, eminent environmental scholars like Bernard Debarbieux and Ken Conca on REG (Balsiger and

VanDeveer 2012) onto regional conflicts/diasporas/ecologies/franchises/media/networks/migrations/sports/TOC etc.

Likewise, curiously, despite MENA being one of the least institutionalized of recognized regions (Harders and Legrenzi 2008, Korany 2011), its series of social movements at the turn of the decade suggest at least informal, civil society communication in the Arab/Islamic world.

In turn, hitherto hegemonic EU perspectives on regional development are being challenged by the recognition by Alex Warleigh-Lack *et al.* (2011) of the relevance of new regionalisms for today's Europe of 27 given the Euro crisis concentrated in the PIIGS. See also the advocacy of a more rigorous comparative regionalisms methodology by an innovative group of UNU-CRIS analysts – Philippe de Lombaerde, Fredrik Soderbaum, Luk Van Langenhove and Francis Baert – in Finn Laursen (2010: 21-39). Similarly, *RIS* has had several special issues or sections devoted to related issues around burgeoning regional relations (Fawn 2009)/powers (Nel and Nolte 2010) etc.

Such reflections lead towards the recognition of compatible/competitive regionalisms exacerbated by the global crisis at the decade's turn given overlaps in membership, function etc (see Mace, Cooper and Shaw 2011).

Before the end of the first decade of the 21st century, Acharya and Johnston (2007: 9-10) had mounted an attack on new regionalisms:

> [T]he new regionalism literature challenged the rationalist bias of neo-liberal institutionalism. Compared to the earlier regional integration literature, the literature on 'new regionalism' viewed regionalism to be a more multifaceted and comprehensive phenomenon, taking into account the role of both state and non-state actors as well as the whole range of political, economic, strategic, social, demographic and ecological interactions within regions. It shifted the focus away from formal institutions toward studying informal sectors, parallel economies, and non-state coalitions [...] its focus [...] might have lessened the importance of institutional features of regionalism.

In turn, as the BRICs/BRICS increase by one to five, with the invitation/inclusion of RSA at the end of 2010 who will host the fifth Summit, the last of the first half-decade round in March 2013, building on the IBSA experience amongst a trio of emerging democracies, there are interesting distinctions to be recognized and debated among the notions of regional powers/economies/markets/societies/companies etc. RSA is not in the Goldman Sachs Next-11 (N-11) (www2.goldmansachs.com/ideas/global) even if it is a part of VISTA, of the BASIC ginger group around COP 15/16/17 and of BCG's corporate 'African Challengers' (www.bcg.com).

So do the five BRICS constitute more an alliance of emerging regional powers than of emerging markets? They now comprise 25% of the G20 (Cooper and Subacchi 2010), constituting the core of the new 'second world' (Khanna 2009). Together they bring their heterogeneous regional networks/hubs and supply chains to bear along with diasporas like those of China in Southeast Asia (Chu 2010) or India's around the Indian Ocean Rim. But how important are such regional dimensions to emerging (global) powers? Nel and Nolte (2010) treat regional powers rather than, say, emerging powers or societies, or regional development or integration. And some regional powers' ambitions may lead away from rather than towards regional cohesion or consensus (Mace, Cooper and Shaw 2011).

Meanwhile, why did the original quad of BRICs not borrow from ASEAN plus or the G8 Heiligendamm Process and just add a handful of special invitations – 'outreach' – to their third and subsequent summits at the start of the second decade of the 21st century (Cooper and Antkiewicz 2008)? Why the formal invitation to RSA to join at the end of 2010 notwithstanding the limitations in its stature or the competing claims of others in the N-11/VISTA rankings?

So, in terms of explaining context, there is a need to problematize similarities among/difference between distinct emphases/genres or 'disciplines' symbolized by *emerging* economies/societies/powers/companies etc (Pieterse and Rehbein 2009: 1-3): more/less business, economics, political science, sociology etc; and also more/less orthodoxy, radicalism, realism, revisionism etc.

And in turn we also need to recognize *varieties* of capitalisms/companies/civil societies/states etc as in Overbeek and Van Apeldoorn (2012). Such varieties are themselves in flux as rebalancing occurs, including significant shifts in capital, governance, networks, supply chains, technologies etc, symbolized by the metamorphosis of G8 into G20 at the turn of the decade. As Cooper argues:

> As a direct consequence of the 'Great Recession' of 2009-9 and the continuing instability left in its wake, the G20 has moved into a putative position of premier forum for global economic governance. (Cooper and Subacchi 2010: 741)

But at the start of the second decade of the 21st century, no such governance can transpire without an association with novel forms of private, transnational governance or transnational transfers (Brown 2011): onto hybrid governance. Cadman (2011: 1-24 and 193-205) and Gale and Haward (2011: 1-47 and 259-266) have advanced case studies and comparative analyses of such non- or extra-state governance in the case of forestry and fisheries, as have Ben Richardson (2009: 1-40 and 194-212) for sugar and Adam Sneyd (2010) for cotton.

The evolution of novel forms of multilateralism – global 'private' governance? – involving a range of heterogeneous actors, not just 200 states, is marked by OP and KP, ETI and EITI etc as outlined in Klaus Dingwerth (2008). Such 'initiatives' or 'processes' incorporate a flexible, dynamic range of actors and interests compatible with varieties of capitalisms, corporations and civil societies; in 2011, Hale and Held (2011) identified over 50 heterogeneous versions of such transnational governance worthy of a thumb-nail sketch. As Pieterse (2011: 43) suggests:

> In treating capitalism in the singular, unilinear theories of capitalism, from Marx to world-system theory, view variation mainly as variation over time. [...] Capitalism survives thanks to the diversity of capitalisms: 'the flexibility of capitalism derives from capitalisms and regional variation.'

This original, innovative, cross-regional collection with its core in the Global South advances such promising interdisciplinary contemporary approaches. These are ever more necessary in a world – conceptual as well as existential – in flux as the 'global' crisis continues to reverberate through exponential rebalancing and restructuring.

We conclude by highlighting a half-dozen conceptual and existential trends, each of which is impacted by the balance among states, companies and societies:

1. Expansion and/or contraction of the two emerging regional poles – EU and the BRICS – assuming the hegemon in decline – the US – fails to pull itself out of its historic nose dive;
2. Similarly, the expansion and/or contraction of the second tier of regional developments, especially the East Asian Summit, UNASUR and/or Africa's FTA;
3. Rise/fall of distinctive sectors as global political economy develops: diasporas, energy, environment, finance, informal/illegal, resources, social policy, technology and tourism including the extension of transnational governance into areas not previously open such as SALW and ATT;
4. More/less regional conflict so more/less regional R2P, from GLR to Central Asia/Europe, Korean Peninsula etc;
5. More/less innovation in regional governance such as certification, corridors, initiatives, peace parks, processes, valleys, zones etc as advocated by Trademark in Eastern and Southern Africa;
6. In short, more/less regional agency by the end of the decade. At the start of the second decade of the 21st century, the EU seems to have less agency than before, and the BRICS more, symbolized by the establishment of a S-S development bank by the BRICS in Durban in March 2013. It would have been unthinkable to have had a collection on 'African agency' until 2010 (Lorenz and Rempe 2013).

The move up from regional to global for the commission on drugs offers an optimistic scenario: the Latin American Commission on Drugs and Democracy (www.drogsedemocracia.org) has evolved into the Global Commission on Drug Policy (www.globalcommissionondrugs.org). Such a scenario was less likely when NETRIS began at the end of the last, first decade than when it ended at the start of the second decade of the 21st century. Regional analysis and policy need to take such changes into account when contrasting agency with dependency, resilience with vulnerability. We conclude with the words of Amitav Acharya (2012: 14):

'it is the field of comparative regionalism [...] whose time has come. Its growing diversity and pluralism is a cause for celebration'.

References

Acharya, A. 2007. Review Article: the emerging regional architecture of world politics. *World Politics*, 59(4), 629-652.

Acharya, A. 2012. Comparative Regionalisms: a field whose time has come? *International Spectator*, 47(1), 3-15.

Acharya, A. and Johnston A.I. (eds.) 2007. *Crafting Cooperation: regional international institutions in comparative perspective*. Cambridge: CUP.

Acharya, A. and Buzan B. 2007. Why is There no Non-Western IR Theory? *International Relations of the Asia-Pacific*, 7(3), 285-438.

Balsiger, J. and Vandeveer S.D. 2012. Navigating Regional Environmental Governance. *Global Environmental Politics*. 12(3), iii-145.

Brown, S. 2011. *Transnational Transfers and Global Development*. London: Palgrave Macmillan.

Cadman, T. 2011. *Quality and Legitimacy of Global Governance: case lessons from forestry*. London: Palgrave Macmillan.

Chang, K-S., Fine, B. and Weiss, L. (eds.) 2012. *Developmental Politics in Transition: the neoliberal era and beyond.* London: Palgrave Macmillan.

Cheru, F. and Obi, C. (eds.) 2010. *The Rise of China and India in Africa*. London: Zed for NAI.

Chu, Y-W. (ed.) 2010. *Chinese Capitalisms: historical emergence and political implications*. London: Palgrave Macmillan.

Cooper, A.F. and Antkiewicz, A. (eds.) 2008. *Emerging Powers in Global Governance: lessons from the Heiligendamm Process*. Waterloo: WLU Press for CIGI.

Cooper, A.F. and Subacchi, P. 2010. Global Economic Governance in Transition. *International Affairs,* 86(3), 607-757.

Cornelissen, S., Cheru, F. and Shaw, T.M. (eds.) 2012. *Africa and International Relations in the 21st Century: still challenging theory?* London: Palgrave Macmillan.

Deacon, B. 2012. *World-Regional Social Policy and Global Governance*. Abingdon: Routledge.

Deacon, B. *et al.* (eds.) 2009. *World-Regional Social Policy and Global Governance: new research and policy agendas in Africa, Asia, Europe and Latin America*. Abingdon: Routledge.

Dingwerth, K. 2008. Private Transnational Governance and the Developing World: a comparative perspective. *International Studies Quarterly*, 52(3), 607-634.

The Economist. 2011. The Lion Kings? *The Economist, 398 (8715)*, 8 January: 72-73.

Fawn, R. 2009. Special Issue: globalizing the regional, regionalizing the global. *Review of International Studies*, 35, 1-261.

Gale, F. and Haward, M. 2011. *Global Commodity Governance: state responses to sustainable forest and fisheries certification*. London: Palgrave Macmillan.

Hale, T. and Held, D. (eds.) 2011. *Handbook of Transnational Governance: institutions and innovations*. Cambridge: Polity.

Harders, C. and Legrenzi, M. (eds.) 2008. *Beyond Regionalism? Regional cooperation, regionalism and regionalization in the Middle East*. Aldershot: Ashgate.

Hartzenberg, T. *et al.* (ed.) 2012. *The Tripartite Free Trade Area: towards a new African integration paradigm*. Stellenbosch: TRALAC.

Khanna, P. 2009. *The Second World: how emerging powers are redefining global competition in the twenty-first century*. New York: Random House.

Laursen, F. (ed.) 2010. *Comparative Regional Integration: Europe and beyond*. Farnham: Ashgate.

Lorenz, U. and Rempe, M. (eds.) 2013 (forthcoming). *Comparing Regions in Africa: mapping agency*. Farnham: Ashgate.

Mace, G., Cooper, A.F. and Shaw, T.M. (eds.) 2011. *Inter-American Cooperation at a Crossroads*. London: Palgrave Macmillan.

Nel, P. and Nolte, D. 2010. Regional Powers in a Changing Global Order. *Review of International Studies*, 36(4), 877-974.

Overbeek, H. and van Apeldoorn, B. (eds.) 2012. *Neoliberalism in Crisis*. London: Palgrave Macmillan.

Pieterse, J.N. 2011. Global Rebalancing: crisis and the East-South turn. *Development and Change*, 42(1): 22-48.

Pieterse, J.N. and Rehbein, B. (eds.) 2009. *Globalization and Emerging Societies: development and inequality*. London: Palgrave Macmillan.

Phillips, N. and Weaver, C. (eds.) 2010. *International Political Economy: debating the past, present and future*. Abingdon: Routledge.

Ravenhill, J. 2010. Special Section: the "new East Asian regionalism". *Review of International Political Economy*, 19(2), 173-318.

Richardson, B. 2009. *Sugar: refined power in a global regime*. London: Palgrave Macmillan.

Robertson, J. (ed.) 2008. *Power and Politics after Financial Crises: rethinking foreign opportunism in emerging markets*. London: Palgrave Macmillan.

Shaw, T.M. 2012. Africa's Quest for Developmental States: renaissance for whom? *Third World Quarterly*, 33(5): 837-851.

Shaw, T.M., Grant, J.A. and Cornelissen, S. (eds.) 2011. *Ashgate Research Companion to Regionalisms*. Farnham: Ashgate.

Sneyd, A. 2011. *Governing Cotton: globalization and poverty in Africa*. London: Palgrave Macmillan.

Tickner, A.B. and Waever, O. (eds.) 2009. *International Relations Scholarship around the World: worlding beyond the West*. Abingdon: Routledge.

UNECA and AU. 2011a. *Economic Report on Africa 2011: governing development in Africa – the role of the state in economic transformation*. Addis Ababa: UNECA.

UNECA and AU. 2011b. *Minerals and Africa's Development: the international study group report on Africa's mineral regimes*. Addis Ababa: UNECA.

Utting, P., Razavi, S. and Buchholz, R. (eds.) 2011. *The Global Crisis and Transformative Social Change*. London: Palgrave Macmillan for UNRISD.

Van Langenhove, L. 2011. *Building Regions: the regionalisation of the world order*. Farnham: Ashgate.

Warleigh-Lack, A., Robinson, N. and Rosamond, B. (eds.) 2011. *New Regionalism and the EU: dialogues, comparisons and new research directions*. Abingdon: Routledge.

Yeates, N. 2007. Special Issue on the Social Policy Dimensions of World-Regionalism. *Global Social Policy*, 7(3): 249-385.

Appendix

Project Name: Network of Regional Integration Studies (NETRIS)

Website: www.netris-acp.org

Project Period: Three years (2009-2011)

Project Funding Arrangement: NETRIS is a project funded by Edulink (www.acp-edulink.eu). Edulink is a regional initiative of the European Union (www.europa.eu) and implemented by the African, Caribbean and Pacific (ACP) secretariat (www.acpsec.org).

Project Objectives: The overall objective of the project is to support and foster regional integration and capacity building in the field of higher education through institutional networking.

Project Partners: The NETRIS partners included Addis Ababa University (AAU) (Ethiopia), Institute des Relations Internationales du Cameroun (IRIC) (Cameroun), Université Cheikh Anta Diop (UCAD) (Senegal), University of Dar es Salaam (UDSM) (Tanzania), University of KwaZulu-Natal (UKZN) (South Africa), University of South Pacific (USP) (Fiji), University of the West Indies (IIR/UWI) (Trinidad and Tobago) and two associated partners: European Centre for Development Policy Management (ECDPM) (Maastricht, The Netherlands), Southern Africa Political Economy Series (SAPES) Trust (Harare, Zimbabwe). **The organizing partners** – United Nations University Institute on Comparative Regional Integration Studies (UNU-CRIS) and the College of Europe (CoE) (Belgium).

Project Conferences: The first NETRIS conference, hosted by the University of the West Indies (IIR/UWI) in March 2010, focused on ***Researching and Advancing the Good Governance Dimension of Regional Integration***. The University of KwaZulu-Natal (UKZN) School of Economics and Finance hosted the second NETRIS conference, ***Prospects for Trade and Economic Integration in ACP countries: Challenges Facing Regionalism and Regional Integration Arrangements***, in September 2010. The third NETRIS conference took place at the University of Cheikh Anta Diop (UCAD) in March 2011 and addressed ***Regional Integration and Migration Policies in ACP countries***. The fourth finale in Addis Ababa in November 2011 took stock of past and relevant contributions made by the NETRIS-ACP higher education partner institutions and associates in the field of comparative regional integration. Academics' and policy-makers' contributions to the four conferences covered a number of significant regional integration issues (theoretical, empirical and policy-related) within the ACP region.

NETRIS Tanzania kick-off meeting (Dar es Salaam 2009)

Project participants:
AAU: T. Tilahun; S. Regassa; and F. Afewerk
IRIC: N. Kombi and J. Kenfack
UCAD: S. Sall and S. Tall
UDSM: B. Sanyagi and S. Othman
UKZN: V. Tang
USP: S. Kahsai and S. Kumar
UWI: T. Shaw and M. Kirton
ECDPM: A. Walker
SAPES: I. Mandaza
UNU-CRIS/CoE: L. Van Langenhove; E. Maertens and M. Macovei
External Participants:
EC: X. Marchal
EU: K. Vervaeke

NETRIS Trinidad and Tobago Conference (St Augustine 2010), *Researching and Advancing the Good Governance Dimension of Regional Integration*

Project Participants:
AAU: G. Estiphanos
IRIC: K. Mouelle
UCAD: S. Dieng
UDSM: P. Kabudi and J. Tesha
UKZN: V. Tang
USP: S. Kumar and K. Kahsai
UWI: C. Sankat, N. Girvan, T. Shaw, M. Kirton and J. Cooblal
ECDPM: K.Van Hove
SAPES: I. Mandaza
UNU-CRIS/CoE: L. Van Langenhove; E. Maertens and R. Tavares
External Participants:
EC: S. Ulos

NETRIS South Africa Conference (Durban 2010), *Prospects for Trade and Economic Integration in ACP countries: Challenges Facing Regionalism and Regional Integration Arrangements*

Project Participants:
AAU: G. Estiphanos and S. Yifredew
IRIC: J. Kenfack
UCAD: S. Tall and S. Dieng
UDSM: J. Kabudi and J. Tesha
UKZN: J. Mubangizi, T. Jones, M. Holden, V. Tang, R. Simson, T. Nichola, P. Koch and D. Mahadea
USP: S. Kumar and K. Kahsai
UWI: T. Shaw and M. Kirton
ECDPM: K. Van Hove
SAPES: C. Chipeta
UNU-CRIS/CoE: S. Kingah and E. Maersten

NETRIS Senegal Seminar (Dakar 2011), *Regional Integration and Migration Policies in ACP countries*

Project Participants:
AAU: G. Estiphanos
IRIC: J. Kenfack
UCAD: S. Ndiaye, S. Tall, A. Seydi, N. Kebe and G. Bitjoka
UDSM: J. Tesha and J. Kabudi
UKZN: J. Fairburn and M. Mutenje
USP: S. Kumar, H. Chen and T. Muliaina
UWI: T. Shaw and M. Kirton
ECDM: H. Klavert and K. Van Hove
SAPES: I. Mandaza
CoE/UNU-CRIS: E. Maertens, M. Macovei and E. Fanta
External Participants:
UNDP: B. Djibo
EC: D. Dellicour

NETRIS Ethiopia Conference (Addis Ababa 2011), *NETRIS Final Conference on Regional Integration Studies in the ACP*

Project Participants:
AAU: F. Anania, G. Estiphanos, S. Yifredew and M. Tedla
IRIC: J. Kenfack and Y. Mandjem
UCAD: S. Tall, S. Dieng and A. Diagne
UDSM: J. Kabudi and J-B. Ngendahimana
UKZN: J. Fairburn, R. Simson and V. Tang

USP: S. Kumar, H. Chen and T. Muliaina
UWI: T. Shaw, M. Kirton and K. Haraksingh
ECDPM: K. Van Hove and M. Dalleau
UNU-CRIS/CoE: E. Maertens, M. Macovei, S. Kingah and E. Fanta
External Participants:
EC: X. Marchal
EU: K. Vervaeke
UNECA: S. Mevel

List of Websites

www.acs-aec.org
www.africaminingvision.org
www.bcg.com
www.caic.org.tt
www.canari.org
www.caricom.org
www.caricomimpacs.org
www.cfatf-gafic.org
www.cgdev.org
www.cop17durban.com
www.cris.unu.edu
www.csgr.org
www.ddiglobal.org
www.drogsedemocracia.org
www.ecdpm.org
www.eclac.org
www.economist.com/theworldin/2012
www.eiti.org
www.fatf-gafi.org
www.foreignpolicy.com
www.garnet-eu.org
www.giga-hamburg.de
www.globalcommissionondrugs.org
www.globaldialogue.info
www.globalwitness.org
www.grandlacs.net
www.iansa.org
www.icbl.org
www.interpol.int
www.kimberleyprocess.com
www.leadinggroup.org
www.mckinsey.com
www.netris-acp.org
www.normangirvan.info
www.organized-crime.org
www.smallarmssurvey.org
www.thecropperfoundation.org
www.tralac.org
www.uncaccoalition.org
www.undp.org
www.unodc.org
www.uwi.edu
www.wdr2011.worldbank.org
www2.goldmansachs.com/ideas/global

Index

THE INTERNATIONAL POLITICAL ECONOMY OF NEW REGIONALISMS SERIES

Other titles in the series

The New Democracy Wars
The Politics of North American Democracy Promotion in the Americas
Neil A. Burron

The European Union after Lisbon
Polity, Politics, Policy
Edited by Søren Dosenrode

Roads to Regionalism
Genesis, Design, and Effects of Regional Organizations
Edited by Tanja A. Börzel, Lukas Goltermann, Mathis Lohaus and Kai Striebinger

New Regionalism or No Regionalism?
Emerging Regionalism in the Black Sea Area
Edited by Ruxandra Ivan

Our North America
Social and Political Issues beyond NAFTA
Edited by Julián Castro-Rea

Community of Insecurity
SADC's Struggle for Peace and Security in Southern Africa
Laurie Nathan

Global and Regional Problems
Towards an Interdisciplinary Study
Edited by Pami Aalto, Vilho Harle and Sami Moisio

The Ashgate Research Companion to Regionalisms
Edited by Timothy M. Shaw, J. Andrew Grant and Scarlett Cornelissen

Asymmetric Trade Negotiations
Sanoussi Bilal, Philippe De Lombaerde and Diana Tussie

The Rise of the Networking Region
The Challenges of Regional Collaboration in a Globalized World
Edited by Harald Baldersheim, Are Vegard Haug and Morten Øgård

Shifting Geo-Economic Power of the Gulf Oil, Finance and Institutions
Edited by Matteo Legrenzi and Bessma Momani

Building Regions
The Regionalization of the World Order
Luk Van Langenhove

National Solutions to Trans-Border Problems?
The Governance of Security and Risk in a Post-NAFTA North America
Edited by Isidro Morales

The Euro in the 21st Century
Economic Crisis and Financial Uproar
María Lorca-Susino

Crafting an African Security Architecture
Addressing Regional Peace and Conflict
in the 21st Century
Edited by Hany Besada

Comparative Regional Integration
Europe and Beyond
Edited by Finn Laursen

The Rise of China
and the Capitalist World Order
Edited by Li Xing

The EU and World Regionalism
The Makability of Regions
in the 21st Century
*Edited by Philippe De Lombaerde
and Michael Schulz*

The Role of the European Union in Asia
China and India as Strategic Partners
*Edited by Bart Gaens, Juha Jokela
and Eija Limnell*

China and the Global Politics
of Regionalization
Edited by Emilian Kavalski

Clash or Cooperation of Civilizations?
Overlapping Integration and Identities
Edited by Wolfgang Zank

New Perspectives on Globalization
and Antiglobalization: Prospects for a
New World Order?
Edited by Henry Veltmeyer

Governing Regional Integration for
Development: Monitoring Experiences,
Methods and Prospects
*Edited by Philippe De Lombaerde,
Antoni Estevadeordal and Kati Suominen*

Europe-Asia Interregional Relations
A Decade of ASEM
Edited by Bart Gaens

Cruising in the Global Economy
Profits, Pleasure and Work at Sea
Christine B.N. Chin

Beyond Regionalism?
Regional Cooperation, Regionalism and
Regionalization in the Middle East
*Edited by Cilja Harders
and Matteo Legrenzi*

The EU-Russian Energy Dialogue
Europe's Future Energy Security
Edited by Pami Aalto

Regionalism, Globalisation
and International Order
Europe and Southeast Asia
Jens-Uwe Wunderlich

EU Development Policy
and Poverty Reduction
Enhancing Effectiveness
Edited by Wil Hout

An East Asian Model for Latin
American Success
The New Path
Anil Hira

European Union and New Regionalism
Regional Actors and Global Governance
in a Post-Hegemonic Era.
Second Edition
Edited by Mario Telò

Regional Integration and Poverty
*Edited by Dirk Willem te Velde
and the Overseas Development Institute*

Redefining the Pacific?
Regionalism Past, Present and Future
Edited by Jenny Bryant-Tokalau
and Ian Frazer

Latin America's Quest for Globalization
The Role of Spanish Firms
Edited by Félix E. Martín
and Pablo Toral

Exchange Rate Crises
in Developing Countries
The Political Role of the Banking Sector
Michael G. Hall

Globalization and Antiglobalization
Dynamics of Change in the
New World Order
Edited by Henry Veltmeyer

Twisting Arms and Flexing Muscles
Humanitarian Intervention and
Peacebuilding in Perspective
Edited by Natalie Mychajlyszyn
and Timothy M. Shaw

Asia Pacific and Human Rights
A Global Political Economy Perspective
Paul Close and David Askew

Demilitarisation and Peace-Building
in Southern Africa
Volume I – Concepts and Processes
Edited by Peter Batchelor
and Kees Kingma

Demilitarisation and Peace-Building
in Southern Africa
Volume II – National and
Regional Experiences
Edited by Peter Batchelor
and Kees Kingma

Persistent Permeability?
Regionalism, Localism, and Globalization
in the Middle East
Edited by Bassel F. Salloukh
and Rex Brynen

The New Political Economy of
United States-Caribbean Relations
The Apparel Industry and the
Politics of NAFTA Parity
Tony Heron

The Nordic Regions and the European Union
Edited by Søren Dosenrode
and Henrik Halkier